FDR's
FIRESIDE CHATS

FDR's
FIRESIDE CHATS

Edited by
Russell D. Buhite
and
David W. Levy

University of Oklahoma Press
Norman and London

Also by Russell D. Buhite

Nelson T. Johnson and American Policy Toward China, 1925–1941
  (East Lansing, 1968)
Patrick J. Hurley and American Foreign Policy (Ithaca, 1973)
(ed.) *The Dynamics of World Power: A Documentary History of U. S.
  Foreign Policy, 1945–1973 (The Far East)* (New York, 1973)
Soviet-American Relations in Asia, 1945–1954 (Norman, 1981)
Decisions at Yalta: An Appraisal of Summit Diplomacy (Wilmington, 1986)

Also by David W. Levy

(ed., with Melvin I. Urofsky) *The Letters of Louis D. Brandeis* (Albany,
  1972–78)
Herbert Croly of the New Republic (Princeton, 1985)
The Debate Over Vietnam (Baltimore, 1991)
(ed., with Melvin I. Urofsky) *"Half Brother, Half Son": The Letters of Louis D.
  Brandeis to Felix Frankfurter* (Norman, 1991)

Text design by Bill Cason

Library of Congress Cataloging-in-Publication Data

Roosevelt, Franklin D. (Franklin Delano), 1882–1945.
    FDR's fireside chats / edited by Russell D. Buhite and David W. Levy.
— 1st ed.
      p.   cm.
    Includes bibliographical references and index.
    ISBN 0-8061-2370-2 (alk. paper)
      1. United States—Politics and government—1933–1945. 2. United
States—Foreign relations—1933–1945. 3. Roosevelt, Franklin D.
(Franklin Delano), 1882–1945—Political and social views.
    I. Buhite, Russell D. II. Levy, David W., 1937– . III. Title.
    E742.5.R65   1992
    973.917'092—dc20   91-50299
                                                                                    CIP

The paper in this book meets the guidelines for permanence and durability
of the Committee on Production Guidelines for Book Longevity of the
Council on Library Resources, Inc.∞

To Merle Curti
and
Paul Varg

scholars, teachers, gentlemen, friends

CONTENTS

Part II The Foreign Policy Fireside Chats

INTRODUCTION

IF THE FOUNDING FATHERS could return to America in the closing years of the twentieth century to inspect the political system they had created in the closing years of the eighteenth, they would find a great many things that would surprise them. The writers of the Constitution would surely catch their breath at the sheer size of the federal bureaucracy. They would marvel at the power of the judiciary, the importance of political parties in making the system function, the magnitude of the defense establishment, the relative loss of power suffered by the individual states—at these and a hundred other developments. They would be entirely unprepared for the long list of responsibilities that the central government had assumed—everything from conserving natural resources to stipulating a minimum wage, from supervising the racial integration of the schools to safeguarding people's bank deposits. Despite the fact that the nation still thought of itself as being governed by their Constitution, despite the fact that they would notice with satisfaction that many of their mechanisms were still in place and functioning effectively, who could blame them if they came away feeling that a very different sort of government had somehow supplanted the one they had devised two centuries before?

No changes would be more stunning than those surrounding the presidency. The Founders had assumed that the legislative branch of the government, and especially the House of Representatives, would reflect and summarize and enact the will of the people. Congress was to be the chief initiating force, the proposer and maker of new laws, the formulator of public policy. Any feelings of intimacy between everyday Americans and their political leaders would naturally be directed toward the local representative who came from the neighborhood, studied the wishes and dispositions of the people back home, and, along with those from other neighborhoods, provided the motive energy behind the American government. The president was expected to execute and administer the laws that Congress passed. But like the independent judges, the chief executive was also to restrain and correct, to temper and, when necessary, to veto the errors, the excesses, the sometimes turbulent passions and whimsical impulses of an occasionally unreliable democracy. Alexander Hamilton, in Federalist Paper no. 71, worried about "the tendency of the legislative authority to absorb every other," and warned that "in governments purely republican, this tendency is almost irresistible."

The returned Founding Fathers would be astonished to observe that by the end of the twentieth century these roles had, somehow, been extensively reversed. In our own time, Congress seems largely reduced to weighing and tinkering with presidential suggestions; to many citizens the House of Representatives is less the seat of the democratic spirit than it is the home of the special interests. Today most Americans believe that it is the president who summarizes the popular will, who provides the energy behind public policy, who embodies the democratic impulse and suggests and justifies new laws. The president not only has become preeminent in the American system of government, he is also the focus of whatever feelings of intimacy average Americans have toward that system. How many people know (or care) where or when their congressional representative vacations, whether he or she prefers golf or fishing or horseback riding, whether the spouse is affable and what the children are like, when the last medical checkup took place or how it turned out?

Not surprisingly, these two aspects in the development of the presidency—the concentration of power in the office and the concentration of interest in the person—have gone hand-in-hand; Americans have cared more about the officeholder precisely as the office itself came to exercise greater and greater influence on their lives. These trends, therefore, have related, if rather uneven histories. The growth of presidential power can be traced through such "strong" presidents as Thomas Jefferson, Andrew Jackson, Abraham Lincoln, Theodore Roosevelt, and Woodrow Wilson. These men—driven by wars or by a program or by temperament—did not hesitate to use or to increase the power of the office. They were willing to be party leaders, to present proposals, to manipulate patronage and bully the Congress, to appeal directly to the people "over the heads" of local representatives. It is not accidental that they were also the presidents who commanded the most interest. These were the personalities that drew the deepest affection and the bitterest ire, the ones schoolchildren knew about and for whom, very often, their schools were named.

To a remarkable extent the possibilities in the office of the presidency were summarized and institutionalized by Franklin Delano Roosevelt. Before him, the growth of presidential power was sporadic. Arthur Schlesinger, Jr., points out that although Jackson revolutionized the office, "the precedents he created were not systematically employed by any successor in time of peace for nearly three quarters of a century."[1] William Howard Taft made no attempt to emulate the flamboyance of his predecessor, Theodore Roosevelt; nor did Harding, Coolidge, or Hoover mimic, let alone build upon, the activism of Wilson. But since Franklin Roosevelt, every president has felt the pressure of his example. In 1983, the historian William E. Leuchtenburg devoted an entire book, *In the Shadow of FDR: From Harry Truman to Ronald Reagan*, to exploring the many ways he shaped the modern presidency. Those who followed after him, Leuchtenburg wrote, "had a vivid sensation of being watched." Their critics

asked not whether Roosevelt's successors dealt adequately with contemporary problems but whether they equalled FDR. They were required not merely to quote Roosevelt and replicate his policies but to do so with conspicuous ardor, not only to put through a program of similar magnitude but to carry it off with the same flair. Each was expected to have a rubric—to be known by three initials like FDR, to be the progenitor of a catch phrase like *New Deal*. When they ran for office, it was asked why they fell so far short of the Great Campaigner, and at the end of each successor's first hundred days, observers compared the score with FDR's. . . . [T]he men who succeeded him found one question inescapable: How did they measure up to FDR?[2]

If the Founding Fathers wanted to point to a culprit—the single individual who had most transformed and modernized the presidency and upset, beyond anything they could have imagined, the relations between that institution and the Congress—the choice would not have been hard to make.

[1] Arthur M. Schlesinger, Jr., "Foreword," in William M. Goldsmith, *The Growth of Presidential Power: A Documented History* (New York and London: Chelsea House, 1974), 1 : xx.

[2] William E. Leuchtenburg, *In the Shadow of FDR: From Harry Truman to Ronald Reagan* (Ithaca and London: Cornell University Press, 1983), x.

Franklin Roosevelt's impact on the presidency may be accounted for by the fortuitous coming together of two factors. First, it fell to him to confront both the greatest domestic crisis and the greatest international crisis of the twentieth century; and second, he was able to bring to those enormous tasks a set of personal attributes and talents marvelously fitted to the needs of the hour.

To a considerable extent the historical reputations of presidents have depended on the seriousness of the challenges they were called upon to face—this is why so few Americans remember very much about Millard Fillmore or Benjamin Harrison or Calvin Coolidge. Great difficulties can call forth the highest qualities of those who, otherwise, might have contentedly spent their terms in a more or less relaxed and ceremonial discharge of their duties. But adversity also tends to awaken in a confused and anxious citizenry a desperate need, a longing for decisive and effective leadership. If the leader responds well, these popular feelings can easily be transformed into deep admiration, intense loyalty, and genuine trust and affection. Thus, however trying the Great Depression and World War II were for millions of Americans, they allowed the president his chance to shine.

By temperament and talent, by energy and shrewd political instinct, Roosevelt appeared ready for the opportunity. By the time he moved into the White House, in 1933, his personal style was well established. Franklin Roosevelt was nothing if he was not attractive: big, handsome, genial, gregarious, outgoing, always grinning, always on the move. Compared to the aloof and dour Hoover, Roosevelt seemed like a breath of fresh air; he was so robust, so vital, so confident and optimistic, so warm and lighthearted, so utterly charming. It is little wonder that many Americans came to imagine him as a personal friend or that they elected him to the highest office in the land four times. His personality was usually enough to obscure the fact that his mind, while nimble and active, was very far from analytic or profound. Even more remarkable, the Roosevelt charm enabled him to overcome two handicaps that would have proved fatal to almost any other democratic politician. In his case, neither the aristocratic heritage, the fact that he had been raised as a pampered young squire in upstate New York, nor the physical disability, the fact that he had been forced to rely on wheelchair and crutches since contracting poliomyelitis in 1921, seemed to matter.

Among all of the traits and skills that made up his persona, none was more important to him or put to better service than his unique ability to communicate to the American people. Roosevelt had a gift for effective language, for anecdote and metaphor and witticism. He seemed to recognize this gift and genuinely to enjoy addressing the public in one way or another. Hoover met with representatives of the press 66 times during his presidency; Roosevelt held 337 press conferences in his first term and 374 in his second. To a reporter from the *St. Louis Post Dispatch*, it seemed that he had taken "the comatose institution" of the press conference and made it into "a distinctly American device for informing the nation of what the President is contemplating."[3] Walter Johnson, a perceptive student of the modern presidency, pointed out that "the personality—the voice, the expression, the gesture, the influence of the face—gained greater and greater importance during Roosevelt's day as against the formally constructed sentence, the sharpened definition, and the grandiose idea."[4] Roosevelt knew how to strike a pose for the new tribe of candid photographers; and he knew how to deliver an effective speech to a roaring mob of supporters in some crowded stadium. But it was in his use of the radio that he was at his very best. His mastery of that medium enabled him to make his most memorable impact on public opinion.

He was fifteen and a student at the aristocratic Groton School when Guglielmo Marconi took out his English patent for the "wireless telegraph." The radio and the boy came to maturity together. By the time Roosevelt was a law student at Columbia, it was possible to transmit the human voice across the airwaves. On the night he was defeated for the vice-presidency in 1920, the election results were actually broadcast to around a thousand homes in Pittsburgh. Thereafter the radio industry expanded with unbelievable speed. Perhaps three hundred thousand people heard the blow-by-blow account of the Dempsey-Carpentier fight in July 1921. By 1924 there were almost six hundred radio stations broadcasting sports events, music, news, and drama to perhaps three million receiving sets around the nation. Both the National Broadcasting Company and the Columbia Broadcasting System (CBS) were networking stations before Roosevelt entered the White House, and both the Mutual Broad-

[3] Raymond P. Brandt, "The President's Press Conference," *Survey Graphic*, July 1939; cited in Walter Johnson, *1600 Pennsylvania Avenue: Presidents and the People, 1929–1959* (Boston and Toronto: Little, Brown, 1960), 189.

[4] Johnson, *1600 Pennsylvania Avenue*, 190.

casting System and the American Broadcasting Company were formed during his presidency.

The political uses of radio were recognized early. In 1924 both major conventions were broadcast, as were many speeches by candidates for various offices; perhaps fifteen million people heard Coolidge's inaugural address when it was carried over twenty-one radio stations, coast to coast. All the major political figures of the 1920s used the medium, but with varied success. As a general rule, those who tried to transfer to the airwaves the style and techniques of platform oratory—Warren Harding, William Jennings Bryan, Robert La Follette, Alfred Smith—were not terribly successful. Those, like Coolidge, who adopted a tone and style more suitable to radio, more relaxed and conversational, did better. There was also considerable discussion about the effect of this new tool on the ancient art of politics. John W. Davis, the Democratic candidate in 1924, theorized that "the radio will completely change campaign methods. . . . I believe it will make the long speech impossible or inadvisable, and that the short speech will be the vogue. Otherwise your audience might tune out on you without your knowing it. It's just a matter of turning a knob."[5] Others thought that radio would reward facts, not style; and some, like La Follette, argued that the radio would counter reactionary newspapers—conservative editors would not be so likely to twist the words of politicians whom millions had heard for themselves.

At the 1924 Democratic convention, Roosevelt's nomination speech for Al Smith had been broadcast and was widely praised. During his years as governor of New York, 1929–33, he used the radio often, two or three times a month, to speak to the people of the state and to pressure the legislature in Albany. By the time he became president, it is arguable that Franklin Roosevelt understood the essence of the medium better than any major political figure. He knew that there was a world of difference between speaking to a crowd in the traditional manner and talking on the radio. In the former setting, the speaker had an audience more or less trapped in its seats. In addition, the atmosphere of the crowd, its self-reinforcing moods and the contagion of its emotions, lent itself to dramatic oratory and gestures. People listened to the radio in fami-

---

[5] Quoted in G. Joseph Wolfe, "Some Reactions to the Advent of Campaigning by Radio," *Journal of Broadcasting,* 13 (Summer 1969): 307.

lies or in groups of two or three; boring speeches could be ended with a flick of the wrist; and, as Roosevelt clearly realized, when you came into people's living rooms or joined them at the kitchen table, relaxed and informal conversation, neighbor to neighbor, was infinitely more appropriate and effective. "That's perhaps the dominating factor that has put grandiloquence out of joint," wrote an editorialist for the *New York Times*. "The radio audiences like to feel that the speaker has dropped into its [*sic*] parlor for an informal chat."[6] (That this rule was not ironclad was being demonstrated by Hitler and Mussolini in Europe; their strident, shrill, frenzied radio speeches were also extremely effective. But it must be remembered that while Roosevelt's purpose was to allay fears, to calm and assure and comfort, the purpose of the fascist dictators was to anger and arouse the mass audience.)

The term "Fireside Chat" was not coined by Roosevelt, but by Harry Butcher of CBS, who used the two words in a network press release before the speech of May 7, 1933. The term was quickly adopted by press and public, and the president himself later used it. The official edition of *The Public Papers and Addresses of Franklin D. Roosevelt,* a thirteen-volume compilation made by Samuel I. Rosenman, labels twenty-seven of Roosevelt's radio talks Fireside Chats. Other authorities list twenty-eight, insisting that the speech of November 14, 1937, was not called a Fireside Chat merely because of editorial oversight. In 1973, tape recordings of all but three of the Fireside Chats were issued by Mass Communications, Inc. (MCI), which asserted that there were actually thirty-one of Roosevelt's radio addresses that should be considered Fireside Chats. To the list of twenty-eight, MCI added the speech of May 27, 1941, the State of the Union Address of 1944, which he delivered over the radio on the evening of January 11; and the summary of the State of the Union Address for 1945, which he presented to the radio audience on January 6. In compiling this edition of the Fireside Chats we have elected to reprint the thirty-one speeches used by MCI.

Roosevelt was aided by at least a dozen talented speech writers during his years in the White House. Especially influential was Samuel Rosenman himself, who had been an adviser and speech writer for Roosevelt since the Albany days and who, despite his duties as

---

[6] Quoted in Wolfe, "Some Reactions to the Advent of Campaigning by Radio," 309.

a New York Supreme Court judge, served as a sort of "chief" of speech writing at the White House. Other men who contributed to the process at various stages of the presidency included close advisers and friends such as Harry Hopkins, Hugh Johnson, Raymond Moley, Rexford Tugwell, Benjamin Cohen, Thomas Corcoran, Donald Richberg, Adolf Berle, and a handful of others. Two illustrious writers also lent a hand during World War II: Archibald MacLeish, the Pulitzer Prize–winning poet and Librarian of Congress, and the playwright and writer Robert E. Sherwood, who won four Pulitzer Prizes before his death. Accounts of how Roosevelt's speeches got written tell a fascinating story of arduous labor: a sea of papers spread across the big table of the Cabinet room; coffee, cokes, bourbon, and sandwiches at 2 A.M.; bleary-eyed typists standing by upstairs, awaiting the latest version; seven, nine, sometimes a dozen drafts of particularly important addresses; clearing this paragraph with George Marshall and that one with Cordell Hull and a third with Leon Henderson; getting approval of the minutest of changes from "the Boss" the next morning.

But there is general agreement that the moving spirit behind the speech-writing enterprise was the president himself. He took an intense interest in every part of it. He dictated early drafts and read aloud each revised version, until he had practically memorized the speech before delivering it. Charley Michelson, a veteran ghost writer, remembered the time that Roosevelt asked him, Hugh Johnson, and Ray Moley for a speech. Each of the three came with one prepared. Roosevelt listened and then

> stretched himself on a couch and with his eyes on the ceiling dictated his own version, occasionally using one of our phrases but generally culling the best ideas that had been submitted and putting them in his own way. So far as I know, this was the practice with every speech. . . . Take it from one rather experienced in the formation and presentation of speeches: Franklin Roosevelt is a better phrase maker than anybody he ever had around him.[7]

Rosenman gives the best description of the interplay between the writers and "the Boss" in his book *Working with Roosevelt* where he describes how the Fireside Chat of February 23, 1942, was written by

---

[7] Charles Michelson, *The Ghost Talks* (New York: G. P. Putnam's Sons, 1944), 12–13.

Hopkins, Sherwood, and himself. Roosevelt "had dictated parts of a first draft several days ago, and had just carefully read over and revised the fifth draft. We had each written some inserts for this fifth draft which had been submitted to him. Some had found their way into the draft—and some into the wastebasket."

> "Too bad, Bob, he cut out that stuff of yours on page three; it sounded pretty good to me as he read it out loud. I wonder why," I murmured as I reached for another sandwich.
>
> "I think he thought it was too optimistic and promised too much good news too soon," said Harry, pouring himself a highball. "One thing the President does not want to do is to kid the American people into believing that this is anything but a tough son-of-a-bitch of a war against the toughest and cruelest bastards on earth. He wants them to realize right at the start what they are up against.". . . .
>
> [Sherwood] grinned. Although he had been doing this kind of work only a little over a year, he had already become quite accustomed to seeing passages that had taken hours to write ruthlessly discarded in a minute.
>
> "I'm glad we were able to convince the Boss to cut out those pages eight and nine that he dictated yesterday," I said as I read through the draft. "That kind of vindictiveness about the old isolationists is out of place now, even though they did often say that there was no chance of Germany or Japan ever attacking us."

And so it went, through the night; the president may have gone off to bed, but he was nevertheless a presence in the room. And Rosenman's conclusion, like Michelson's, was emphatic: "the speeches as finally delivered were his—and his alone—no matter who the collaborators were. . . . No matter how frequently the speech assistants were changed through the years, the speeches were always Roosevelt's. They all expressed the personality, the convictions, the spirit, the mood of Roosevelt. No matter who worked with him in the preparation, the finished product was always the same—it was Roosevelt himself."[8]

The Fireside Chats, as readers of them will quickly see, employed certain techniques, certain rhetorical devices with great effectiveness. Roosevelt and his speech writers chose the simplest possible language, language that average Americans could understand ("he looked for words that he would use in an informal conversation with

[8]Samuel I. Rosenman, *Working with Roosevelt* (New York: Harper and Brothers, 1952), 5–6.

one or two of his friends," Judge Rosenman recalled[9]). He talked about himself as "I" and often referred to the American people as "you." He used concrete examples and everyday analogies to illustrate his points. In many of the speeches he united the audience by calling attention to some enemy, some small minority of the perverse or wrongheaded, whose pernicious ideas the rest of us had to resist at all costs: "the few men, who might thwart this great common purpose by seeking selfish advantage"; "the professional economists who insist that things must run their course and that human agencies can have no influence on economic ills"; the "chiselers in every walk of life, [and] those in every industry who are guilty of unfair practices"; the isolationists; the cowards; the hoarders; the pessimists. The strategem of finding and naming an enemy signaled to average Americans what attitudes and actions were unpatriotic; but the device also served the larger purpose of instilling in listeners feelings of unity with the vast majority of their fellow citizens ("Well at least *I'm* no fatalistic professional economist, no chiseler, no coward"). Almost every speech makes some patriotic reference to the hallowed traditions of the American past, a memory of Lincoln or Jackson, a solemn recollection of the glorious days of the Revolution or the tragic days of the Civil War—and the patriotic mood was reinforced with the playing of "The Star-Spangled Banner" after every speech. Almost every speech ends with some appeal to God, to the kindly Providence that has watched over the nation. These artifices were simple enough, but they were enormously potent.

Roosevelt was also perfectly capable of modifying a speech while delivering it, changing a word here and there, adding a phrase, omitting a sentence. "The advance text of a prepared address, which was almost always released to the press before the President began speaking, was seldom, if ever followed by the President word for word when he spoke," observed Rosenman. "He loved to 'ad lib,' and, in many cases, his 'ad libbing' improved the prepared text."[10] This has resulted in discrepancies between the official version of the speeches, as printed in *The Public Papers and Addresses*, and what the American people actually heard over their radios as they tuned in the president. In this volume, we have departed from the

[9]Rosenman, *Working with Roosevelt*, 92–93.
[10]Samuel I. Rosenman, "Foreword," to *The Public Papers and Addresses of Franklin D. Roosevelt* (New York: Harper and Brothers, 1950), 10:ix.

printed texts and have given the version that Franklin Roosevelt actually spoke. In the rare cases where he stumbled over a word or substituted an unintended word for the one he clearly meant to say, we have ignored his mistake and resorted to the printed version. In a few cases, where the changes or omissions seem significant, we have indicated the differences in a footnote. We have also taken the liberty of "modernizing" a few spellings, the use of capital letters, and the punctuation of the printed version. We have, finally, affixed to each address a short, descriptive title—we intend these as aids to readers, but it should be understood that these titles are ours and not Roosevelt's. Otherwise, we have kept our editorial intrusions to a minimum, confining ourselves to identifying persons, events, and allusions that were familiar to listeners of the 1930s and 1940s but that might not be so well known to modern readers.

The Fireside Chats were normally delivered from a room on the first floor of the White House, the president sitting behind a desk loaded with microphones. Almost all of the speeches were given in the evening and more than a third of them on a Sunday. Secretary of Labor Frances Perkins remembered these radio talks.

> His voice and his facial expression as he spoke were those of an intimate friend. After he became President, I often was at the White House when he broadcast, and I realized how unconscious he was of the twenty or thirty of us in that room and how clearly his mind was focused on the people listening at the other end. As he talked his head would nod and his hands would move in simple, natural, comfortable gestures. His face would smile and light up as though he were actually sitting on the front porch or in the parlor with them. People felt this, and it bound them to him in affection.[11]

Once again, the classic description is given by Samuel Rosenman:

> The President sat before a desk on which were bunched three or four microphones, a reading light, a pitcher of water, and glasses. Equipment and machinery had to be brought in which would enable sixty or seventy million people to join in the scene and hear what was being said. There were some thirty uncomfortable folding chairs for those who had been invited to listen—usually friends, house guests, and selected public officials. The audience was seated about ten minutes past ten for a ten-thirty broadcast (the usual hour), and the President was wheeled in

[11] Frances Perkins, *The Roosevelt I Knew* (New York: Viking Press, 1946), 72.

at about ten-twenty, carrying his reading-copy book and the inevitable cigarette.

Radio announcers for the major broadcasting chains would huddle about, testing their microphones. The radio engineers would test their equipment, which was spread all over the room from wall to wall, making it difficult to move about. . . .

The President, once seated at his desk, exchanged greetings and pleasantries for a few moments with the guests and the announcers. As the minute of ten-thirty approached the atmosphere got more tense. The President would put out his cigarette, arrange his reading copy, and take a drink of water, as nervously as when he was about to address a visible audience. Then, on signal, complete silence, a nod from the chief radio engineer, the usual announcement from each announcer stating tersely that the broadcast was coming from the White House and introducing "The President of the United States"—and finally the clear, resonant voice: "My friends." [12]

It always, somehow, came back to that clear and resonant voice. Beyond the elaborate process by which the speeches were constructed, beyond the rhetorical devices and the physical arrangements, was the speaker himself. Taking the American people into his confidence. Instilling in them hope. Making them feel that it was their government, their country. That voice emanating from a cramped room in Washington, D.C., and spreading, by some miracle, into thirty million American homes. Walter Johnson told of a nameless soldier who, when informed of the president's death, thought that "America will seem a strange, empty place without his voice talking to the people whenever great events occur." [13] A few days later, a New York writer and folklorist, Carl Lamson Carmer, wrote a poem that summed up the feelings of many Americans:

> . . . I never saw him—
> But I *knew* him. Can you have forgotten
> How, with his voice, he came into our house,
> The President of the United States,
> Calling us friends. . . . [14]

[12] Rosenman, *Working with Roosevelt,* 93.
[13] Johnson, *1600 Pennsylvania Avenue,* 194–95.
[14] Quoted in Johnson, *1600 Pennsylvania Avenue,* 195.

PART I

THE DOMESTIC FIRESIDE CHATS

THE CRISIS AT HOME

THE GREAT DEPRESSION, which struck the United States with full force during the first years of the 1930s, presented itself to average Americans in two related but distinct ways. In the first place, it was the worst economic disaster since the coming of industrialization to the Western world. America had known hard economic times before— in the late 1830s, in the late 1850s, and throughout much of the last three decades of the nineteenth century. There had also been recessions in the twentieth century (in 1907, in 1913, and in 1921 as part of the aftermath of the First World War). On those occasions too there had been widespread suffering and dislocation. But there had never been anything quite like this before, and nothing in the economic history of the nation could have prepared Americans for the catastrophe they faced during the early 1930s. In the second place, the Great Depression resulted in something like a genuine spiritual crisis for the American people, a troubling and uncharacteristic weakening of confidence, not only in the current crop of political leadership, but in the very political and economic system itself. Any program or any leader that did not recognize and address both aspects of the catastrophe would be woefully inadequate.

An optimistic and innocent faith in America's limitless growth prevailed in the 1920s, and it blinded most Americans to some real weaknesses in the economy. Hardships in the agricultural sector, already severe before 1929, seriously limited the ability of farmers and their families to sustain the general prosperity by purchasing industrial goods. A badly skewed distribution of wealth, in which the wealthiest 5 percent of the population garnered approximately a third of all personal income, encouraged unstable luxury spending and speculation. The wild flurry of gambling on the stock market in the late 1920s diverted capital from sound investment and encouraged some corporations to increase production beyond the capacity of people to consume, given their incomes; this irrational activity on

3

Wall Street was inadequately supervised, even abetted in some ways, by the policies of the Federal Reserve Board. The new mania for installment buying stimulated an overproduction that quickly led to huge inventories and drastic layoffs of workers once the panic started. America's status as a creditor nation, with exports far exceeding imports, required a steady outflow of overseas loans and investments so that foreigners could continue to buy our goods; time would soon reveal how precarious was the base upon which international commerce rested. Certain important industries such as cotton textiles, bituminous coal, and residential construction were far from healthy. Both the banking and the corporate systems of the nation were riddled with structural weaknesses.

Of course it proved much easier to notice these economic infirmities in retrospect, once the disaster had exposed them for all to see, than it was to take them seriously in the midst of the general prosperity of the 1920s. Economists, business leaders, and Republican politicians joined in celebrating the miracle of American abundance, filling the air with predictions that the old business cycles of boom and bust had at last been conquered, that prosperity was permanent, that the nation had entered upon a New Era. It should be quickly noted that the American people were not difficult to persuade. They could see evidence of progress all around them: improvements in machinery, advances in scientific management, a steady climb in both the gross national product (GNP) and in the real wages of workers, and spectacular growth in the automobile, home appliance, chemical, and entertainment industries. Perhaps understandably, they chose to concentrate on the positive news and ignore the negative. They flung themselves into the orgy of materialism to whatever extent their means allowed, and, tempted by the expansion of easy credit and the lures of modern advertising, often beyond.

The dramatic stock market collapse in the autumn of 1929 did not "cause" the Great Depression (there had been many stock market panics in American history that did not lead to a general downturn of the economy), but the crash set into motion forces that led in the direction of serious economic trouble. Banks suddenly found that the value of their vast holdings of common stock, which they had thought to represent both a profitable investment of their depositors' money and an ample cushion of safety, had shrunk in value disastrously. They curtailed their new lending and called in their loans, domestic and foreign. The tightening of credit had a doubly detrimental impact: it retarded the prospects for continued economic expansion at home, and, together with the remarkably perverse tariff policy of the Hoover administration, helped to bring international trade to an almost complete standstill. After many banks failed and closed their doors, hundreds of thousands of Americans, whose savings were suddenly wiped away, were prevented from the kind of spending that was so necessary to the maintenance of prosperity. The stock market crash was also responsible for a crippling loss of confidence on the part of businessmen and consumers alike: maybe it would be better not to build that new wing on the factory just now; maybe we can make do with the old Ford for a couple more years. Spending declined; orders for new goods evaporated; businesses went under and workers were dismissed; prices and wages fell; and the world sank deeper and deeper into the worst economic calamity in history.

The course of the Great Depression in the United States can be told coldly and efficiently by means of a few statistics. Between 1929 and 1933 the GNP fell from $103.1 billion to $55.6 billion; each American's share of the GNP dropped from $847 to $442. Between 1929 and 1932 more than one hundred thousand American businesses failed, the total net profits of private corporations dropped from $8.4 to $3.4 billion, and total industrial productivity fell off 51 percent. From 1929 to 1932 the value of both American imports and American exports declined by more than two thirds. The income of farmers, already hard hit during the 1920s, fell from $11 to $5 billion. Perhaps most troubling of all were the unemployment figures. In 1929, according to the government, 3.2 percent of the work force was unemployed; in 1930, that figure had more than doubled to 8.9 percent; in 1931, it doubled again to 16.3 percent; in 1932, 24.1 percent of American workers were out of a job and in 1933, 25.2 percent. At the depth of the depression, therefore, one out of every four American workers had no work to do. Nongovernmental agencies reported unemployment figures to be even higher. Those terrifying numbers fail to tell us how many of the employed had suffered crippling cuts in their earnings or how many skilled workers and once-prosperous professionals were doing menial tasks just to stay alive.

Translating the pain represented by these figures into understandable human terms is almost impossible. The Great Depression touched the lives of millions of Americans. It made itself felt among those who had known prosperity and comfort, but who now faced the bleak prospects of unemployment, vanished savings, ruined businesses, and frighteningly reduced circumstances. Middle-class Americans found they could not send their children to college as they had always planned, that they could not retire and take it easy the way they had always hoped, that they needed to make room in their homes for desperate relatives who had to "double up" to save the rent money. Young people graduating from college found that there was little chance of finding the sort of work they had trained so hard for. Those wishing to marry and start new families were forced to postpone—the birth rate plummeted during the early thirties as young couples calculated whether they could afford another mouth to feed. School teachers, paid from a local tax base that had suddenly dried up, found that the state or local governments cut the school year drastically, reduced their paychecks, and, in some places, paid them with dubious promissory notes rather than with real money.

And if the depression was a disaster for millions of the once comfortable, what must it have been like for those who had been poor even before the trouble started? For America's already destitute, the economic disaster of the 1930s brought nightmares of deprivation and suffering. Every large city had its long breadlines and shabby soup-kitchens, but no credible observer suggested that existing charitable resources were even remotely equal to the crushing need. Many surveys reported widespread hunger and malnutrition. Every night, summer and winter, city parks and subways filled with the homeless, dressed in rags, and looking for some empty bench to sleep on. On the outskirts of almost every American city there arose clusters of desperate shacks, little "Hoovervilles" built of spare boards and crates and cardboard, where the poor stayed while they carried on their futile search for work. Thousands took to the road. Some, who had been foreclosed for back rent or taxes, went as families (like the famous Okies who headed for California); others wandered the countryside as individuals, hoboes begging door-to-door for chores to do in exchange for something to eat, eager for the chance to pick other people's crops for pitiful wages, thumbing rides along the highways or hopping passing freight trains in order to try their luck in some other place. Blacks, who had previously done the menial jobs, found themselves displaced by whites who suddenly no longer found such work to be beneath them.

Looking at the period right before Franklin Roosevelt's inauguration, the historian David Shannon wrote,

> Many have said that during those four terrible months "capitalism almost failed." It "almost" failed only if one defines failure as the economy's grinding to an utter stop. If however, one defines failure as inability to provide a minimum standard of living for a large part of the population, an opportunity for profitable investment of capital, and security for savings and other funds already invested, then the economy did not "almost" fail; it did fail.[1]

This panorama of suffering inevitably affected the mood of the country. Even those fortunate Americans who were relatively unscathed by the economic fallout of the depression were required to ponder its moral and spiritual meaning. No thoughtful observer could fail to see that some of the oldest and strongest faiths of the nation were being tested and questioned as never before. Most Americans had always assumed, for example, that free-enterprise capitalism, if not directly ordained by a benevolent deity, was at the very least based on the eternal principles of natural law. Their economic system, they instinctively knew, rested firmly on the most basic truths about human nature, justice, and morality. Any difficulties within the economic system, they believed, were bound to be temporary; they would soon be corrected by the automatic and self-adjusting mechanisms of the free market, by the innate hardiness of American individualism, and, when necessary, by the generosity of private charities. Governmental interference in the workings of the economy was to be avoided at all costs; the bureaucrats might be well meaning, but they were inevitably inefficient, usually counterproductive, and very often corrupt. Most Americans had always assumed, furthermore, that poverty was a sign of laziness, drunkenness, plain incompetence, or some other moral, physical, or intellectual defect in its victims. The idea that healthy, intelligent, and industrious Americans might find themselves utterly destitute through no fault of their own was almost as foreign to Americans as the idea that monarchy was the best form of government.

[1]David A. Shannon, *Between the Wars: America, 1919–1941* (Boston: Houghton Mifflin, 1965), 109.

All of these ancient faiths, as well as others—that the United States was a land of limitless opportunities; that anyone could get ahead by hard work; that traditional democratic processes were entirely adequate to handle even the most complex problems; that poor nations should model their economies on America's; that there was nothing at all redeeming in socialism or communism; that accepting help from others, going on the dole, receiving welfare was a badge of shame; that nothing happening overseas could possibly touch the health and prosperity of American society—fell under serious strain during the years of the Great Depression. It was impossible that so pervasive and sharp an attack on American beliefs, bolstered as it was by clear evidence of the system's failures, could fail to weaken the normal confidence of the American people. Indeed, to some historians of the early 1930s, the wonder is not that a spiritual malaise and a weakening of faith should have accompanied a cataclysm of such vast proportions. The real wonder is that so much of the traditional political and economic system was able to survive, that the strenuous efforts of homegrown revolutionaries and radicals should have made such little headway despite the natural discontent bred by the collapse.

It would obviously be ascribing far too much influence to a single individual to argue that it was Franklin Roosevelt who frustrated the radicals and preserved so much of the American political and economic tradition. But it seems very clear that he was at least partly responsible. He was somehow able to address both aspects of the Great Depression, to give the necessary assurances as regarded both the economic and the spiritual crisis confronting the nation. And he was persuasive enough on both scores to forestall the sweeping changes that some were demanding but that he hated and feared as much as anyone.

Roosevelt was the governor of New York when the stock market crashed and the depression started, one of the few Democrats to have won election in 1928, when the general prosperity swept the Republicans back into office across the country. After the economic troubles started, his record of activity in Albany contrasted favorably with the apparent inactivity of Hoover in Washington; and after his triumphant reelection to the governorship in 1930, Roosevelt was clearly the frontrunner for the Democratic nomination in 1932.

Once it was clear that Hoover's unpopularity would assure the presidency to whomever the Democrats nominated, a warm contest developed, but Roosevelt emerged victorious from the Chicago convention of 1932 and set out to convince Americans to vote for him in November. The campaign was not notable for thorough discussions of the issues or for presentation of a comprehensive plan of action against the depression. The candidate seemed content to blast Hoover, to talk in optimistic generalities, and to let his energy and personality contrast with the lethargic and colorless campaign of Herbert Hoover. It was a foregone conclusion that he would win. He received 57.4 percent of the vote to Hoover's 39.7 percent, and he got 472 votes in the electoral college to Hoover's 59.

On the basis of his bland campaign, few Americans would have predicted that the ascendancy of Franklin Roosevelt to the White House would result in either the revolutionizing of the presidency or the headlong flurry of antidepression legislation that was about to follow. That legislation took its designation, "the New Deal," from a phrase in his Chicago acceptance speech. And it was the various segments of this program that Roosevelt set out to explain and justify to the nation in the first thirteen of his Fireside Chats. As will be seen from an examination of these talks, Roosevelt wanted to make it appear that the laws Congress was passing at his instigation constituted a coherent and unified program and that this program was effective. In short, the president tried, by means of these radio talks, to assure the nation that the first aspect of the Great Depression—the difficult economic crisis that had caused so much genuine hardship for American families—was being addressed sensibly and with good results.

Historians have been skeptical of these claims. To most of them it now seems as if the New Deal was a lot less coherent and unified than Franklin Roosevelt liked to pretend. On such important matters as the control of big business and a balanced budget, the New Deal seemed to lack a consistent policy. Much of the legislation now seems to have been the product of Roosevelt's desire to solve immediate problems or to appease particular groups within the population—something for farmers, something for business, something for labor, something for bankers. The various measures also seem to reveal the influence of particular and sometimes conflicting groups of his advisers; some, like the relief measures, seem designed to stamp out brush fires while others, like the Tennessee Valley Authority (TVA) or the Federal Deposit Insurance Corporation (FDIC) or the social security system, seem designed to attempt permanent reforms.

Historians also raise questions about the New Deal's ultimate effectiveness in combatting the economic downturn. While giving high marks to some New Deal programs (social security, conservation, regulation of the stock exchanges, and insurance of the safety of bank deposits), and while acknowledging that the New Deal's relief and public works measures provided much needed help to many thousands of American families, these historians point out the uneven record of economic recovery achieved by Roosevelt and the New Deal. At the end of the New Deal, no one could rightly claim that the poorest denizens of the slums, the migrant workers and the sharecroppers, or black Americans had experienced very much genuine advance. In 1939 the unemployment rate in the United States still hovered around 20 percent and the wealthiest 5 percent of Americans still garnered a quarter of the personal income. In the end it was the economic boom caused by the Second World War, not Roosevelt's New Deal, that finally cured the Great Depression. Only the massive government infusions for war matériel succeeded in raising the level of industrial productivity above the predepression level, and it was not until 1943 that unemployment again sank below what it had been in 1929.

As far as the second aspect of the Great Depression was concerned, however, Roosevelt's achievement is almost universally praised. That part of the catastrophe that cannot be told in statistics, that part that was finally measured in popular attitudes and moods, the president addressed with masterly skill. As these Fireside Chats will show, Roosevelt tried very hard to dispel the damaging unease of the spirit, the self-doubt and loss of faith that was also a part of these troubled years. In a greater measure than might have been expected, he succeeded. By talking candidly, confidently, and naturally to the people of America, he did much to restore their hope and rebuild their self-assurance. Thus if he could not cure the disease that was gripping the nation, he did help to soothe some of the pain and to persuade those who would listen that there was no need to despair because better times were ahead.

THE BANKING CRISIS [1]

AT THE VERY MOMENT that Franklin Roosevelt was taking his oath of office, on March 4, 1933, the nation was in the midst of a terrifying financial crisis—the virtual collapse of the country's banking system. The ultimate cause of this collapse was the radical uncertainty, felt by thousands of Americans, about the safety of the money they had deposited in their banks. Bank "runs," when panic-stricken depositors suddenly appeared to demand their savings, were not uncommon even during the late 1920s—especially in agricultural regions and small towns. But the pace of bank closings picked up dramatically after the stock market crash of October 1929: in 1929, 642 banks closed; in 1930, 1,345; and in 1931, a stunning 2,298. Between the time of Roosevelt's election in November 1932 and his inauguration in March 1933, the disease became an epidemic. State governors began, by proclamation, to close their banks protectively by declaring temporary banking "holidays." The first occurred in Nevada in October 1932 and others followed (seventeen states closed their banks the day before the inauguration). Early on the morning of March 4, all remaining states declared their banks to be officially closed.

Before federal deposit insurance, the closing of a bank very often meant that a family's hard earned savings were suddenly wiped away. The careful plans of thousands of Americans—for buying a new car, sending the kids to college, enjoying a secure retirement, meeting the mortgage payments, caring for elderly parents, or having some money set aside in case of some unexpected emergency—exploded into fragments. Besides being an immense personal tragedy, the destruction of the banking system also had deleterious effects on an already staggering economy, an economy in which the index of industrial production was already at an all-time low.

[1] The titles of this address and of all the others in this volume were added by the editors as an aid to readers; President Roosevelt did not employ such titles.

On the day after his inauguration, Roosevelt called for a special session of Congress, to convene on March 9. (This was the session that accomplished the famous "First Hundred Days" avalanche of relief and recovery legislation.) Before Congress gathered, however, Roosevelt moved energetically to meet the banking crisis. On March 6, he issued a proclamation declaring a four-day national banking holiday and other measures relating to the banking system. The Congress assembled on the ninth and approved Roosevelt's actions on that very day. The Senate's vote was 77 to 7 and the House was unanimous. Banks were divided into four groups on the basis of their health, and the process of reopening them began quickly. Half the banks (representing 90 percent of the deposits) opened by March 15, and nearly all of the others soon followed. The reopenings relaxed the fears of the American people and they began to return their hoarded deposits to their banks. The problem, which had been met temporarily by resolute action from the president and the Congress, would not be permanently solved until the Glass-Steagall Banking Act in June 1933, which established the Federal Deposit Insurance Corporation.

On Sunday evening, March 12, Roosevelt went on the radio to explain to the American people what had been done. That speech was his first Fireside Chat.

MY FRIENDS, I want to talk for a few minutes with the people of the United States about banking—to talk with the comparatively few who understand the mechanics of banking, but more particularly with the overwhelming majority of you who use banks for the making of deposits and the drawing of checks. I want to tell you what has been done in the last few days, and why it was done, and what the next steps are going to be. I recognize that the many proclamations from the state capitals and from Washington, the legislation, the Treasury regulations and so forth, couched for the most part in banking and legal terms, ought to be explained for the benefit of the average citizen. I owe this in particular because of the fortitude and the good temper with which everybody has accepted the inconvenience and the hardships of the banking holiday. And I know that when you understand what we in Washington have been about I shall continue to have your cooperation as fully as I have had your sympathy and your help during the past week.

First of all, let me state the simple fact that when you deposit money in a bank the bank does not put the money into a safe deposit vault. It invests your money in many different forms of credit—in bonds, in commercial paper, in mortgages, and in many other kinds of loans. In other words, the bank puts your money to work to keep the wheels of industry and of agriculture turning round. A comparatively small part of the money that you put into the bank is kept in currency—an amount which in normal times is wholly sufficient to cover the cash needs of the average citizen. In other words, the total amount of all the currency in the country is only a comparatively small proportion of the total deposits in all the banks of the country.

What, then, happened during the last few days of February and the first few days of March? Because of undermined confidence on the part of the public, there was a general rush by a large portion of our population to turn bank deposits into currency or gold—a rush so great that the soundest banks couldn't get enough currency to meet the demand. The reason for this was that on the spur of the moment it was, of course, impossible to sell perfectly sound assets of a bank and convert them into cash except at panic prices far below their real value.

By the afternoon of March 3, a week ago last Friday, scarcely a bank in the country was open to do business. Proclamations closing them in whole or in part had been issued by the governors in almost all of the states.

It was then that I issued the proclamation providing for the national bank holiday, and this was the first step in the government's reconstruction of our financial and economic fabric.

The second step, last Thursday, was the legislation promptly and patriotically passed by the Congress confirming my proclamation and broadening my powers so that it became possible in view of the requirement of time to extend the holiday and lift the ban of that holiday gradually in the days to come. This law also gave authority to develop a program of rehabilitation of our banking facilities, and I want to tell our citizens in every part of the nation that the national Congress—Republicans and Democrats alike—showed by this action a devotion to public welfare and a realization of the emergency and the necessity for speed that it is difficult to match in all our history.

The third stage has been the series of regulations permitting the banks to continue their functions to take care of the distribution of food and household necessities and the payment of payrolls.

This bank holiday, while resulting in many cases in great inconvenience, is affording us the opportunity to supply the currency necessary to meet the situation. Remember that no sound bank is a dollar worse off than it was when it closed its doors last week. Neither is any bank which may turn out not to be in a position for immediate opening. The new law allows the twelve federal reserve banks to issue additional currency on good assets and thus banks that reopen will be able to meet every legitimate call. The new currency is being sent out by the Bureau of Engraving and Printing in large volume to every part of the country. It is sound currency because it is backed by actual, good assets.

Another question that you will ask is this: why are all the banks not to be reopened at the same time? The answer is simple, and I know you will understand it. Your government does not intend that the history of the past few years shall be repeated. We do not want and will not have another epidemic of bank failures.

As a result, we start tomorrow, Monday, with the opening of banks in the twelve federal reserve bank cities—those banks which on first examination by the Treasury have already been found to be all right. That will be followed on Tuesday by the resumption of all other functions by banks already found to be sound in cities where there are recognized clearing houses. That means about 250 cities of the United States. In other words, we are moving as fast as the mechanics of the situation will allow us.[2]

On Wednesday and succeeding days banks in smaller places all through the country will resume business, subject, of course, to the government's physical ability to complete its survey. It is necessary that the reopening of banks be extended over a period in order to permit the banks to make applications for the necessary loans, to obtain currency needed to meet their requirements, and to enable the government to make commonsense checkups.

Please let me make it clear to you that if your bank does not open

[2] This sentence was added by Roosevelt as he delivered the speech.

the first day, you are by no means justified in believing that it will not open. A bank that opens on one of the subsequent days is in exactly the same status as the bank that opens tomorrow.

I know that many people are worrying about state banks that are not members of the Federal Reserve System. There is no occasion for that worry.[3] These banks can and will receive assistance from member banks and from the Reconstruction Finance Corporation[4] and of course they are under the immediate control of the state banking authorities.[5] These state banks are following the same course as the national banks except that they get their licenses to resume business from the state authorities, and these authorities have been asked by the secretary of the treasury to permit their good banks to open up on the same schedule as the national banks. And so I am confident that the state banking departments will be as careful as the national government in the policy relating to the opening of banks and will follow the same broad theory.

It is possible that when the banks resume a very few people who have not recovered from their fear may again begin withdrawals. Let me make it clear to you that the banks will take care of all needs except of course the hysterical demands of hoarders—and it is my belief that hoarding during the past week has become an exceedingly unfashionable pastime in every part of our nation. It needs no prophet to tell you that when the people find that they can get their money—that they can get it when they want it for all legitimate purposes—the phantom of fear will soon be laid. People will again be glad to have their money where it will be safely taken care of and where they can use it conveniently at any time. I can assure you, my friends, that it is safer to keep your money in a reopened bank than it is to keep it under the mattress.

The success of our whole national program depends, of course, on the cooperation of the public—on its intelligent support and its use of a reliable system.

Remember that the essential accomplishment of the new legislation is that it makes it possible for banks more readily to convert

---

[3] This sentence was also added by Roosevelt spontaneously.

[4] The Reconstruction Finance Corporation had been President Herbert Hoover's response to the depression. This government agency began functioning in February 1932 with a capitalization of $500 million. It loaned money to railroads, insurance companies, and banks, on the theory that shoring up these institutions would stabilize all sectors of the economy.

[5] The words "and of course they are under the immediate control of the state banking authorities" were added by Roosevelt as he delivered the speech.

their assets into cash than was the case before. More liberal provision has been made for banks to borrow on these assets at the reserve banks and more liberal provision has also been made for issuing currency on the security of these good assets. This currency is not fiat currency. It is issued only on adequate security, and every good bank has an abundance of such security.

One more point before I close. There will be, of course, some banks unable to reopen without being reorganized. The new law allows the government to assist in making these reorganizations quickly and effectively and even allows the government to subscribe to at least a part of any new capital that may be required.

I hope you can see, my friends, from this essential recital of what your government is doing that there is nothing complex, nothing radical, in the process.

We had a bad banking situation. Some of our bankers had shown themselves either incompetent or dishonest in their handling of the people's funds. They had used the money entrusted to them in speculations and unwise loans. This was, of course, not true in the vast majority of our banks, but it was true in enough of them to shock the people of the United States for a time into a sense of insecurity and to put them into a frame of mind where they did not differentiate, but seemed to assume that the acts of a comparative few had tainted them all. And so it became the government's job to straighten out this situation and to do it as quickly as possible. And that job is being performed.

I do not promise you that every bank will be reopened or that individual losses will not be suffered, but there will be no losses that possibly could be avoided; and there would have been more and greater losses had we continued to drift. I can even promise you salvation for some at least of the sorely pressed banks. We shall be engaged not merely in reopening sound banks but in the creation of more sound banks through reorganization.

It has been wonderful to me to catch the note of confidence from all over the country. I can never be sufficiently grateful to the people for the loyal support that they have given me in their acceptance of the judgment that has dictated our course, even though all our processes may not have seemed clear to them.

After all, there is an element in the readjustment of our financial system more important than currency, more important than gold, and that is the confidence of the people themselves. Confidence and courage are the essentials of success in carrying out our plan. You people must have faith; you must not be stampeded by rumors or guesses. Let us unite in banishing fear. We have provided the machinery to restore our financial system; and it is up to you to support and make it work.

It is your problem, my friends, your problem no less than it is mine. Together we cannot fail.

PROGRESS MADE DURING
THE NEW DEAL'S FIRST TWO MONTHS

ROOSEVELT'S SECOND FIRESIDE CHAT was delivered more than halfway through the First Hundred Days—sixty days of that historic special session of Congress had already passed, forty enormously productive days still lay ahead. Roosevelt had several purposes in mind for this address. He wanted to apprise the American people of the encouraging progress that had been made in the two months since his inauguration. Even more important, though, he wanted to establish a momentum for crucial bills that he had proposed, but that the Congress had not yet acted upon. Near the end of the talk, Roosevelt also tried to justify the decision taken on April 19 to abandon the gold standard, freeing the country to issue more currency in order to raise commodity prices. He took the opportunity, finally, to say a few words about the international dimension of the depression and the efforts underway to achieve cooperation behind a set of diplomatic objectives. Throughout the speech Roosevelt was particularly anxious to assure the country that, despite this vigorous activity, nothing terribly radical or worrisome was transpiring in the nation's capital. During the process of making his points, the president saw nothing wrong with getting in a few licks at former-President Hoover.

On the evening of the speech, the New Deal could point to only a relatively few measures that had already become laws. Besides the Emergency Banking Relief Act (signed on March 9), there was only the Beer-Wine Revenue Act (March 22) and the Civilian Conservation Corps Act (March 31), both of which the president trumpeted in this talk. He also discussed, however, a number of bills that Congress still had under consideration. The Federal Emergency Relief Act, authorizing half a billion dollars for relief to be distributed through states and municipalities, was signed by Roosevelt only five days after this talk; and the Tennessee Valley Authority became law just a week after that. Two measures to reduce the number of mortgage foreclosures, the Home Owners Refinancing Act, which established the Home Owners

Loan Corporation, and the Farm Credit Act, were signed on June 13 and June 16. The president also mentioned the Railroad Bill, designed to regulate and reinvigorate the nation's railroad system; that law was signed on June 16. But Roosevelt gave greatest attention and most emphasis to two controversial pieces of legislation that would constitute the heart of the recovery program of the early New Deal: the Agricultural Adjustment Act (AAA), which became law on May 12; and the National Industrial Recovery Act, which he signed on June 16. The main purposes of the former were to subsidize farmers while trying to reduce crippling agricultural surpluses; the main purposes of the latter were to encourage industrial self-regulation through industrywide codes of behavior, to reduce unemployment and ensure laborers the right of collective bargaining, and to inaugurate an extensive program of public works. So critical to his plans were these two laws that Roosevelt devoted almost the entirety of his next Fireside Chat, delivered on July 24, to explaining and justifying them to the citizenry.

Roosevelt's remarks about the international aspect of the Great Depression were little more than vague generalities. In the end the president remained unconvinced about the necessity for worldwide cooperation to defeat the depression and unready to pay the price of short-run American disadvantages for the sake of long-run international cooperation in the economic sphere.

ON A SUNDAY NIGHT a week after my inauguration I used the radio to tell you about the banking crisis and about the measures we were taking to meet it. In that way I tried to make clear to the country various facts that might otherwise have been misunderstood and in general to provide a means of understanding which I believe did much to restore confidence.

Tonight, eight weeks later, I come for the second time to give you my report, in the same spirit and by the same means, to tell you about what we have been doing and what we are planning to do.

Two months ago as you know we were facing serious problems. The country was dying by inches. It was dying because trade and commerce had declined to dangerously low levels; prices for basic commodities were such as to destroy the value of the assets of national institutions such as banks, and savings banks, and insurance companies, and others. These institutions, because of their great needs, were foreclosing mortgages, they were calling loans, and they were refusing credit. Thus there was actually in process of destruction the property of millions of people who had borrowed money on that property in terms of dollars which had had an entirely different value from the level of March 1933. That situation in that crisis did not call for any complicated consideration of economic panaceas or fancy plans. We were faced by a condition and not a theory.

There were just two alternatives at that time: The first was to allow the foreclosures to continue, credit to be withheld, money to go into hiding, thus forcing liquidation and bankruptcy of banks and railroads and insurance companies and a recapitalizing of all business and all property on a lower level. That alternative meant a continuation of what is loosely called "deflation," the net result of which would have been extraordinary hardships on all property owners and all bank depositors,[1] and incidentally, extraordinary hardships on all persons working for wages through an increase in unemployment and a further reduction of the wage scale.

It is easy to see that the result of that course would have not only economic effects of a very serious nature, but social results also that might bring incalculable harm. Even before I was inaugurated I came to the conclusion that such a policy was too much to ask the American people to bear. It involved not only a further loss of homes and farms and savings and wages, but also a loss of spiritual values—the loss of that sense of security for the present and the future that is so necessary to the peace and contentment of the individual and of his family. When you destroy those things you find it difficult to establish confidence of any sort in the future. And it is clear that mere appeals coming out of Washington for more confidence and the mere lending of more money to shaky institutions could not stop that downward course. A prompt program applied as quickly as possible seemed to me not only justified but imperative to our national security. The Congress, and when I say the Congress I mean the members of both political parties, fully understood this and gave me generous and intelligent support. The members of the Congress realized that the methods of normal times had to be replaced in the

---

[1] The words "and all bank depositors" were added by the president to his prepared text.

emergency by measures that were suited to the serious and pressing requirements of the moment. There was no actual surrender of power. Congress still retains its constitutional authority to legislate and to appropriate,[2] and no one has the slightest desire to change the balance of these powers. The function of Congress is to decide what has to be done and to select the appropriate agency to carry out its will. That policy it has strictly adhered to. The only thing that has been happening has been to designate the president of the United States as the agency to carry out certain of the purposes of the Congress. This was constitutional and is constitutional, and it is in keeping with the past American tradition.

The legislation that has been passed or is in the process of enactment can properly be considered as part of a well-grounded, well-rounded plan.

First, we are giving opportunity of employment to a quarter of a million of the unemployed, especially the young men who have dependents, to let them go into forestry and flood-prevention work. That is a big task because it means feeding and clothing and caring for nearly twice as many men as we have in the regular Army itself. And in creating this Civilian Conservation Corps we are killing two birds with one stone. We are clearly enhancing the value of our natural resources, and at the same time we are relieving an appreciable amount of actual distress. This great group of men, young men, have entered upon their work on a purely voluntary basis; no military training is involved and we are conserving not only our natural resources, but also our human resources. One of the great values to this work is the fact that it is direct and requires the intervention of very little machinery.

Secondly, I have requested the Congress and have secured action upon a proposal to put the great properties owned by our government at Muscle Shoals to work after long years of wasteful inaction, and with this goes hand-in-hand a broad plan for the permanent improvement of the vast area included in the whole of the Tennessee Valley. It will add to the comfort and to the happiness of hundreds of thousands of people and the incident benefits will reach the entire nation.

Next, the Congress is about to pass legislation that will greatly ease the mortgage distress among the farmers and among the home-

[2]The words "to legislate and to appropriate" were added by Roosevelt.

owners of the nation, by providing for the easing of the burden of debt that now bears so heavily upon millions of our people.

Our next step in seeking immediate relief is a grant of half a billion dollars to help the states and the counties and the municipalities in their duty to care for those who at this time need direct and immediate relief.

In addition to all this, the Congress also passed legislation as you know authorizing the sale of beer in such states as desired it. That has already resulted in considerable reemployment, and incidentally it has provided for the federal government and for the states a much-needed tax revenue.

Now as to the future.

We are planning within a few days to ask the Congress for legislation to enable the government to undertake public works, thus stimulating directly and indirectly the employment of many others in well-considered projects.

Further legislation has been taken up which goes much more fundamentally into our economic problems. The Farm Relief Bill seeks by the use of several methods, alone or together, to bring about an increased return to farmers for their major farm products, seeking at the same time to prevent in the days to come disastrous overproduction, the kind of overproduction that so often in the past has kept farm commodity prices far below a reasonable return. This measure provides wide powers for emergencies and the extent of its use will depend entirely upon what the future has in store.

Well-considered and conservative measures will likewise be proposed, within a few days, that will attempt to give to the industrial workers of the country a more fair wage return, to prevent cutthroat competition, to prevent unduly long hours for labor, and at the same time to encourage each industry to prevent overproduction.

One of our bills falls into the same class, the Railroad Bill. It seeks to provide and make certain a definite planning by the railroads themselves, with the assistance of the government, in order to eliminate the duplication and the waste that now results in railroad receiverships and in continuing operating deficits.

I feel very certain that the people of this country understand and approve the broad purposes behind these new governmental policies relating to agriculture and industry and transportation. We found ourselves faced with more agricultural products than we could possibly consume ourselves and with surpluses which other nations did not have the cash to buy from us except at prices ruin-ously low. We found our factories able to turn out more goods than we could possibly consume, and at the same time we have been faced with a falling export demand. We have found ourselves with more facilities to transport goods and crops than there were goods and crops to be transported. All of this has been caused in large part by a complete lack of planning and a complete failure to understand the danger signals that have been flying ever since the close of the World War. The people of this country have been erroneously en-couraged to believe that they could keep on increasing the output of farm and of factory indefinitely and that some magician would find ways and means for that increased output to be consumed with reasonable profit to the producer.

But today we have reason to believe that things are a little better than they were two months ago. Industry has picked up, railroads are carrying more freight, farm prices are better. But I am not going to indulge in issuing proclamations of overenthusiastic assurance. We cannot ballyhoo ourselves back to prosperity and I am going to be honest at all times with the people of the country. I do not want the people of this country to take the foolish course of letting this improvement come back on another speculative wave. I do not want the people to believe that because of unjustified optimism we can resume the ruinous practice of increasing our crop output and our factory output in the hope that a kind Providence will find buyers at high prices. Such a course may bring us immediate and false pros-perity but it will be the kind of prosperity that will lead us into an-other tailspin.

It is wholly wrong to call the measures that we have taken govern-ment control of farming or government control of industry, or a gov-ernment control of transportation. It is rather a partnership—a part-nership between government and farming, a partnership between government and industry, and a partnership between government and transportation. Not a partnership in profits, because the profits will still go to the private citizen, but rather a partnership in plan-ning, and a partnership to see that the plans are carried out.

Let me illustrate with an example. Take for instance the cotton-goods industry. It is probably true that 90 percent of the cotton man-ufacturers of this country would agree tomorrow to eliminate star-vation wages, would agree to stop long hours of employment, would agree to stop child labor, would agree to prevent an overproduction that would result in unsalable surpluses. But, my friends, what good is such an agreement of the 90 percent if the other 10 percent of the cotton manufacturers pay starvation wages and require long hours and employ children in their mills and turn out burdensome surpluses? The unfair 10 percent could produce goods so cheaply that the fair 90 percent would be compelled to meet the unfair conditions. And that is where government comes in. Government ought to have the right and will have the right, after surveying and planning for an industry, to prevent, with the assistance of the overwhelming majority of that industry, all unfair practices and to enforce that agreement by the authority of government. The so-called antitrust laws were intended to prevent the creation of monopolies and to forbid unreasonable profits to those monopolies. That purpose of the antitrust laws must be continued, but those laws were never intended to encourage the kind of unfair competition that results in long hours and starvation wages and overproduction.

And, my friends, the same principle that is illustrated by that example applies to farm products and to transportation and to every other field of organized private industry.

We are working towards a definite goal, a goal that seeks to prevent the return of conditions which came very close to destroying what we alive call modern civilization. The actual accomplishment of our purposes cannot be attained in a day. Our policies are wholly within the purposes for which our American constitutional government was established 150 years ago.

I know that the people of this country will understand this and that they will also understand the spirit in which we are undertaking that policy. I do not deny that we may make some mistakes of procedure as we carry out this policy. I have no expectation of making a hit every time I come to bat. What I seek is the highest possible batting average, not only for myself but for the team. Theodore Roosevelt once said to me, "If I can be right 75 percent of the time, I shall come up to the fullest measure of my hopes."

Much has been said of late about federal finances and inflation, about the gold standard, and francs and pounds and so forth. I should like to make the facts very simple and to make my policy very clear. In the first place, government credit and government currency are really one and the same thing. Behind government bonds there is only a promise to pay. Behind government currency we have, in addition to the promise to pay, a reserve of gold and a small reserve of silver, neither of them anything like the total amount of the currency.[3] And in this connection it is worthwhile remembering that in the past the government has agreed to redeem nearly 30 billions of its debts and its currency in gold, and private corporations and individuals[4] in this country have agreed to redeem another 60 or 70 billions of securities and mortgages in gold. The government and the private corporations and individuals were making these agreements when they knew full well that all of the gold in the United States amounted to only between 3 and 4 billion and that all of the gold in all of the world amounted to only about 11 billion.

If the holders of these promises to pay were all of them to start in to demand gold the firstcomers would get gold for a few days or a few hours and those firstcomers who would get the gold would amount to about one twenty-fifth of all of the holders of the securities and the currency. The other twenty-four people out of twenty-five, who did not happen to be at the top of the line, would be politely told that there was no more gold left. And so we have decided in Washington to treat all twenty-five people in the same way in the interest of justice and in the exercise of the constitutional powers of this government. We placed everyone on the same basis in order that the general good may be preserved.

Nevertheless, gold, and to a partial extent silver also, are perfectly good bases for currency, and that is why I decided not to let any of the gold now in the country go out of it.

A series of conditions arose three weeks ago which very readily might have meant, first, a drain on our gold by foreign countries, and secondly, as a result of that drain, a flight of American capital itself, in the form of gold, out of our country. And it is not exaggerating the possibility to tell you that such an occurrence might well have taken from us the major part of our gold reserve and might well have resulted in such a further weakening of our government and private credit as to bring on actual panic conditions and the complete stoppage of the wheels of industry.

The administration has the definite objective of raising commodity prices to such an extent that those who have borrowed money will, on the average, be able to repay that money in the same kind of dollar which they borrowed. We do not seek to let them get

---

[3] The words "neither of them anything like the total amount of the currency" were added.
[4] The words "and individuals" were added by Roosevelt both here and a few lines below.

such a cheap dollar that in effect they will be able to pay a great deal less back than they borrowed. In other words, we seek to correct a wrong and not to create another wrong in the opposite direction. That is why powers are being given to the administration to provide, if necessary, for an enlargement of credit, in order to correct the existing wrong. These powers will be used when, as, and if it may be necessary to accomplish the purpose.

Hand in hand with the domestic situation which, of course, is our first concern, is the world situation, and I want to emphasize to you that the domestic situation is inevitably and deeply tied in with the conditions in all of the other nations of the world. In other words, we can get, in all probability, some measure of return of prosperity in the United States, but it will not be permanent unless we can get a return to prosperity all over the world.

In the conferences that we have held and are holding with the leaders of other nations, we are seeking four great objectives: first, a general reduction of armaments and through this the removal of the fear of invasion and of armed attack, and, at the same time, a reduction in armament costs in order to help in the balancing of government budgets and in the reduction of taxation; secondly, a cutting down of the trade barriers, in order to restart the flow of exchange of crops and goods between nations; third, we seek the setting up of a stabilization of currencies, in order that trade and commerce can make contracts ahead; and fourth, we seek the reestablishment of friendly relations and greater confidence between all nations.

Our foreign visitors these past three weeks[5] have responded to these purposes in a very helpful way. All of the nations have suffered alike in this great depression. They have all reached the conclusion that each can best be helped by the common action of all. And it is in this spirit that our visitors have met with us and discussed our common problems. The great international conference of this summer that lies before us must succeed.[6] The future of the world de-

[5] Preparatory to the London Economic Conference (see next note), Roosevelt was visited by representatives from eleven countries.

[6] The London Economic Conference met from June 12 to July 27, 1933. It was a distinct failure, dashing hopes for international economic cooperation and stabilization. A good part of the failure must be attributed to Roosevelt's own decision, cabled to Secretary of State Cordell Hull in early July, rejecting currency stabilization. Roosevelt made this controversial decision because he believed that the American dollar was priced too high on world markets. The

mands it, and we have each of us pledged ourselves to the best joint efforts to that end.

To you, the people of this country, all of us in Washington, the members of the Congress and the members of this administration, owe a profound debt of gratitude. Throughout the depression you have been patient. You have granted us wide powers; you have encouraged us with a widespread approval of our purposes. Every ounce of strength, every resource at our command, we have devoted and we are devoting to the end of justifying your confidence. We are encouraged to believe that a wise and sensible beginning has been made. In the present spirit of mutual confidence, in the present spirit of mutual encouragement we go forward.

And in conclusion, my friends, may I express to the National Broadcasting Company and to the Columbia Broadcasting System my thanks for the facilities which they have made available to me tonight.[7]

---

sinking of the conference signaled an American economic isolationism that would soon have its counterpart in the diplomatic and military realm as well.

[7] This final paragraph, thanking the networks, was added to the prepared text.

PRAISING THE FIRST HUNDRED DAYS AND BOOSTING THE NRA [1]

WITH THE SPECIAL congressional session ended on June 16, the time had come for an assessment of the work of the First Hundred Days. Roosevelt attempted that assessment on July 24 in his third Fireside Chat. He insisted, as usual, that the New Deal had "not been just a collection of haphazard schemes but rather the orderly component parts of a connected and logical whole," trying to create the impression that the program had a unity that was, in fact, never present in it. As the speech progressed, however, its real purpose became obvious: to whip up enthusiasm and support for the National Industrial Recovery Act (NIRA) and for the National Recovery Administration (NRA) that it set up. More than half of the address was devoted to that single program.

The NIRA (called by historian Arthur S. Link "the most pretentious piece of legislation ever presented to Congress to that time") was hastily drawn—in order to head off competing recovery suggestions from labor and the Chamber of Commerce. Roosevelt hoped that the NRA would be able to stabilize the economy by reducing unemployment, paying decent wages to workers so that they could purchase products, limiting overproduction so that prices would rise to a profitable level, and eliminating cutthroat competition. At the insistence of Secretary of Labor Frances Perkins, the law also contained a provision that guaranteed labor the right to collective bargaining.

How were these highly ambitious goals to be accomplished? Each industry would draw up a code that would lay down the guidelines for proper behavior within that industry. These codes were to be arrived at jointly by representatives of management, labor, and the public. They were then submitted for approval to Washington. In the

---

[1] No recording appears to have been made of this speech. For the text, the editors have relied on the transcript made by the White House stenographer from his shorthand notes taken at the time the speech was made. We wish to express our gratitude to the Franklin D. Roosevelt Library at Hyde Park, New York, for providing this transcript.

meantime, the Roosevelt administration drew up a "blanket code" of behavior that would suffice until the industrywide committees could complete their work. The experiment got off to a flying start as hundreds of thousands of employers, covering millions of workers, eagerly subscribed to the blanket code. The whole effort, as can be seen in this Fireside Chat, was accompanied by drummed-up enthusiasm and considerable official publicity. It was fashionable to compare the project to a war and to use military metaphors to describe it; NRA parades were held in countless cities and towns across the country. The slogan We Do Our Part was seen everywhere; so was the chief symbol of the crusade, the Blue Eagle, which was displayed proudly by those who joined the patriotic work of battling the depression by rebuilding the economy through the NRA.

By the time the code-making phase ended (February 1934), the NRA had approved 557 basic codes and 200 supplementary ones, and it did not take very long for critics to see what was wrong with them. Although the codes were supposed to be written jointly by labor, management, and the public, it became obvious that most of the time management had the greatest influence in laying down the rules. Within each industry, moreover, the giants wielded the most influence, and they tended to formulate regulations that favored themselves at the expense of small producers. Old progressives were quick to see, finally, that the NRA permitted businessmen to conspire to restrain trade—a power that reformers had tried to keep out of their hands, through antitrust legislation, since the administration of Benjamin Harrison.

Almost immediately after the initial enthusiasm, therefore, the entire NRA experiment encountered substantial and steadily growing opposition. There were even some within official circles who were not terribly sorry when the United States Supreme Court declared the experiment unconstitutional in May 1935.

AFTER THE ADJOURNMENT of the historical special session of the Congress five weeks ago I purposely refrained from addressing you for two very good reasons.

First, I think that we all wanted the opportunity of a little quiet thought to examine and assimilate in a mental picture the crowding events of the hundred days which had been devoted to the starting of the wheels of the New Deal.

Secondly, I wanted a few weeks in which to set up the new administrative organization and to see the first fruits of our careful planning.

I think it will interest you if I set forth the fundamentals of this planning for national recovery; and this I am very certain will make it abundantly clear to you that all of the proposals and all of the legislation since the fourth day of March have not been just a collection of haphazard schemes but rather the orderly component parts of a connected and logical whole.

Long before inauguration day I became convinced that individual effort and local effort and even disjointed federal effort had failed and of necessity would fail and, therefore, that a rounded leadership by the federal government had become a necessity both of theory and of fact. Such leadership, however, had its beginning in preserving and strengthening the credit of the United States government, because without that no leadership was a possibility. For years the government had not lived within its income. The immediate task was to bring our regular expenses within our revenues. That has been done.

It may seem inconsistent for a government to cut down its regular expenses and at the same time to borrow and to spend billions for an emergency. But it is not inconsistent because a large portion of the emergency money has been paid out in the form of sound loans which will be repaid to the Treasury over a period of years; and to cover the rest of the emergency money we have imposed taxes to pay the interest and the installments on that part of the debt.

So you will see that we have kept our credit good. We have built a granite foundation in a period of confusion. That foundation of the federal credit stands there broad and sure. It is the base of the whole recovery plan.

Then came the part of the problem that concerned the credit of the individual citizens themselves. You and I know of the banking crisis and of the great danger to the savings of our people. On March 6 every national bank was closed. One month later 90 percent of the deposits in the national banks had been made available to the depositors. Today only about 5 percent of the deposits in national banks are still tied up. The condition relating to state banks, while not quite so good on a percentage basis, is showing a steady reduction in the total of frozen deposits—a result much better than we had expected three months ago.

The problem of the credit of the individual was made more difficult because of another fact. The dollar was a different dollar from the one with which the average debt had been incurred. For this reason large numbers of people were actually losing possession of and title to their farms and homes. All of you know the financial steps which have been taken to correct this inequality. In addition the Home Loan Act, the Farm Loan Act, and the bankruptcy act[2] were passed.

It was a vital necessity to restore purchasing power by reducing the debt and interest charges upon our people, but while we were helping people to save their credit it was at the same time absolutely essential to do something about the physical needs of hundreds of thousands who were in dire straits at that very moment. Municipal and state aid were being stretched to the limit. We appropriated half a billion dollars to supplement their efforts and in addition, as you know, we have put 300,000 young men into practical and useful work in our forests and to prevent flood and soil erosion. The wages they earn are going in greater part to the support of the nearly 1 million people who constitute their families.[3]

In this same classification we can properly place the great public works program[4] running to a total of over $3 billion—to be used for highways and ships and flood prevention and inland navigation and thousands of self-sustaining state and municipal improvements. Two points should be made clear in the allotting and administration of these projects—first, we are using the utmost care to choose labor creating quick-acting, useful projects, avoiding the smell of the pork barrel; and secondly, we are hoping that at least half of the money will come back to the government from projects which will pay for themselves over a period of years.

[2] The Glass-Steagall Banking Act was signed on June 16. It guaranteed Americans' bank deposits up to $2,500 through a new Federal Deposit Insurance Corporation. The sum insurable was raised to $5,000 in 1935 and to $10,000 after World War II.

[3] Roosevelt refers here to the Federal Emergency Relief Act of May 12 and to the Civilian Conservation Corps (CCC). Most of the dollar-per-day wages of the young men in the CCC was sent directly home to their families.

[4] Title II of the NIRA, incorporated into the bill at the last minute, created the Public Works Administration (PWA). It was administered by Secretary of the Interior Harold Ickes. The PWA was authorized to distribute $3.3 billion and during its existence undertook more than 30,000 construction projects around the nation.

Thus far I have spoken primarily of the foundation stones—the measures that were necessary to reestablish credit and to head people in the opposite direction by preventing distress and providing as much work as possible through governmental agencies. Now I come to the links which will build us a more lasting prosperity. I have said that we cannot attain that in a nation half-boom and half-broke. If all of our people have work and fair wages and fair profits, they can buy the products of their neighbors and business is good. But if you take away the wages and the profits of half of them, business is only half as good. It doesn't help much if the fortunate half is very prosperous—the best way is for everybody to be reasonably prosperous.

For many years the two great barriers to a normal prosperity have been low farm prices and the creeping paralysis of unemployment. These factors have cut the purchasing power of the country in half. I promised action. Congress did its part when it passed the farm and the industrial recovery acts. Today we are putting these two acts to work and they will work if people understand their plain objectives.

First, the farm act: It is based on the fact that the purchasing power of nearly half our population depends on adequate prices for farm products. We have been producing more of some crops than we consume or can sell in a depressed world market. The cure is not to produce so much. Without our help the farmers cannot get together and cut production, and the farm bill gives them a method of bringing their production down to a reasonable level and of obtaining reasonable prices for their crops. I have clearly stated that this method is in a sense experimental, but so far as we have gone we have reason to believe that it will produce good results.

It is obvious that if we can greatly increase the purchasing power of the tens of millions of our people who make a living from farming and the distribution of farm crops, we will greatly increase the consumption of those goods which are turned out by industry.

That brings me to the final step: bringing back industry along sound lines.

Last autumn, on several occasions, I expressed my faith that we can make possible by democratic self-discipline in industry general increases in wages and shortening of hours sufficient to enable industry to pay its own workers enough to let those workers buy and use the things that their labor produces. This can be done only if we permit and encourage cooperative action in industry because it is obvious that without united action a few selfish men in each competitive group will pay starvation wages and insist on long hours of work. Others in that group must either follow suit or close up shop. We have seen the result of action of that kind in the continuing descent into the economic hell of the past four years.

There is a clear way to reverse that process: If all employers in each competitive group agree to pay their workers the same wages—reasonable wages—and require the same hours—reasonable hours—then higher wages and shorter hours will hurt no employer. Moreover, such action is better for the employer than unemployment and low wages, because it makes more buyers for his product. That is the simple idea which is the very heart of the Industrial Recovery Act.

On the basis of this simple principle of everybody doing things together, we are starting out on this nationwide attack on unemployment. It will succeed if our people understand it—in the big industries, in the little shops, in the great cities and in the small villages. There is nothing complicated about it and there is nothing particularly new in the principle. It goes back to the basic idea of society and of the nation itself that people acting in a group can accomplish things which no individual acting alone could even hope to bring about.

Here is an example. In the cotton textile code and in other agreements already signed, child labor has been abolished. That makes me personally happier than any other one thing with which I have been connected since I came to Washington. In the textile industry—an industry which came to me spontaneously and with a splendid cooperation as soon as the Recovery Act was signed—child labor was an old evil. But no employer acting alone was able to wipe it out. If one employer tried it, or if one state tried it, the costs of operation rose so high that it was impossible to compete with the employers or states which had failed to act. The moment the Recovery Act was passed, this monstrous thing which neither opinion nor law could reach through years of effort went out in a flash. As a British editorial put it, we did more under a code in one day than they in England had been able to do under the common law in eighty-five years of effort. I use this incident, my friends, not to boast of what has already been done but to point the way to you for even greater cooperative efforts this summer and autumn.

We are not going through another winter like the last. I doubt if ever any people so bravely and cheerfully endured a season half so bitter. We cannot ask America to continue to face such needless hardships. It is time for courageous action, and the Recovery Bill gives us the means to conquer unemployment with exactly the same weapon that we have used to strike down child labor.

The proposition is simply this: If all employers will act together to shorten hours and raise wages we can put people back to work. No employer will suffer, because the relative level of competitive cost will advance by the same amount for all. But if any considerable group should lag or shirk, this great opportunity will pass us by and we will go into another desperate winter. This must not happen.

We have sent out to all employers an agreement which is the result of weeks of consultation. This agreement checks against the voluntary codes of nearly all the large industries which have already been submitted. This blanket agreement carries the unanimous approval of the three boards which I have appointed to advise in this, boards representing the great leaders in labor, in industry, and in social service. The agreement has already brought a flood of approval from every state, and from so wide a cross-section of the common calling of industry that I know it is fair for all. It is a plan—deliberate, reasonable, and just—intended to put into effect at once the most important of the broad principles which are being established, industry by industry, through codes. Naturally, it takes a good deal of organizing and a great many hearings and many months to get these codes perfected and signed, and we cannot wait for all of them to go through. The blanket agreements, however, which I am sending to every employer will start the wheels turning now, and not six months from now.

There are, of course, men, a few of them, who might thwart this great common purpose by seeking selfish advantage. There are adequate penalties in the law, but I am now asking the cooperation that comes from opinion and from conscience. These are the only instruments we shall use in this great summer offensive against unemployment. But we shall use them to the limit to protect the willing from the laggard and to make the plan succeed.

In war, in the gloom of night attack, soldiers wear a bright badge on their shoulders to be sure that comrades do not fire on comrades. On that principle, those who cooperate in this program must know each other at a glance. That is why we have provided a badge of honor for this purpose, a simple design with a legend, We Do Our

Part; and I ask that all those who join with me shall display that badge prominently. It is essential to our purpose.

Already all the great, basic industries have come forward willingly with proposed codes, and in these codes they accept the principles leading to mass reemployment. But, important as is this heartening demonstration, the richest field for results is among the small employers, those whose contribution will give new work for from one to ten people. These smaller employers are indeed a vital part of the backbone of the country, and the success of our plans lies largely in their hands.

Already the telegrams and letters are pouring into the White House—messages from employers who ask that their names be placed on this special roll of honor. They represent great corporations and companies, and partnerships and individuals. I ask that even before the dates set in the agreements which we have sent out, the employers of the country who have not already done so—the big fellows and the little fellows—shall at once write or telegraph to me personally at the White House, expressing their intention of going through with the plan. And it is my purpose to keep posted in the post office of every town, a roll of honor of all those who join with me.

I want to take this occasion to say to the twenty-four governors who are now in conference in San Francisco that nothing thus far has helped in strengthening this great movement more than their resolutions adopted at the very outset of their meeting, giving this plan their instant and unanimous approval, and pledging to support it in their states.[5]

To the men and women whose lives have been darkened by the fact or the fear of unemployment, I am justified in saying a word of encouragement because the codes and the agreements already approved, or about to be passed upon, prove that the plan does raise wages, and that it does put people back to work. You can look on every employer who adopts the plan as one who is doing his part, and those employers deserve well of everyone who works for a living. It will be clear to you, as it is to me, that while the shirking employer may undersell his competitor, the saving he thus makes is made at the expense of his country's welfare.

[5] The governors, gathered at their annual conference in California, passed a resolution promising "whole-hearted and active support" of the president's recovery program.

While we are making this great common effort there should be no discord and dispute. This is no time to cavil or to question the standard set by this universal agreement. It is time for patience and understanding and cooperation. The workers of this country have rights under this law which cannot be taken from them, and nobody will be permitted to whittle them away but, on the other hand, no aggression is now necessary to attain those rights. The whole country will be united to get them for you. The principle that applies to the employers applies to the workers as well, and I ask you workers to cooperate in the same spirit.

When Andrew Jackson, "Old Hickory," died, someone asked, "Will he go to heaven?" and the answer was, "He will if he wants to." If I am asked whether the American people will pull themselves out of this depression, I answer, "They will if they want to." The essence of the plan is a universal limitation of hours of work per week for any individual by common consent, and a universal payment of wages above the minimum, also by common consent. I cannot guarantee the success of this nationwide plan, but the people of this country can guarantee its success. I have no faith in "cure-alls" but I believe that we can greatly influence economic forces. I have no sympathy with the professional economists who insist that things must run their course and that human agencies can have no influence on economic ills. One reason is that I happen to know that professional economists have changed their definition of economic laws every five or ten years for a very long time. But I do have faith, and retain faith, in the strength of common purpose, and in the strength of unified action taken by the American people.

That is why I am describing to you the simple purposes and the solid foundations upon which our program of recovery is built. That is why I am asking the employers of the nation to sign this common covenant with me—to sign it in the name of patriotism and humanity. That is why I am asking the workers to go along with us in a spirit of understanding and of helpfulness.

ASSESSING THE NEW DEAL AND MANIPULATING THE CURRENCY [1]

BY THE END of October 1933, most of the major pieces of the early New Deal were in place and functioning. Although prices rose slightly, production figures began to slide downward from mid-summer and into the fall. In this Fireside Chat, nonetheless, the president chose to report encouraging progress all along the line: unemployment was falling; direct relief was continuing to succor the most unfortunate; farms and homes were being saved from foreclosure; the public works program was continuing apace; banks were growing stronger and more stable; and the prices for commodities were slowly but steadily rising. As usual, Roosevelt placed most stress on the AAA and the NRA, two key "pillars" in the structure of economic recovery. In short, the largest part of the address was designed to offset some disappointing economic news by reporting steady advances in many fields, to assure the American people that things were on track and moving forward—even if there was still some way to go in many areas of economic concern.

The news in this Fireside Chat came near the end and touched, once again, upon the highly complicated matter of currency and the gold standard. If limiting production had not succeeded in raising prices quickly enough, perhaps inflating the currency would do the trick. Three days after this speech, President Roosevelt ordered the Reconstruction Finance Corporation to buy gold at a higher price than the current world price (on the theory that commodity prices would also rise); and the gold value of the American dollar was fixed at sixty-six cents, a devaluation that the president hoped would also serve to raise prices. When these hopes did not materialize, Roose-

[1] No recording appears to have been made of this speech. For the text, the editors have relied on the transcript made by the White House stenographer from his shorthand notes taken at the time the speech was made. We wish to express our gratitude to the Franklin D. Roosevelt Library at Hyde Park, New York, for providing this transcript.

velt surrendered any further attempt to cure the depression through manipulating the currency.

IT IS THREE MONTHS since I have talked with the people of this country about our national problems; but during this period many things have happened, and I am glad to say that the major part of them have greatly helped the well-being of the average citizens.

Because, in every step which your government is taking we are thinking in terms of the average of you—in the old words, "the greatest good to the greatest number"—we, as reasonable people, cannot expect to bring definite benefits to every person or to every occupation or business, or industry or agriculture. In the same way, no reasonable person can expect that in this short space of time, during which new machinery had to be not only put to work, but first set up, that every locality in every one of the forty-eight states of the country could share equally and simultaneously in the trend to better times.

The whole picture, however—the average of the whole territory from coast to coast, the average of the whole population of 120,000,000 people—shows to any person willing to look, facts and action of which you and I can be proud.

In the early spring of this year there were actually and proportionately more people out of work in this country than in any other nation in the world. Fair estimates showed 12 or 13 millions unemployed last March. Among those there were, of course, several millions who could be classed as normally unemployed—people who worked occasionally when they felt like it, and others who preferred not to work at all. It seems, therefore, fair to say that there were about 10 millions of our citizens who earnestly, and in many cases hungrily, were seeking work and could not get it. Of these, in the short space of a few months, I am convinced that at least 4 millions have been given employment—or, saying it another way, 40 percent of those seeking work have found it.

That does not mean, my friends, that I am satisfied, or that you are satisfied that our work is ended. We have a long way to go but we are on the way.

How are we constructing the edifice of recovery—the temple which, when completed, will no longer be a temple of money changers or of beggars, but rather a temple dedicated to and maintained for a greater social justice, a greater welfare for America—the habitation of a sound economic life? We are building, stone by stone, the columns which will support that habitation. Those columns are many in number, and though for a moment the progress of one column may disturb the progress on the pillar next to it, the work on all of them must proceed without let or hindrance.

We all know that immediate relief for the unemployed was the first essential of such a structure and that is why I speak first of the fact that three hundred thousand young men have been given employment all through this winter in the Civilian Conservation Corps camps in almost every part of the nation.

So, too, we have, as you know, expended greater sums in cooperation with states and localities for work relief and home relief than ever before—sums which during the coming winter cannot be lessened for the very simple reason that though several million people have gone back to work, the necessities of those who have not yet obtained work is more severe than at this time last year.

Then we come to the relief that is being given to those who are in danger of losing their farms or their homes. New machinery had to be set up for farm credit and for home credit in every one of the 3,100 counties of the United States, and every day that passes is saving homes and farms to hundreds of families. I have publicly asked that foreclosures on farms and chattels and on homes be delayed until every mortgagor in the country shall have had full opportunity to take advantage of federal credit. I make the further request which many of you know has already been made through the great federal credit organizations that if there is any family in the United States about to lose its home or about to lose its chattels, that family should telegraph at once either to the Farm Credit Administration or the Home Owners Loan Corporation in Washington requesting their help.

Two other great agencies are in full swing. The Reconstruction Finance Corporation continues to lend large sums to industry and finance with the definite objective of making easy the extending of credit to industry, commerce, and finance.

The program of public works in three months has advanced to this point: Out of a total appropriated for public works of

$3,300,000,000, $1,800,000,000 has already been allocated to federal projects of all kinds and literally in every part of the United States and work on these is starting forward. In addition, $300 millions have been allocated to public works to be carried out by states, municipalities, and private organizations, such as those undertaking slum clearance. The balance of the public works money—nearly all of it intended for state or local projects—waits only on the presentation of proper projects by the states and localities themselves. Washington has the money and is waiting for the proper projects to which to allot it.

Another pillar in the making is the Agricultural Adjustment Administration. I have been amazed by the extraordinary degree of cooperation given to the government by the cotton farmers in the South, the wheat farmers of the West, the tobacco farmers of the Southeast, and I am confident that the corn-hog farmers of the Middle West will come through in the same magnificent fashion. The problem we seek to solve had been steadily getting worse for twenty years but during the last six months we have made more rapid progress than any nation has ever made in a like period of time. It is true that in July farm commodity prices had been pushed up higher than they are today, but that push came in part from pure speculation by people who could not tell you the difference between wheat and rye, by people who had never seen cotton growing, by people who did not know that hogs were fed on corn—people who have no real interest in the farmer and his problems.

In spite, however, of the speculative reaction from the speculative advance, it seems to be well established that during the course of the year 1933 the farmers of the United States will receive 33 percent more dollars for what they have produced than they received in the year 1932. Put in another way, they will receive $400 in 1933, where they received $300 the year before. That, remember, is for the average of the country, for I have reports that some sections are not any better off than they were a year ago. This applies among the major products, especially to cattle raising and the dairy industry. We are going after those problems as fast as we can.

I do not hesitate to say, in the simplest, clearest language of which I am capable, that although the prices of many products of the farm have gone up and although many farm families are better off than they were last year, I am not satisfied either with the amount or the extent of the rise, and that it is definitely a part of our policy to increase the rise and to extend it to those products which have as yet felt no benefit. If we cannot do this one way we will do it another. Do it, we will.

Standing beside the pillar of the farm—the AAA—is the pillar of industry—the NRA. Its object is to put industry and business workers into employment and to increase their purchasing power through increased wages.

It has abolished child labor. It has eliminated the sweatshop. It has ended sixty cents a week paid in some mills and eighty cents a week paid in some mines. The measure of the growth of this pillar lies in the total figures of reemployment which I have already given you, and in the fact that reemployment is continuing and not stopping. The secret of NRA is cooperation. That cooperation has been voluntarily given through the signing of the blanket codes and through the signing of specific codes which already include all of the greater industries of the nation.

In the vast majority of cases, in the vast majority of localities—the NRA has been given support in unstinted measure. We know that there are chiselers. At the bottom of every case of criticism and obstruction we have found some selfish interest, some private axe to grind.

Ninety percent of complaints come from misconception. For example, it has been said that NRA has failed to raise the price of wheat and corn and hogs; that NRA has not loaned enough money for local public works. Of course, NRA has nothing whatsoever to do with the price of farm products, nor with public works. It has to do only with industrial organization for economic planning to wipe put unfair practices and to create reemployment. Even in the field of business and industry, NRA does not apply to the rural communities or to towns of under twenty-five hundred population, except insofar as those towns contain factories or chain stores which come under a specific code.

It is also true that among the chiselers to whom I have referred, there are not only the big chiselers but also petty chiselers who seek to make undue profit on untrue statements.

Let me cite to you the example of the salesman in a store in a large eastern city who tried to justify the increase in the price of a cotton shirt from one dollar and a half to two dollars and a half by saying to the customer that it was due to the cotton-processing tax.[2] Actually in that shirt there was about one pound of cotton and the processing tax amounted to four and a quarter cents on that pound of cotton.

At this point it is only fair that I should give credit to the 60 or 70 million people who live in the cities and larger towns of the nation for their understanding and their willingness to go along with the payment of even these small processing taxes, though they know full well that the proportion of the processing taxes on cotton goods and on food products paid for by city dwellers goes 100 percent towards increasing the agricultural income of the farm dwellers of the land.

The last pillar of which I speak is that of the money of the country in the banks of the country. There are two simple facts.

First, the federal government is about to spend $1 billion as an immediate loan on the frozen or nonliquid assets of all banks closed since January 1, 1933, giving a liberal appraisal to those assets. This money will be in the hands of the depositors as quickly as it is humanly possible to get it out.

Secondly, the government bank deposit insurance on all accounts up to $2,500 goes into effect on January 1. We are now engaged in seeing to it that on or before that date the banking capital structure will be built up by the government to the point that the banks will be in sound condition when the insurance goes into effect.

Finally, I repeat what I have said on many occasions, that ever since last March the definite policy of the government has been to restore commodity price levels. The object has been the attainment of such a level as will enable agriculture and industry once more to give work to the unemployed. It has been to make possible the payment of public and private debts more nearly at the price level at which they were incurred. It has been gradually to restore a balance in the price structure so that farmers may exchange their products for the products of industry on a fairer exchange basis. It has been and is also the purpose to prevent prices from rising beyond the point necessary to attain these ends. The permanent welfare and security of every class of our people ultimately depends on our attainment of these purposes.

[2] Subsidies to farmers under the Agricultural Adjustment Act came from a tax on processors of certain agricultural products, including cotton. It was the processing tax feature of the AAA that resulted in the act being declared unconstitutional in 1936.

Obviously, and because hundreds of different kinds of crops and industrial occupations in the huge territory that makes up this nation are involved, we cannot reach the goal in only a few months. We may take one year or two years or three years.

No one who considers the plain facts of our situation believes that commodity prices, especially agricultural prices, are high enough yet.

Some people are putting the cart before the horse. They want a permanent revaluation of the dollar first. It is the government's policy to restore the price level first. I would not know, and no one else could tell, just what the permanent valuation of the dollar will be. To guess at a permanent gold valuation now would certainly require later changes caused by later facts.

When we have restored the price level, we shall seek to establish and maintain a dollar which will not change its purchasing and debt-paying power during the succeeding generation. I said that in my message to the American delegation in London last July. And I say it now once more.

Because of conditions in this country and because of events beyond our control in other parts of the world, it becomes increasingly important to develop and apply the further measures which may be necessary from time to time to control the gold value of our own dollar at home.

Our dollar is now altogether too greatly influenced by the accidents of international trade, by the internal policies of other nations, and by political disturbance in other continents. Therefore the United States must take firmly in its own hands the control of the gold value of our dollar. This is necessary in order to prevent dollar disturbances from swinging us away from our ultimate goal, namely, the continued recovery of our commodity prices.

As a further effective means to this end, I am going to establish a Government market for gold in the United States. Therefore, under the clearly defined authority of existing law, I am authorizing the Reconstruction Finance Corporation to buy gold newly mined in the United States at prices to be determined from time to time after consultation with the secretary of the treasury and the president. Whenever necessary to the end in view, we shall also buy or sell gold in the world market.

My aim in taking this step is to establish and maintain continuous control.

This is a policy and not an expedient.

It is not to be used merely to offset a temporary fall in prices. We are thus continuing to move towards a managed currency.

You will recall the dire predictions made last spring by those who did not agree with our common policies of raising prices by direct means. What actually happened stood out in sharp contrast with those predictions. Government credit is high, prices have risen in part. Doubtless prophets of evil still exist in our midst. But government credit will be maintained and a sound currency will accompany a rise in the American commodity price level.

I have told you tonight the story of our steady but sure work in building our common recovery. In my promises to you both before and after March 4, I made two things plain: First, that I pledged no miracles and, second, that I would do my best.

I thank you for your patience and your faith. Our troubles will not be over tomorrow, but we are on our way and we are headed in the right direction.

ANSWERING THE CRITICS[1]

THE PERFORMANCE of the Seventy-third Congress between January and June, 1934, was almost as extraordinary as had been its performance during the First Hundred Days. In this Fireside Chat the president summarizes the record of the Congress, praises its wisdom and courage, and reviews the achievements of the New Deal thus far, under the headings of relief, recovery, reform, and reconstruction.

The most notable aspect of this speech, however, may be that the president felt forced to respond to recent criticisms. There could be no doubt that complaints about both the New Deal and the president himself were growing steadily. The objections were being raised in part by those on the left who felt that the government had not done enough for the truly destitute. Perhaps Roosevelt's reference, in this speech, to his developing plans for "social insurance" was a subtle request for patience from these reformers and their followers.

But the most stinging abuse of his legislative program came from conservatives and from the business community in particular. One of the most irritating voices belonged to Herbert Hoover. The former president was busy assailing the New Deal in speeches around the country, and his book, *The Challenge to Liberty*, to be published in September, summarized much of the conservative critique. These complaints were institutionalized with the formation of the Liberty League in August. The message of these critics was simple: President Roosevelt had accumulated far too much power; the federal government was rapidly and dangerously invading areas of America's economic and social life where it had never gone before; and in this process, free enterprise, traditional American initiative, and sacred individual freedoms were in grave danger of being uprooted. Solemn

---

[1]No recording appears to have been made of this speech. For the text, the editors have relied on the transcript made by the White House stenographer from his shorthand notes taken at the time the speech was made. We wish to express our gratitude to the Franklin D. Roosevelt Library at Hyde Park, New York, for providing this transcript.

warnings against excessive national "regimentation" were issued, and cautionary comparisons to Italian Fascism, Stalinist Communism, and German Nazism were drawn.

Roosevelt's answer, as can be seen clearly in this Fireside Chat, came in two ways. First, he charged that the criticism was coming from those selfish and interested individuals who hoped to recover lost political or economic power, those "comparative few who seek to retain or to gain position or riches or both by some shortcut which is harmful to the greater good." Second, Roosevelt vehemently insisted that everything that the government had done to combat the depression was done well within the traditional boundaries of the American political system. Whether measured against the sacred guarantees of the Bill of Rights or by any other standard, normal American freedoms were as safe as they had ever been; indeed, Roosevelt declared, "what we are doing today is a necessary fulfillment of what Americans have always been doing—a fulfillment of old and tested American ideals."

Both the president and his critics, of course, had their eye on the coming congressional elections, only four months away.

IT HAS BEEN several months since I have talked with you concerning the problems of government. Since January, those of us in whom you have vested responsibility have been engaged in the fulfillment of plans and policies which had been widely discussed in previous months. It seemed to us our duty not only to make the right path clear but also to tread that path.

As we review the achievements of this session of the Seventy-third Congress, it is made increasingly clear that its task was essentially that of completing and fortifying the work it had begun in March 1933. That was no easy task, but the Congress was equal to it. It has been well said that while there were a few exceptions, this Congress displayed a greater freedom from mere partisanship than any other peacetime Congress since the administration of President Washington himself. The session was distinguished by the extent and variety of legislation enacted and by the intelligence and good-will of debate upon these measures.

I mention only a few of the major enactments. It provided for the readjustment of the debt burden through the Corporate and Municipal Bankruptcy Acts and the Farm Relief Act. It lent a hand to industry by encouraging loans to solvent industries unable to secure adequate help from banking institutions. It strengthened the integrity of finance through the regulation of securities exchanges. It provided a rational method of increasing our volume of foreign trade through reciprocal trading agreements. It strengthened our naval forces to conform with the intentions and permission of existing treaty rights. It made further advances towards peace in industry through the labor adjustment act. It supplemented our agricultural policy through measures widely demanded by farmers themselves and intended to avert price destroying surpluses. It strengthened the hand of the federal government in its attempts to suppress gangster crime. It took definite steps toward a national housing program through an act which I signed today designed to encourage private capital in the rebuilding of the homes of the nation. It created a permanent federal body for the just regulation of all forms of communication, including the telephone, the telegraph, and the radio. Finally, and I believe most important, it reorganized, simplified, and made more fair and just our monetary system, setting up standards and policies adequate to meet the necessities of modern, economic life, doing justice to both gold and silver as the metal bases behind the currency of the United States.[2]

In the consistent development of our previous efforts toward the saving and safeguarding of our national life, I have continued to recognize three related steps. The first was relief, because the primary concern of any government dominated by the humane ideals of democracy is the simple principle that in a land of vast resources no one should be permitted to starve. Relief was and continues to be our first consideration. It calls for large expenditures and will continue in modified form to do so for a long time to come. We may as well recognize that fact. It comes from the paralysis that arose as the aftereffect of that unfortunate decade characterized by a mad

[2] These are the new laws to which President Roosevelt refers in this paragraph: the Corporate Bankruptcy Act (June 7); the Municipal Bankruptcy Act (May 24); the Farm Mortgage Refinancing Act (January 31); the Securities Exchange Act (June 6); the Vinson Naval Parity Act (March 27); the Labor Disputes Joint Resolution (June 19); the Jones-Connally Farm Relief Act, the Bankhead (Cotton Control) Act, and the Jones-Costigan Sugar Act (April 7 and 21, and May 9); the Crime Control Acts (May 18); the National Housing Act (June 28); the Communications Act (June 19); the Gold Reserve Act of 1934 (January 30) and the Silver Purchase Act (June 19).

chase for unearned riches and an unwillingness of leaders in almost every walk of life to look beyond their own schemes and speculations. In our administration of relief we follow two principles: First, that direct giving shall, wherever possible, be supplemented by provision for useful and remunerative work and, second, that where families in their existing surroundings will in all human probability never find an opportunity for full self-maintenance, happiness, and enjoyment, we will try to give them a new chance in new surroundings.

The second step was recovery, and it is sufficient for me to ask each and every one of you to compare the situation in agriculture and in industry today with what it was fifteen months ago.

At the same time we have recognized the necessity of reform and reconstruction: reform because much of our trouble today and in the past few years has been due to a lack of understanding of the elementary principles of justice and fairness by those in whom leadership in business and finance was placed; reconstruction because new conditions in our economic life as well as old but neglected conditions had to be corrected.

Substantial gains well known to all of you have justified our course. I could cite statistics to you as unanswerable measures of our national progress—statistics to show the gain in the average weekly pay envelope of workers in the great majority of industries, statistics to show hundreds of thousands reemployed in private industries and other hundreds of thousands given new employment through the expansion of direct and indirect government assistance of many kinds; although, of course, there are those exceptions in professional pursuits whose economic improvement, of necessity, will be delayed. I also could cite statistics to show the great rise in the value of farm products—statistics to prove the demand for consumers' goods, ranging all the way from food and clothing to automobiles and of late to prove the rise in the demand for durable goods, statistics to cover the great increase in bank deposits and to show the scores of thousands of homes and of farms which have been saved from foreclosure.

But the simplest way for each of you to judge recovery lies in the plain facts of your own individual situation. Are you better off than you were last year? Are your debts less burdensome? Is your bank account more secure? Are your working conditions better? Is your faith in your own individual future more firmly grounded?

Also, let me put to you another simple question: have you as an individual paid too high a price for these gains? Plausible self-seekers and theoretical diehards will tell you of the loss of individual liberty. Answer this question also out of the facts of your own life. Have you lost any of your rights or liberty or constitutional freedom of action and choice? Turn to the Bill of Rights of the Constitution, which I have solemnly sworn to maintain and under which your freedom rests secure. Read each provision of that Bill of Rights and ask yourself whether you personally have suffered the impairment of a single jot of these great assurances. I have no question in my mind as to what your answer will be. The record is written in the experiences of your own personal lives.

In other words, it is not the overwhelming majority of the farmers or manufacturers or workers who deny the substantial gains of the past year. The most vociferous of the doubting Thomases may be divided roughly into two groups: First, those who seek special political privilege and, second, those who seek special financial privilege. About a year ago I used as an illustration the 90 percent of the cotton manufacturers of the United States who wanted to do the right thing by their employees and by the public but were prevented from doing so by the 10 percent who undercut them by unfair practices and un-American standards. It is well for us to remember that humanity is a long way from being perfect and that a selfish minority in every walk of life—farming, business, finance, and even government service itself—will always continue to think of themselves first and their fellow being second.

In the working out of a great national program which seeks the primary good of the greater number, it is true that the toes of some people are being stepped on and are going to be stepped on. But these toes belong to the comparative few who seek to retain or to gain position or riches or both by some shortcut which is harmful to the greater good.

In the execution of the powers conferred on it by Congress, the administration needs and will tirelessly seek the best ability that the country affords. Public service offers better rewards in the opportunity for service than ever before in our history—not great salaries, but enough to live on. In the building of this service there are coming to us men and women with ability and courage from every part of the union. The days of the seeking of mere party advantage through the misuses of public power are drawing to a close. We are increasingly demanding and getting devotion to the public service on the part of every member of the administration, high and low.

The program of the past year is definitely in operation and that operation month by month is being made to fit into the web of old and new conditions. This process of evolution is well illustrated by the constant changes in detailed organization and method going on in the National Recovery Administration. With every passing month we are making strides in the orderly handling of the relationship between employees and employers. Conditions differ, of course, in almost every part of the country and in almost every industry. Temporary methods of adjustment are being replaced by more permanent machinery and, I am glad to say, by a growing recognition on the part of employers and employees of the desirability of maintaining fair relationships all around.

So also, while almost everybody has recognized the tremendous strides in the elimination of child labor, in the payment of not less than fair minimum wages, and in the shortening of hours, we are still feeling our way in solving problems which relate to self-government in industry, especially where such self-government tends to eliminate the fair operation of competition.

In this same process of evolution we are keeping before us the objectives of protecting on the one hand industry against chiselers within its own ranks, and on the other hand, the consumer through the maintenance of reasonable competition for the prevention of the unfair skyrocketing of retail prices.

But, in addition to this our immediate task, we must still look to the larger future. I have pointed out to the Congress that we are seeking to find the way once more to well-known, long-established, but to some degree forgotten ideals and values. We seek the security of the men, women, and children of the nation.

That security involves added means of providing better homes for the people of the nation. That is the first principle of our future program.

The second is to plan the use of land and water resources of this country to the end that the means of livelihood of our citizens may be more adequate to meet their daily needs.

And, finally, the third principle is to use the agencies of government to assist in the establishment of means to provide sound and adequate protection against the vicissitudes of modern life—in other words, social insurance.

Later in the year I hope to talk with you more fully about these plans.

A few timid people, who fear progress, will try to give you new and strange names for what we are doing. Sometimes they will call it "Fascism," sometimes "Communism," sometimes "regimentation," sometimes "Socialism." But, in so doing, they are trying to make very complex and theoretical something that is really very simple and very practical.

I believe in practical explanations and in practical policies. I believe that what we are doing today is a necessary fulfillment of what Americans have always been doing—a fulfillment of old and tested American ideals.

Let me give you a simple illustration:

While I am away from Washington this summer, a long-needed renovation of and addition to our White House office building is to be started. The architects have planned a few new rooms built into the present all-too-small one-story structure. We are going to include in this addition and in this renovation modern electrical wiring and modern plumbing and modern means of keeping the offices cool in the hot Washington summers. But the structural lines of the old Executive Office Building will remain. The artistic lines of the White House buildings were the creation of master builders when our republic was young. The simplicity and the strength of the structure remain in the face of every modern test. But within this magnificent pattern, the necessities of modern government business require constant reorganization and rebuilding.

If I were to listen to the arguments of some prophets of calamity who are talking these days, I should hesitate to make the alterations. I should fear that while I am away for a few weeks the architects might build some strange new Gothic tower or a factory building or perhaps a replica of the Kremlin or of the Potsdam Palace. But I have no such fears. The architects and builders are men of common sense and of artistic American tastes. They know that the principles of harmony and of necessity itself require that the building of the new structure shall blend with the essential lines of the old. It is this combination of the old and the new that marks orderly peaceful progress—not only in building buildings but in building government itself.

Our new structure is a part of and a fulfillment of the old.

All that we do seeks to fulfill the historic traditions of the American people. Other nations may sacrifice democracy for the transitory stimulation of old and discredited autocracies. We are restoring confidence and well-being under the rule of the people themselves. We remain, as John Marshall[3] said a century ago, "emphatically and truly, a government of the people." Our government "in form and in substance ... emanates from them. Its powers are granted by them, and are to be exercised directly on them, and for their benefits."

Before I close, I want to tell you of the interest and pleasure with which I look forward to the trip on which I hope to start in a few days.[4] It is a good thing for everyone who can possibly do so to get away at least once a year for a change of scene. I do not want to get into the position of not being able to see the forest because of the thickness of the trees.

I hope to visit our fellow Americans in Puerto Rico, in the Virgin Islands, in the canal zone, and in Hawaii. And, incidentally, it will give me an opportunity to exchange a friendly word of greeting to the presidents of our sister republics, Haiti, Colombia, and Panama.

After four weeks on board ship, I plan to land at a port in our Pacific Northwest, and then will come the best part of the whole trip, for I am hoping to inspect a number of our new great national projects on the Columbia, Missouri, and Mississippi rivers, to see some of our national parks and, incidentally, to learn much of actual conditions during the trip across the continent back to Washington.

While I was in France during the war our boys used to call the United States "God's country." Let us make it and keep it "God's country."

---

[3] John Marshall (1755–1835), the illustrious chief justice of the Supreme Court from 1801 until his death, was undoubtedly the central figure in the formation of federal law and judicial practice before the Civil War.

[4] Roosevelt left from Annapolis on July 1, aboard the USS *Houston*. The 10,000-mile tour ended with his return to the capital on August 10.

GOVERNMENT
AND MODERN CAPITALISM

FIVE WEEKS BEFORE the congressional elections, Roosevelt addressed the nation on the topic of America's industrial situation. More than other Fireside Chats, this one had a single and concentrated focus: the relations between capital, labor, and the government in a free society. And more than other Fireside Chats, this one frankly revealed a thoughtful philosophy about how those relations should be conducted.

With the election so close, the president was naturally eager to point out the gains that had been made by both labor and management because of the New Deal. He reminded workers of the growth in the number of jobs, the elimination of child labor, the shortening of the workweek, and the establishment of a minimum wage in many industries. He reminded businessmen of the federal loans that had kept many enterprises afloat, of the elimination of evils in banks and stock exchanges, and of the growth in profits; he also pledged his continuing faith in a system of free enterprise and individual initiative. To both halves of the industrial equation he pointed out that there was a long distance still to travel, and he registered a plea for reasonable cooperation in an effort to achieve industrial peace and harmony. Nevertheless, it is hard to read this speech and conclude that Roosevelt was being perfectly evenhanded in his treatment of labor and business. He chided labor for not using fully the governmental mechanisms available for settling disputes (while insisting that he had no desire to abolish the traditional weapons of industrial warfare). But he threatened business with genuine reforms of the NRA codes, reforms that would uproot the decidedly probusiness aspects of the experiment and that were very likely to upset the business community. (It was not a mere coincidence that throughout the late summer of 1934 businessmen were growing increasingly critical of Roosevelt and the New Deal.) The president hinted darkly that the government would review the pricing agreements in many of the

53

codes, the evasion of the antitrust laws, the limitation of production, and the whole matter of a fair annual (rather than a mere hourly) wage. Roosevelt was beginning to move toward the left—partly out of irritation with business ingratitude ("Now that these people are coming out of their storm cellars, they forget that there ever was a storm"), and partly to undercut angry voices from the left, like those of Upton Sinclair, Huey Long, and Francis Townsend, who were complaining about the New Deal's timidity and ineffectiveness. Within another twelve months few could doubt the leftward drift of Roosevelt's program.

In this address Roosevelt also made explicit the underlying economic philosophy of the New Deal. He argued that unregulated free enterprise capitalism had shown its inability to manage without government assistance and regulation, "lest it destroy not only itself but also our processes of civilization." In short, government was going to be a permanent presence in the management of the economic life of the nation. At the same time, the president stated his rejection of "the theory that business should and must be taken over into an all-embracing government." In other words, the New Deal would endeavor to find some happy middle ground between socialism and laissez-faire capitalism, a third way that would retain the benefits and blessings of economic liberty while safeguarding the public interest through firm but reasonable regulation.

THREE MONTHS HAVE PASSED since I talked with you shortly after the adjournment of the Congress. Tonight I continue that report, though, because of the shortness of time, I must defer a number of subjects to a later date.

Recently the most notable public questions that have concerned us all have had to do with industry and labor, and with respect to these, certain developments have taken place that I consider of great importance. I am happy to report that after years of uncertainty, culminating in the collapse of the spring of 1933, we are bringing order out of the old chaos with a greater certainty of the employment of labor at a reasonable wage and of more business at a fair profit. These governmental and industrial developments hold promise of new achievements for the nation.

Men may differ as to the particular form of governmental activity with respect to industry and business, but nearly all men are agreed that private enterprise in times such as these cannot be left without assistance and without reasonable safeguards lest it destroy not only itself but also our processes of civilization. The underlying necessity for such activity is indeed as strong now as it was years ago when Elihu Root[1] said the following very significant words:

> Instead of the give and take of free individual contract, the tremendous power of organization has combined great aggregations of capital in enormous industrial establishments working through vast agencies of commerce and employing great masses of men in movements of production and transportation and trade, so great in the mass that each individual concerned in them is quite helpless by himself. The relations between the employer and the employed, between the owners of aggregated capital and the units of organized labor, between the small producer, the small trader, the consumer, and the great transporting and manufacturing and distributing agencies, all present new questions for the solution of which the old reliance upon the free action of individual wills appears quite inadequate. And in many directions, the intervention of that organized control which we call government seems necessary to produce the same result of justice and right conduct which obtained through the attrition of individuals before the new conditions arose.

It was in this spirit thus described by Secretary Root that we approached our task of reviving private enterprise in March 1933. And our first problem was, of course, the banking situation because, as you know, the banks had collapsed. Some banks could not be saved but the great majority of them, either through their own resources or with government aid, have been restored to complete public confidence. This has given safety to millions of depositors in these banks. Closely following this great constructive effort we have, through various federal agencies, saved debtors and creditors alike in many other fields of enterprise, such as loans on farm mortgages and home mortgages, loans to the railroads and insurance companies, and, finally, help for homeowners and for industry itself.

In all of these efforts the government has come to the assistance

---

[1] Elihu Root (1845–1937) was for two generations a leading Republican statesman and officeholder. He served as secretary of war under McKinley and Theodore Roosevelt, and the latter appointed him secretary of state in 1905.

of business and with the full expectation that the money used by the government to assist these enterprises will eventually be repaid. I believe it will be.

The second step we have taken in the restoration of normal business enterprise has been to clean up thoroughly unwholesome conditions in the field of investment. In this we have had assistance from many bankers and businessmen, most of whom recognize the past evils in the banking system, evils in the sale of securities, evils in the deliberate encouragement of stock gambling, evils in the sale of unsound mortgages, evils in many other ways in which the public lost literally billions of dollars. They saw that without changes in the policies and methods of investment there could be no recovery of public confidence in the security of savings. The country now enjoys the safety of bank savings under the new banking laws, the careful checking of new securities under the Securities Act, and the curtailment of rank stock speculation through the Securities Exchange Act. I sincerely hope that as a result people will be discouraged in unhappy efforts to get rich quick by speculating in securities. For the average person almost always loses. Only a very small minority of the people of this country believe in gambling as a substitute for the old philosophy of Benjamin Franklin that the way to wealth is through work.

In meeting the problems of industrial recovery the chief agency of the government has been the National Recovery Administration. Under its guidance, trades and industries covering over 90 percent of all industrial employees have adopted codes of fair competition, which have been approved by the president. And under these codes, in the industries covered, child labor has been eliminated. The workday and the workweek have been shortened. Minimum wages have been established and other wages adjusted towards a rising standard of living.[2] For the emergency purpose of the NRA was to put men to work and since its creation more than 4 million persons have been reemployed, in great part through the cooperation of American business brought about under the codes.

Benefits of this industrial recovery program have come, not only

[2] Both the blanket code, drawn up in Washington, and the industry-specific codes, approved through February 1934, provided for the abolition of child labor. Most codes established a workweek of forty hours, and each provided a minimum wage, usually ranging from thirty to forty cents per hour.

to labor in the form of new jobs, in relief from overwork, in relief from underpay, but also to the owners and managers of industry because, together with a great increase in the payrolls, there has come at the same time a substantial rise in the total of industrial profits—a rise from a deficit figure in the first quarter of 1933 to a level of sustained profits within one year after the inauguration of NRA.

Now it should not be expected of course that even employed labor and capital would be completely satisfied with present conditions. Employed workers have not by any means all of them enjoyed a return to the earnings of prosperous times, although millions of hitherto underprivileged workers are today far better paid than ever before. Also, billions of dollars of invested capital have today a greater security of present and future earning power than before. This is because of the establishment of fair, competitive standards and because of relief from unfair competition in wage cutting which of course depresses markets and destroys purchasing power. But it is an undeniable fact that the restoration of other billions of sound investments to a reasonable earning power could not be brought about in one year. There is no magic formula, no economic panacea, which could simply revive overnight, for example, the heavy industries and the trades that are dependent upon them.

Nevertheless, my friends, the gains of trade and industry, as a whole, have been substantial and everybody knows it. In these gains and in the policies of the administration there are assurances that hearten—hearten all forward-looking men and women with the confidence that we are definitely rebuilding our political and economic system on the lines laid down by the New Deal—lines which, as I have so often made clear, are in complete accord with the underlying principles of orderly popular government which Americans have demanded since the white man first came to these shores. We count, in the future as in the past, on the driving power of individual initiative, on the incentive of fair private profit, strengthened of course with the acceptance of those obligations to the public interest which rest upon us all. We have the right to expect that this driving power will be given patriotically and wholeheartedly to our nation.

We have passed through the formative period of code making in the National Recovery Administration, and we have effected a reorganization of the NRA suited to the needs of the next phase, which is, in turn, a period of preparation for legislation which will determine its permanent form.[3]

In this recent reorganization we have recognized three distinct functions: first, the legislative or policymaking function; and second, the administrative function of code making and revision; and third, the judicial function, which includes enforcement, and consumer complaints and the settlement of disputes between employers and employees and between one employer and another.

We are now prepared to move into this second phase, to move into it on the basis of our experience in the first phase under the able and energetic leadership of General Johnson.[4]

We shall watch carefully the working of this new machinery for the second phase of NRA, modifying it where it needs modification and finally making recommendations to the Congress, in order that the functions of NRA which have proved their worth may be made a part of the permanent machinery of government.

Let me call your attention to the fact that the National Industrial Recovery Act gave businessmen the opportunity they had sought for years to improve business conditions through what has been called self-government in industry. If the codes which have been written have been too complicated, if they have gone too far in such matters as price fixing and limitation of production, let it be remembered that so far as possible, consistent with the immediate public interest of this past year and consistent with the vital necessity of improving labor conditions, the representatives of trade and industry were permitted to write their own ideas into the codes. It is now time to review these actions as a whole to determine through deliberative means in the light of experience, from the standpoint of the good of the industries themselves, as well as the general public interest, whether the methods and the policies adopted in the emergency have been best calculated to promote industrial recovery and a permanent improvement of business and labor conditions. There

[3] Roosevelt refers here to a shake-up at the NRA that had occurred the week before. On September 24, he had accepted the resignation of General Hugh S. Johnson (see next note) and replaced his one-man rule with a National Industrial Recovery Board of five men. The president's reference to determining the NRA's "permanent form" reflects his conviction that the Congress would renew the experiment, which was scheduled to expire in June 1935. In May 1935, the Supreme Court declared the NRA unconstitutional.

[4] General Hugh Samuel Johnson (1882–1942) had been appointed administrator of the NRA from the agency's inception. Johnson was deeply committed to the effort and worked hard to make it a success. But his colorful, dramatic, and impulsive personality made it increasingly difficult for others to work with him, causing Roosevelt finally to force him out.

may be a serious question as to the wisdom of many of those devices to control production, or to prevent destructive price cutting which many business organizations have insisted were necessary, or whether their effect may have been to prevent that volume of production which would make possible lower prices and increased employment. Another question arises as to whether in fixing minimum wages on the basis of an hourly or weekly wage we have reached into the heart of the problem which is to provide such annual earnings, earnings throughout the year, for the lowest paid worker—such earnings as will meet his minimum needs. And we question also the wisdom of extending code requirements suited to the great industrial centers and suited to large employers—to extend those to the great number of small employers in the smaller communities.

During the last twelve months, you and I know that our industrial recovery has been to some extent retarded by strikes, including a few of major importance. I would not minimize the inevitable losses to employers and employees and to the general public through such conflicts. But I would point out that the extent and severity of labor disputes during this period have been far less than in any previous comparable period.

When the businessmen of the country were demanding the right to organize themselves adequately to promote their legitimate interests, when the farmers were demanding legislation which would give them opportunities and incentives to organize themselves for a common advance, it was natural that the workers should seek and obtain a statutory declaration of their constitutional right to organize themselves for collective bargaining, the right embodied in Section 7A of the National Industrial Recovery Act.

Machinery set up by the federal government has provided some new methods of adjustment.[5] Both employers and employees must share the blame of not using them as fully as they should. The employer who turns away from impartial agencies of peace, who denies freedom of organization to his employees, or fails to make every reasonable effort at a peaceful solution of their differences, that employer is not fully supporting the recovery effort of his government.

[5]On June 19, the government had created the National Labor Relations Board—partly in response to the wave of strikes that Roosevelt mentioned two paragraphs above. This three-man board could require union elections for purposes of the collective bargaining that was guaranteed under Section 7A of the NIRA.

And the workers who turn away from these same impartial agencies and decline to use their good offices to gain their ends, those workers likewise are not fully cooperating with their government.

It is time that we made a clean-cut effort to bring about that united action of management and labor, which is one of the high purposes of the Recovery Act. We have passed through more than a year of education. Step by step we have created all the government agencies necessary to ensure, as a general rule, industrial peace, with justice for all those willing to use these agencies whenever their voluntary bargaining fails to produce a necessary agreement.

There should be at least a full and fair trial, a trial given to these means of ending industrial warfare; and in such an effort we should be able to secure for employers and employees and consumers the benefits that all derive from the continuous, peaceful operation of our essential enterprises.

Accordingly, I propose to confer within the coming month with small groups of those people who are truly representative of large employers of labor and those people who are truly representative of large groups of organized labor, in order to seek their cooperation in establishing what I may describe as a specific trial period of industrial peace.

From those who are willing to join in establishing this hoped-for period of peace, from them I shall seek assurances of the making and the maintenance of agreements, which can be mutually relied upon, under which wages and hours and working conditions may be determined and any later adjustments may be made either by agreement or, in case of disagreement, through the mediation or arbitration of state or federal agencies. I shall not ask either employers or employees permanently to lay aside the weapons common to industrial war. But, I shall ask both groups to give a fair trial to peaceful methods of adjusting their conflicts of opinion and interest, and to experiment for a reasonable time with measures suitable to civilize our industrial civilization.

Closely allied to the NRA is the program of public works. The program provided for in the same act and designed to put more men back to work, both directly on the public works themselves, and indirectly in the industries supplying the materials for these public works. To those people who say that our expenditures for public works and for other means for recovery are a waste that we cannot afford, I answer that no country, however rich, can afford the waste of its human resources. Demoralization caused by vast unemployment is our greatest extravagance. Morally, it is the greatest menace to our social order. Some people try to tell me that we must make up our minds that for the future we shall permanently have millions of unemployed just as other countries have had them for over a decade. What may be necessary for those other countries is not my responsibility to determine. But as for this country, I stand or fall by my refusal to accept as a necessary condition of our future a permanent army of unemployed. On the contrary, we must make it a national principle that we will not tolerate a large army of unemployed, that we will arrange our national economy to end our present unemployment as soon as we can and then to take wise measures against its return. I do not want to think that it is the destiny of any American to remain permanently on relief rolls.

Those, fortunately few in number, who are frightened by boldness, who are cowed by the necessity for making decisions, complain that all we have done is unnecessary and that all we have done is subject to great risks. Now that these people are coming out of their storm cellars, they forget that there ever was a storm. They point for example to England. They would have you believe that England has made progress out of her depression by a do-nothing policy, by letting nature take her course. England has her peculiarities and we have ours, but I do not believe any intelligent observer can accuse England of undue orthodoxy in the present emergency.

Did England let nature take her course? No. Did England hold to the gold standard when her reserves were threatened? No. Has England gone back to the gold standard today? No. Did England hesitate to call in $10 billion of her war bonds bearing 5 percent interest, to issue new bonds therefor bearing only 3½ percent interest, thereby saving the British Treasury $150 million a year in interest alone? Of course not. And let it be recorded, my friends, that the British bankers helped their government. Is it not a fact that ever since the year 1909, Great Britain in many ways has advanced further along lines of social security than the United States? Is it not a fact that relations between capital and labor on the basis of collective bargaining are much further advanced in Great Britain than in the United States? It is perhaps not strange that the conservative British press has told us with pardonable irony that much of our New Deal program is only an attempt to catch up with English reforms that go back ten years or more.

I believe that nearly all Americans are sensible and calm people. We do not get greatly excited, nor is our peace of mind disturbed, whether we be businessmen or workers or farmers, by awesome pronouncements concerning the unconstitutionality of some of our measures of recovery and relief and reform. We are not frightened by reactionary lawyers or by political editors. All of these cries have been heard before. More than twenty years ago, when Theodore Roosevelt and Woodrow Wilson were attempting to correct abuses in our national life, the great Chief Justice White[6] said this:

> There is great danger it seems to me to arise from the constant habit which prevails where anything is opposed or objected to, of referring without rhyme or reason to the Constitution as a means of preventing its accomplishment, thus creating the general impression that the Constitution is but a barrier to progress instead of being the broad highway through which alone true progress may be enjoyed.

In our efforts for recovery we have avoided, on the one hand, the theory that business should and must be taken over into an all-embracing government. We have avoided, on the other hand, the equally untenable theory that it is an interference with liberty to offer reasonable help when private enterprise is in need of help. The course we have followed fits the American practice of government, a practice of taking action step by step, of regulating only to meet concrete needs, a practice of courageous recognition of change. I believe, with Abraham Lincoln, that "The legitimate object of government is to do for a community of people whatever they need to have done but cannot do at all or cannot do so well for themselves in their separate and in their individual capacities."

My friends, I still believe in ideals. I am not for a return to that definition of liberty under which for many years a free people were being gradually regimented into the service of the privileged few. I prefer and I am sure you prefer that broader definition of liberty under which we are moving forward to greater freedom, to greater security for the average man than he has ever known before in the history of America.

---

[6] Edward Douglass White (1845–1921) joined the Supreme Court in 1894 and became chief justice in 1910, serving in that office until his death.

DEFENDING THE WPA AND PRESSING FOR SOCIAL SECURITY

PRESIDENT ROOSEVELT had not delivered a Fireside Chat to the American people for a full seven months, but this speech at the end of April 1935 sounded many of the same notes as the earlier ones: that the rush of New Deal laws did not represent a scattered and incoherent program, but parts of a well-considered whole; that there was steady and gratifying progress in the recovery from the dislocations of the Great Depression; and that the American people must continue to beware of unscrupulous critics and immoral chiselers. In addition to reiterating old themes, however, Roosevelt had two special purposes for this radio address.

In the first place, he was anxious to explain and defend the immense program of public works that the Congress had approved just twenty days before. As part of the Emergency Relief Appropriation Act, the Congress had established the Works Progress Administration (WPA). That agency lasted until 1943 (with a change of name to Works Projects Administration in 1939) and spent around $11 billion, more than 80 percent of it in direct wages to those in need of work. The WPA constructed thousands of parks, buildings, bridges, airports, and roads; it also employed artists, writers, photographers, musicians, and actors. It was administered by one of the president's most intimate advisers, Harry L. Hopkins. As can be seen in this speech, Roosevelt took pains to assure Americans that this immense effort was necessary in order to reduce unemployment, that it was carefully conceived, and that it would operate according to a set of fixed and perfectly fair principles. He also tried to anticipate and defuse the chief criticism that he (accurately) saw looming ahead: that the WPA would be inefficient, that it would waste millions of dollars, and that it would be a refuge for the lazy and the corrupt. Despite Roosevelt's efforts to assure his listeners, it was not very long before these very charges filled the air, and accusations about shiftless men "leaning on their shovels" while drawing taxpayers' money for it became a stock weapon of opponents of the New Deal.

The second purpose of this Fireside Chat was to acquaint the public with a series of laws that presently lay before the Congress, but which that body had not yet passed. He laid special stress upon the Social Security Act that would provide both old age pensions and unemployment compensation (signed into law on August 14). He also devoted a major part of this section of his speech to the highly controversial and hotly debated Public Utility Holding Company Act (signed on August 28). That law forbade the "pyramiding" of utility companies, thereby trying to limit the evils of monopoly in the power industry. In passing, Roosevelt also urged support for the renewal of the NRA—an appeal that the Supreme Court rendered unnecessary four weeks after this talk when it found the NRA unconstitutional; for the Banking Act of 1935 (signed on August 23), which modified and increased the powers and organization of the Federal Reserve System; and for the Motor Carrier Act (signed on August 3), which placed buses and trucks under the regulatory power of the Interstate Commerce Commission.

MY FRIENDS, since my annual Message to the Congress on January 4 last, I have not addressed the general public over the air. In the many weeks since that time the Congress has devoted itself to the arduous task of formulating legislation necessary to the country's welfare. It has made and is making distinct progress.

Before I come to any of the specific measures, however, I want to leave in your minds one clear fact. The administration and the Congress are not proceeding in any haphazard fashion in this task of government. Each of our steps has a definite relationship to every other step. The job of creating a program for the nation's welfare is, in some respects, like the building of a ship. At different points on the coast where I often visit they build great seagoing ships, and when one of these ships is under construction and the steel frames have been set in the keel, it is difficult for a person who does not know ships to tell how it will finally look when it is sailing the high seas. It may seem confused to some, but out of the multitude of detailed parts that go into the making of the structure, the creation of a useful instrument for man ultimately comes.

It is that way with the making of a national policy. The objective of the nation has greatly changed in three years. Before that time individual self-interest and group selfishness were paramount in public thinking. The general good was at a discount.

Three years of hard thinking have changed the picture. More and more people, because of clearer thinking and a better understanding, are considering the whole rather than a mere part, a part relating to one section, or to one crop, or to one industry, or to one individual private occupation. That is a tremendous gain for the principles of democracy. For the overwhelming majority of people in this country know how to sift the wheat from the chaff in what they hear and in what they read. They know that the process of the constructive rebuilding of America cannot be done in a day or a year, but that it is being done in spite of the few who seek to confuse them and to profit by their confusion. Americans as a whole are feeling a lot better—a lot more cheerful than for many, many years.

The most difficult place in the world to get a clear and open perspective of the country as a whole is Washington, and I am reminded sometimes of what President Wilson once said: "So many people come to Washington who know things that are not so, and so few people who know anything about what the people of the United States are thinking about." That is why I occasionally leave this scene of action for a few days to go fishing or to go back home to Hyde Park so that I can have a chance to think quietly about the country as a whole. "To get away from the trees," as they say, "and to look at the whole forest." This duty of seeing the country in a long-range perspective is one which, in a very special manner, attaches to this office to which you have chosen me. Did you ever stop to think that there are, after all, only two positions in the nation that are filled by the vote of all of the voters—the presidency and the vice-presidency? That makes it particularly necessary for the vice-president and for me to conceive of our duty toward the entire country. I speak, therefore, tonight to and of the American people as a whole.

My most immediate concern is in carrying out the purposes of the great work program just enacted by the Congress. Its first objective is to put men and women now on the relief rolls to work and, incidentally, to assist materially in our already unmistakable march toward recovery. I shall not confuse my discussion by a multitude of figures. So many figures are quoted to prove so many things. Sometimes it depends on what paper you read or what broadcast you listen in on. Therefore, let us keep our minds on two or three simple essential facts in connection with this problem of unemployment. It is true that while business and industry are definitely better our relief rolls are still too large. However, for the first time in five long years the relief rolls have declined instead of increased during the winter months. And they are still declining. The simple fact is that many millions more people have private work today than two years ago today or one year ago today and every day that passes offers more chances to work for those who want to work. In spite of the fact that unemployment remains a serious problem here as in every other nation, we have come to recognize the possibility and the necessity of certain helpful remedial measures. These measures are of two kinds. The first is to make provisions intended to relieve, to minimize, and to prevent future unemployment; the second is to establish the practical means to help those who are unemployed in this present emergency. Our social security legislation that I have spoken about before is an attempt to answer the first of these questions; our work relief program, the second.

The program for social security that is now pending before the Congress is a necessary part of the future unemployment policy of the government. While our present and projected expenditures for work relief are wholly within the reasonable limits of our national credit resources, it is obvious that we cannot continue to create governmental deficits for that purpose year after year after year. We must begin now to make provision for the future and that is why our social security program is an important part of the complete picture. It proposes, by means of old-age pensions, to help those who have reached the age of retirement to give up their jobs and thus give to the younger generation greater opportunities for work and to give to all, old and young alike, a feeling of security as they look toward old age.

The unemployment insurance part of the legislation will not only help to guard the individual in future periods of lay-off against dependence upon relief, but it will, by sustaining the purchasing power of the nation, cushion the shock of economic distress. Another helpful feature of unemployment insurance is the incentive that it will give to employers to plan more carefully in order that unemployment may be prevented by stabilizing employment itself.

Provisions for social security, however, are protections for the future. Our responsibility for the immediate necessities of the unemployed has been met by the Congress through the most comprehensive work plan in the history of the nation. Our problem is to put to work three and one-half million employable persons, men and women, who are now on the relief rolls. It is a problem quite as much for private industry as for the government.

We are losing no time in getting the government's vast work relief program under way and we have every reason to believe that it should be in full swing by the autumn. I think it will interest you if I tell you what we propose to do in directing it. I shall recognize six fundamental principles for this work relief program:

First, the projects should be useful.

Secondly, the projects should be of a nature that a considerable proportion of the money spent will go into wages for labor.

Third, projects that promise ultimate return to the federal Treasury of a considerable proportion of the costs will be sought as far as possible.[1]

Fourth, funds allotted for each project should be actually and promptly spent and not held over until later years for the spending.

Fifth, in all cases projects must be of a character to give employment to those on the relief rolls first.

And finally, projects will be allocated to the localities or to the relief areas in relation to the number of workers on the relief rolls in those areas.

Next, I think it will interest you to know exactly how we shall direct the work as a federal government.

First, I have set up a division of application and information to which division all proposals for the expenditure of money must go for preliminary study and consideration.

Secondly, after this division of application and information has sifted the projects and studied them,[2] they will be sent to an allotment division composed of representatives of the more important government agencies charged with carrying on the work relief pro-

---

[1] In delivering the speech, Roosevelt added "as far as possible."
[2] In delivering the speech, Roosevelt added "and studied them."

jects. And this group will also include representatives of the cities, representatives of labor and farming and banking and industry. This allotment division will consider all of the recommendations submitted to it and such projects as they approve will be next submitted to the president, who under the act is required to make the final allocations.

The next step will be to notify the proper government agency in whose field the project falls, and also to notify another agency which I am creating—a progress division. This division will have the duty of coordinating the purchase of materials and supplies and of making certain that people who are employed will be taken from the relief rolls. It will also have the responsibility of determining work payments in various localities, of making full use of existing employment services and to assist people engaged in relief work to move as rapidly as possible back into private employment when such employment becomes available. Moreover, and very importantly, this division of progress will be charged with keeping the projects moving on scheduled time.

Finally, I have felt it to be essentially wise and prudent to avoid, as far as possible, the creation of new governmental machinery for supervising this work. The national government now has at least sixty different agencies, most of them dating back many years[3]— agencies with the staff and the experience and the competence necessary to carry on the 250 or 300 different kinds of work that will be undertaken. These agencies of the government, therefore, will simply be doing on a somewhat enlarged scale, the same sort of things that they have been doing in the past. This will make certain that the largest possible portion of the funds allotted will be spent actually creating new work and not for building up an expensive overhead organization here in the capital city of the nation.

For many months preparations have been underway. The allotment of funds for desirable projects has already begun. The key men responsible for the major portion of the task already have been selected. I well realize that the country is expecting before this year is out to see the "dirt fly," as they say, in carrying on the work, and I assure my fellow citizens that no energy will be spared in using these funds effectively to make a major attack upon the problem of unemployment.

[3] Roosevelt added the phrase "most of them dating back many years" as he read the speech.

Our responsibility is to all of the people in this country. This is a great national crusade, a crusade to destroy enforced idleness which is an enemy of the human spirit generated by this depression. Our attack upon these enemies must be without stint and without discrimination. No sectional, no political distinctions can be permitted.

It must, however, be recognized, and I know you will recognize it, that when an enterprise of this character is extended over more than 3,100 counties throughout the nation, there may be occasional instances of inefficiency, bad management, or misuse of funds. When cases of that kind occur, there will be those, of course, who will try to tell you that the exceptional failure is characteristic of the entire endeavor. It should be remembered that in every big job there are some imperfections. There are chiselers in every walk of life, there are those in every industry who are guilty of unfair practices; every profession has its black sheep; but long experience in government has taught me that the exceptional instances of wrongdoing in government are probably less numerous than in almost every other line of endeavor. My friends, the most effective means of preventing such evils in this work relief program will be the eternal vigilance of the American people themselves. I call upon my fellow citizens everywhere to cooperate with me in making this the most efficient and the cleanest example of public enterprise the world has ever seen.

It is time to provide a smashing answer for those cynical men who say that a democracy cannot be honest, cannot be efficient. If you will help, this can be done. I therefore hope you will watch the work in every corner of the nation. Feel free to criticize. Tell me of instances where work can be done better, or where improper practices prevail. Neither you nor I want criticism conceived in a purely fault-finding or partisan spirit, but I am jealous of the right of every citizen to call to the attention of his or her government examples of how the public money can be more effectively spent for the benefit of the American people.

I now come, my friends, to a part of the remaining business before the Congress. It has under consideration many measures which provide for the rounding out of the program of economic and social reconstruction with which we have been concerned for two years and to which I have often referred. I can only mention a few of these measures tonight, but I do not want my mention of these few to be interpreted as a lack of interest in or as disapproval of many other important proposals that are pending.

The National Industrial Recovery Act expires on the sixteenth of June this year. After careful consideration, I have asked the Congress to extend the life of this useful agency of government. As we have proceeded with the administration of the act, we have found from time to time more and more useful ways of promoting its legitimate purpose. No reasonable person wants to abandon our present gains—we must continue to protect children, to enforce minimum wages; to prevent excessive hours; to safeguard, define, and enforce collective bargaining; and, while retaining fair competition, to eliminate, so far as humanly possible, the kinds of unfair practices by selfish minorities which unfortunately did more than anything else to bring about the recent collapse of industry.

There is likewise pending before the Congress legislation to provide for the elimination of unnecessary holding companies in the public utility field.

I consider this legislation a positive recovery measure. Power production in this country is virtually back to the 1929 peak. The operating companies in the gas and electric utility field are by and large in excellent condition. But, under holding company domination the utility industry has long been hopelessly at war within itself and at war with public sentiment. By far the greater part of the general decline in utility securities had occurred before I was inaugurated. The absentee management of unnecessary holding company control has lost touch with, and has lost the sympathy of, the communities it pretends to serve. Even more significantly, it has given to the country as a whole an uneasy apprehension of overconcentrated economic power in the hands of a very few.[4]

You and I know that a business that loses the confidence of its customers and the goodwill of the public cannot long continue to be a good risk for the investor. This legislation will serve the investor by ending the conditions that have caused that lack of confidence and goodwill. It will put the public utility operating industry on a sound basis for the future, both in its public relations and in its internal relations.

This legislation will not only in the long run result in providing lower electric and gas rates to the consumer but it will protect the

---

[4] Roosevelt added the phrase "in the hands of a very few."

actual value, the actual earning power of properties now owned by thousands of investors who have little protection under the old laws against what used to be called frenzied finance. And remember that it will not destroy legitimate value.

Not only business recovery, but the general economic recovery of the nation will be greatly stimulated by the enactment of another kind of legislation—that designed to improve the status of our transportation agencies. There is need for legislation providing for the regulation of interstate transportation by buses and trucks, to regulate transportation by water, and new provisions for strengthening our Merchant Marine and our air service, measures for the strengthening of the Interstate Commerce Commission to enable it to carry out a rounded conception of the national transportation system in which the benefits of private ownership are retained while the public stake in these important services is protected by the public's own government.

And finally, the reestablishment of public confidence in the banks of the nation is one of the most hopeful results of our efforts as a nation to reestablish public confidence in private banking. We all know, we should all remember, that private banking actually exists by virtue of the permission of and regulation by the people as a whole, speaking through their national government and their state governments.[5] Wise public policy, however, requires not only that banking be safe but that the resources of banking must be most fully utilized in the economic life of the country. To that end it was decided more than twenty years ago that the government should assume the responsibility of providing a means by which the credit of the nation might be controlled, not by a few private banking institutions, but by a body with public prestige and authority. And the answer to that demand was the Federal Reserve System. Twenty years of experience with that system have justified the efforts made to create it, but these twenty years have shown by experience definite possibilities for great improvement. Certain proposals made to amend the Federal Reserve Act deserve prompt and favorable action by the Congress. They are a minimum of wise readjustments of our Federal Reserve System in the light of past experience and in the light of present needs.

[5] The phrase "and their state governments" was also added by Roosevelt as he read his speech.

These measures that I have mentioned are, in large part, the program which under my constitutional duty I have recommended to the Congress. They are essential factors in that rounded program for national recovery to which I have referred. They contemplate the enrichment of our national life by a sound and rational ordering of its various elements and wise provisions for the protection of the weak against the strong.

Never since my inauguration in March 1933 have I felt so unmistakably the atmosphere of American recovery. But it is more than the recovery of the material basis of our individual lives. It is the recovery of confidence in our democratic processes, our republican institutions. We have survived all of the arduous burdens and the threatening dangers of a great economic calamity. We have in the darkest moments of our national trials retained our faith in our own ability to master our own destiny. Fear is vanishing. Confidence is growing on every side, renewed faith in the vast possibilities of human beings to improve their material and spiritual status through the instrumentality of the democratic form of government. That faith is receiving its just reward. For that we can be thankful to the God who watches over America.

A PRE-ELECTION APPEAL TO FARMERS AND LABORERS

IT HAD BEEN sixteen months since Roosevelt last addressed the nation in a Fireside Chat, months that had been filled with frantic legislative and reform activity. Now, two months before the November elections, he decided to use the radio once again—and he addressed himself particularly to two of the largest and most politically potent groups in the United States: farmers and laborers.

Farmers in America's midsection had been hard hit by the second drought in three years. While not as disastrous as the calamity of 1934, the 1936 drought was serious enough to reduce crop yields by 20 percent, cover the land with horrifying dust storms, and cause widespread suffering and dislocation. The president went West to examine the damage, and in the first part of his speech, he movingly described the hardships facing the farmers of the Great Plains. He then reviewed the steps being taken to provide help before the winter came, help in the form of increased works projects, close cooperation with appropriate state agencies, and the provision of expert help toward the conservation of soil and water. With the Supreme Court's declaring unconstitutional the attempts of the Agricultural Adjustment Act to pay farmers to reduce surpluses, the New Deal moved to accomplish both goals by a program of soil conservation. The Soil Conservation and Domestic Allotment Act had been passed back in February, and the emphasis in this talk on conservation reflected the changed focus of the administration.

As far as labor was concerned, Roosevelt took the occasion of the Labor Day holiday to praise the fortitude and determination of American workers (in much the same way as he had just praised the farmers). He also reviewed the steps taken by the New Deal to alleviate the continuing distress and pointed with pride to the good results so far.

This Fireside Chat is most notable for the bold effort Roosevelt made to convince both farmers and workers of how much they needed one another. The president, trying to form an alliance that politicians had been hoping in vain to cement at least since the days of the Populists, pointed out that farmers had to earn enough money to buy manufactured products and that labor had to earn enough to consume the agricultural goods being produced on the nation's farms. A lack of purchasing power in either sector of the economy, he argued, would spell quick and inevitable disaster for the other sector too.

Roosevelt could not make this alliance between urban workers and farmers a permanent one—the two groups were divided by too many serious economic, ethnic, religious, and social differences for there ever to be lasting political cooperation between them. But in the short run the attempt seemed to work just fine. Eight weeks after this speech, Franklin Roosevelt carried every agricultural state in America and every urbanized state as well, losing only Vermont and Maine to his Republican challenger, Alfred M. Landon of Kansas.

MY FRIENDS, I have been on a journey of husbandry. I went primarily to see at first hand conditions in the drought states, to see how effectively federal and local authorities are taking care of pressing problems of relief and also how they are to work together to defend the people of this country against the effects of future droughts.

I saw drought devastation in nine states.

I talked with families who had lost their wheat crop, lost their corn crop, lost their livestock, lost the water in their well, lost their garden and come through to the end of the summer without one dollar of cash resources, facing the winter without feed or food— facing a planting season without seed to put in the ground.

That was the extreme case, but there are thousands and thousands of families on western farms who share the same difficulties.

I saw cattlemen who because of lack of grass or lack of winter feed have been compelled to sell all but their breeding stock and will need help to carry even these through the coming winter. I saw livestock kept alive only because water had been brought to them long distances in tank cars. I saw other farm families who have not lost everything but who, because they have made only partial crops, must have some form of help if they are to continue farming next spring.

I shall never forget the fields of wheat so blasted by heat that they cannot be harvested. I shall never forget field after field of corn stunted, earless, stripped of leaves, for what the sun left the grasshoppers took. I saw brown pastures that would not keep a cow on fifty acres.

Yet I would not have you think for a single minute that there is permanent disaster in these drought regions, or that the picture I saw meant depopulating these areas. No cracked earth, no blistering sun, no burning wind, no grasshoppers are a permanent match for the indomitable American farmers and stockmen and their wives and children who have carried on through desperate days, and inspire us with their self-reliance, their tenacity, and their courage. It was their fathers' task to make homes; it is their task to keep these homes; and it is our task to help them win their fight.

First, let me talk for a minute about this autumn and the coming winter. We have the option, in the case of families who need actual subsistence, of putting them on the dole[1] or putting them to work. They do not want to go on the dole and they are one thousand percent right. We agree, therefore, that we must put them to work, work for a decent wage; and when we reach that decision we kill two birds with one stone, because these families will earn enough by working, not only to subsist themselves, but to buy food for their stock and seed for next year's planting. And into this scheme of things there fit of course the government lending agencies which next year, as in the past, will help with production loans.

Every governor with whom I have talked is in full accord with this program of providing work for these farm families, just as every governor agrees that the individual states will take care of their unemployables, but that the cost of employing those who are entirely able and willing to work must be borne by the federal government.

If then we know, as we do today, the approximate number of farm families who will require some form of work relief from now on through the winter, we face the question of what kind of work they ought to do. Let me make it clear that this is not a new question

---

[1]The "dole" was any outright gift of aid to the needy without requiring anything in return. The term had a highly unfavorable connotation during the 1930s, and accepting the dole, instead of working for pay, was felt by many to be disreputable.

because it has already been answered to a greater or less extent in every one of the drought communities. Beginning in 1934, when we also had a serious drought condition, the state and federal governments cooperated in planning a large number of projects, many of them directly aimed at the alleviation of future drought conditions. In accordance with that program, for example, literally thousands of ponds or small reservoirs have been built in order to supply water for stock and to lift the level of the underground water to protect wells from going dry. Thousands of wells have been drilled or deepened; community lakes have been created and irrigation projects are being pushed.

Water conservation by means such as these is being expanded as a result of this new drought all through the Great Plains area, the western corn belt, and in the states that lie further south. In the Middle West water conservation is not so pressing a problem. And here the work projects run more to soil erosion control and the building of farm-to-market roads.

Spending like this is not waste. It would spell future waste if we did not spend for such things now. These emergency work projects provide money to buy food and clothing for the winter; they keep the livestock on the farm; they provide seed for a new crop, and, best of all, they will conserve soil and water in the future in those areas that are most frequently hit by drought.

If, for example, in some local place the water table continues to drop and the topsoil to blow away, the land values will disappear with the water and the soil. People on the farms will drift into nearby cities; the cities will have no farm trade and the workers in the city factories and stores will have no jobs. Property values in those cities will decline. If, on the other hand, the farms within that area remain as farms with better water supply and no erosion, the farm population will stay on the land and prosper and the nearby cities will prosper too. Property values will increase instead of disappearing. That is why it is worth our while as a nation to spend money in order to save money.

I have, however, used this argument in relation only to a small area. But, it holds good in its effect on the nation as a whole. Every state in the drought area is now doing and always will do business with every state outside it. The very existence of the men and women working in the clothing factories of New York, making clothes worn by farmers and their families; of the workers in the steel mills in Pittsburgh and Gary, in the automobile factories of Detroit, and in the harvester factories of Illinois, depend upon the farmers' ability to purchase the commodities that they produce. In the same way it is the purchasing power of the workers in these factories in the cities that enables them and their wives and children to eat more beef, more pork, more wheat, more corn, more fruit and more dairy products, and to buy more clothing made from cotton and wool and leather. In a physical and in a property sense, as well as in a spiritual sense, we are members one of another.

I want to make it clear that no simple panacea can be applied to the drought problem in the whole of the drought area. Plans have to depend on local conditions, for these vary with all kinds of things like annual rainfall, soil characteristics, altitude, and topography. Water and soil conservation methods may differ in one county from those in an adjoining county. Work to be done in the cattle and sheep country differs, of course, in type from work in the wheat country or work in the corn belt.

The Great Plains Drought Area Committee has given me its preliminary recommendations for a long-time program for the Great Plains region. Using that report as a basis, we are cooperating successfully and in entire accord with the governors and state planning boards. As we get this program into operation the people more and more will be able to maintain themselves securely on the land. That will mean a steady decline in the relief burdens that the federal government and the states have had to assume in time of drought; but, more important, it will mean a greater contribution to general national prosperity by these regions that have been hit by drought. It will conserve and improve not only property values, but human values. The people in the drought area do not want to be dependent on federal, or state, or any other kind of charity. They want for themselves and their families an opportunity to share fairly by their own efforts in the progress of America.

The farmers of America want a sound national agricultural policy in which a permanent land use program will have an important place. They want assurance against another year like 1932, a year when they made good crops but had to sell them for prices that meant ruin just as surely as did the drought. Sound policy must maintain farm prices in good crop years as well as in bad crop years.

It must function when we have drought, but it must also function when we have bumper crops.

The maintenance of a fair equilibrium between farm prices and the prices of industrial products is an aim that we must keep ever before us, just as we must give constant thought to the sufficiency of the food supply of the nation even in bad years. Our modern civilization can and should devise a more successful means by which the excess supplies of bumper years can be conserved for use in lean years.

On this trip of mine I have been deeply impressed with the general efficiency of those agencies of the federal and state and local governments which have moved in on the immediate task created by this drought. In 1934 none of us had preparation; we worked without blueprints, and we made the mistakes of inexperience. Hindsight shows us this. But as time has gone on we have been making fewer and fewer mistakes. Remember that the federal and state governments have done only broad planning. Actual work on a given project originates in the local community. Local needs are listed from local information. Local projects are decided on only after obtaining the recommendations and the help of those in the local community who are best able to give it. And it is worthy of note that on my entire trip, though I asked the question dozens of times, I heard no complaint against the character of a single works relief project.

The elected heads of the states concerned, together with their state officials and their experts from agricultural colleges and state planning boards, have shown cooperation with and approval of the work which the federal government has headed up. I am grateful to them and I am grateful also to the men and women in all those states who have accepted leadership in the work in their locality.

In the drought area people are not afraid to use new methods to meet changes in nature, and to correct mistakes of the past. If overgrazing has injured range lands, they are willing to reduce the grazing. If certain wheat lands should be returned to pasture, they are willing to cooperate. If trees should be planted as windbreaks or to stop erosion, they will work with us. If terracing or summer fallowing or crop rotation is called for, they will carry them out. They stand ready to fit, not to fight, the ways of nature.

We are helping, and shall continue to help the farmer, to do those things, through local soil conservation committees and other cooperative local, state, and federal agencies of government.

I wish I had the time tonight to deal with other and more comprehensive agricultural policies but that must wait till a later time.[2]

With this fine help we are tiding over the present emergency. We are going to conserve soil, conserve water, and conserve life. We are going to have long-time defenses against both low prices and drought. We are going to have a farm policy that will serve the national welfare. That is our hope for the future.

There are two reasons why I want to end tonight by talking about reemployment. Tomorrow is Labor Day. The brave spirit with which so many millions of working people are winning their way out of depression deserves respect and admiration. It is like the courage of the farmers in the drought areas.

That is my first reason. The second is that healthy employment conditions stand equally with healthy agricultural conditions as a buttress of national prosperity. Dependable employment at fair wages is just as important to the people in the towns and cities as good farm income is to agriculture. Our people must have the ability to buy the goods they manufacture and the crops they produce. Thus city wages and farm buying power are the two strong legs that carry the nation forward.

I am glad to say that reemployment in industry is proceeding fairly rapidly. Government spending was in large part responsible for keeping industry going and putting it in a position to make this reemployment possible. Government orders were the backlog of heavy industry; government wages turned over and over again to make consumer purchasing power and to sustain every merchant in the community. Businessmen with their businesses, small and large, had to be saved. Private enterprise is necessary to any nation which seeks to maintain the democratic form of government. In their case, just as certainly as in the case of drought-stricken farmers, government spending has saved. Government having spent wisely to save it, private industry begins to take workers off the rolls of the government relief program. Until this administration we had no free employment service, except in a few states and cities; and because there was no unified employment service, the worker, forced to move as industry moved, often traveled over the country, wandering after jobs which seemed always to travel just a little faster than he

---

[2] Roosevelt added the phrase "but that must wait till a later time" as he was delivering this speech.

did. He was often victimized by fraudulent practices of employment clearing houses, and the facts of employment opportunities were at the disposal neither of himself nor of the employer.

In 1933 the United States Employment Service was created[3]—a cooperative state and federal enterprise, through which the federal government matches dollar for dollar the funds provided by the states for registering the occupations and the skills of workers and for actually finding jobs for these registered workers in private industry. The federal-state cooperation has been splendid. Already employment services are operating in thirty-two states, and the areas not covered by them are served by the federal government.

We have developed a nationwide service with 700 district offices, and 1,000 branch offices, thus providing facilities through which labor can learn of jobs available and employers can find workers.

Last spring, in March, I expressed the hope that employers would realize their deep responsibility to take men off the relief rolls and give them jobs in private enterprise. Subsequently I was told by many employers that they were not satisfied with the information available concerning the skill and the experience of the workers on the relief rolls. On August 25 I allocated a small sum to the employment service for the purpose of getting better and more recent information in regard to those now actively at work on WPA projects—information as to their skills and their previous occupations—and to keep the records of such men and women up-to-date for maximum service in making them available to industry. Tonight I am announcing the allocation of two and a half million dollars more to enable the Employment Service to make an even more intensive search than it has yet been equipped to make, to find opportunities in private employment for workers registered with it.

And so tonight I urge the workers to cooperate with and take full advantage of this intensification of the work of the Employment Service. This does not mean that there will be any lessening of our efforts under our WPA and PWA and other work relief programs until all workers have decent jobs in private employment at decent wages. We do not surrender our responsibility to the unemployed. We have had ample proof that it is the will of the American people that those who represent them in national, state, and local govern-

---

[3] This agency was created by the National Employment System Act as part of the First Hundred Days. It was signed into law by Roosevelt on June 6, 1933.

ment should continue as long as necessary to discharge that responsibility. But it does mean that the government wants to use every resource to get private work for those now employed on government work, and thus to curtail to a minimum the government expenditures for direct employment.

And tonight I ask employers, large and small, throughout the nation, to use the help of the state and federal Employment Service whenever in the general pick-up of business they require more workers.

Tomorrow is Labor Day. Labor Day in this country has never been a class holiday. It has always been a national holiday. It has never had more significance as a national holiday than it has now. In other countries the relationship of employer and employee has been more or less accepted as a class relationship not readily to be broken through. In this country we insist, as an essential of the American way of life, that the employer-employee relationship should be one between free men and equals. We refuse to regard those who work with hand or brain as different from or inferior to those who live from their own property. We insist that labor is entitled to as much respect as property. But our workers with hand and brain deserve more than respect for their labor. They deserve practical protection in the opportunity to use their labor at a return adequate to support them at a decent and constantly rising standard of living, and to accumulate a margin of security against the inevitable vicissitudes of life.

The average man must have that twofold opportunity if we are to avoid the growth of a class-conscious society in this country.

There are those who fail to read both the signs of the times and American history. They would try to refuse the worker any effective power to bargain collectively, to earn a decent livelihood, and to acquire security. It is those shortsighted ones, not labor, who threaten this country with that class dissension which in other countries has led to dictatorship and the establishment of fear and hatred as the dominant emotions in human life.

All American workers, brain workers and manual workers alike, and all the rest of us whose well-being depends on theirs, know that our needs are one in building an orderly economic democracy in which all can profit and in which all can be secure from the kind of faulty economic direction which brought us to the brink of common ruin seven years ago.

There is no cleavage between white-collar workers and manual workers, between artists and artisans, musicians and mechanics, lawyers and accountants and architects and miners.

Tomorrow, Labor Day, belongs to all of us. Tomorrow, Labor Day, symbolizes the hope of all Americans. Anyone who calls it a class holiday challenges the whole concept of American democracy.

The Fourth of July commemorates our political freedom—a freedom which without economic freedom is meaningless indeed. Labor Day symbolizes our determination to achieve an economic freedom for the average man which will give his political freedom reality.

DEFENDING THE PLAN TO
"PACK" THE SUPREME COURT

THE FIRESIDE CHAT of March 9, 1937, will be remembered as one of Roosevelt's most dramatic, as well as one of his best-crafted speeches.

On February 5, he had rocked the nation with a "bombshell"—a stunning announcement that caught nearly everyone, including Congress and some close advisers, by surprise. The president proposed to alter radically the composition of the Supreme Court of the United States, as well as that of the lower federal courts, by appointing an additional judge for each one who had reached the age of seventy and had refused to retire. This would mean, among other things, appointing six new justices to the highest court in the land (presuming those presently over seventy refused to retire). Opponents lost little time in denouncing the scheme, charging that Roosevelt had gone "power mad" and that he was trying to "pack" the Court. One of the major unintended effects of the president's move was the strengthening of a conservative congressional coalition composed of Republicans and Democrats opposed to the New Deal.

No one could deny, of course, that the Court had been giving Roosevelt and his New Deal a very hard time. It had struck down a number of antidepression experiments, including the Frazier-Lemke Farm Bankruptcy Act, the Municipal Bankruptcy Act, the Railroad Retirement Act of 1934, and both of the centerpieces of the early New Deal—the Agricultural Adjustment Act and the National Recovery Administration. The Court also invalidated a number of progressive state statutes. To Roosevelt it seemed clear that these "nine old men" stood opposed to the democratic will of the American people, speaking through their president and their elected representatives.

This Fireside Chat saw Roosevelt at his aggressive best, taking the offensive, criticizing the conservative justices in harsh terms, stating the case for change as persuasively and tellingly as he possibly could. The speech was also delivered with unusual skill—even for

Roosevelt. But there can be no doubt that he had, in this instance, made one of his very rare political miscalculations. The debate over the "Court-packing" proposal raged through the end of July. The Democrats split over the issue and a vigorous opposition was mounted in Congress. The assurance of Chief Justice Hughes that the Court was not behind in its work undercut Roosevelt's claim that he wanted to improve the efficiency of the body; and the unexpected death of Senator Joseph Robinson of Arkansas, who was leading the fight for the measure in the Senate, took much of the steam out of Roosevelt's crusade. In the end, the American people, upon whom the president was counting for support, seemed unready to accede to his wishes in this particular matter. Partly this reluctance was the product of reverence for the constitutional balance of powers; partly, no doubt, of the traditional American fear of too much power in any person's hands—even a person so firmly enshrined in the nation's affection that he had, less than half a year before, carried forty-six of the forty-eight states.

Nonetheless, Roosevelt's move might have had its desired effect. One arch-conservative, Justice Willis Van Devanter, announced his resignation two months after this speech. And even more important, the Supreme Court handed down, during the spring of 1937, a series of pro–New Deal decisions—including ones that approved both the Social Security Act and the Wagner Labor Relations Act. In the end, nature took its course and Franklin Roosevelt had his chance to reshape the Court. Before his death, he named eight new justices: Hugo Black (1937), Stanley Reed (1938), Felix Frankfurter (1939), William O. Douglas (1939), Frank Murphy (1940), James Byrnes (1941), Robert Jackson (1941), and Wiley Rutledge (1943).

MY FRIENDS, last Thursday I described in detail certain economic problems which everyone admits now face the nation.[1] For the many

---

[1] Roosevelt had addressed a rousing Democratic victory celebration at the Mayflower Hotel on March 4. The conclusion of the speech consisted of the president listing, one at a time, the pressing economic problems of the country, following each item with the shout "Now!"

messages which have come to me after that speech, and which it is physically impossible to answer individually, I take this means of saying thank you. Tonight, sitting at my desk in the White House, I make my first radio report to the people in my second term of office.[2]

I am reminded of that evening in March, four years ago, when I made my first radio report to you. We were then in the midst of the great banking crisis.

Soon after, with the authority of the Congress, we asked the nation to turn over all of its privately held gold, dollar for dollar, to the government of the United States.

Today's recovery proves how right that policy was.

But when, almost two years later, it came before the Supreme Court its constitutionality was upheld only by a five-to-four vote.[3] The change of one vote would have thrown all the affairs of this great nation back into hopeless chaos. In effect, four justices ruled that the right under a private contract to exact a pound of flesh was more sacred than the main objectives of the Constitution to establish an enduring nation.

In 1933 you and I knew that we must never let our economic system get completely out of joint again—that we could not afford to take the risk of another Great Depression.

We also became convinced that the only way to avoid a repetition of those dark days was to have a government with power to prevent and to cure the abuses and the inequalities which had thrown that system out of joint.

We then began a program of remedying those abuses and inequalities—to give balance and stability to our economic system, to make it bomb-proof against the causes of 1929.

Today we are only part-way through that program—and recovery is speeding up to a point where the dangers of 1929 are again becoming possible, not this week or month perhaps, but within a year or two.

[2] Perhaps it should be pointed out that because of the Twentieth Amendment to the Constitution, Roosevelt's second term had begun on January 20, making him the first president to be inaugurated on a date other than March 4.

[3] The cases upholding the government's nullification of the gold clause (June 5, 1933) were U.S. v. Bankers Trust Co. and Norman v. Baltimore & Ohio Railroad Co., both at 294 U.S. 240, Perry v. U.S., 294 U.S. 330, and Nortz v. U.S., 294 U.S. 317. The four dissenting votes Roosevelt refers to were cast by the Court's conservatives, Justices McReynolds, Van Devanter, Butler, and Sutherland. Voting to uphold the government were Chief Justice Hughes and Justices Brandeis, Cardozo, Roberts, and Stone.

National laws are needed to complete that program. Individual or local or state effort alone cannot protect us in 1937 any better than ten years ago.

It will take time—and plenty of time—to work out our remedies administratively even after legislation is passed. To complete our program of protection in time, therefore, we cannot delay one moment in making certain that our national government has power to carry through.

Four years ago action did not come until the eleventh hour. It was almost too late.

If we learned anything from the depression, we will not allow ourselves to run around in new circles of futile discussion and debate, always postponing the day of decision.

The American people have learned from the depression. For in the last three national elections an overwhelming majority of them voted a mandate that the Congress and the president begin the task of providing that protection—not after long years of debate, but now.

The courts, however, have cast doubts on the ability of the elected Congress to protect us against catastrophe by meeting squarely our modern social and economic conditions.

We are at a crisis, a crisis in our ability to proceed with that protection. It is a quiet crisis. There are no lines of depositors outside closed banks. But to the farsighted it is far-reaching in its possibilities of injury to America.

I want to talk with you very simply tonight about the need for present action in this crisis—the need to meet the unanswered challenge of one-third of a nation ill-nourished, ill-clad, ill-housed.

Last Thursday I described the American form of government as a three-horse team provided by the Constitution to the American people so that their field might be plowed. The three horses are, of course, the three branches of government—the Congress, the executive, and the courts. Two of the horses, the Congress and the executive, are pulling in unison today; the third is not. Those who have intimated that the president of the United States is trying to drive that team, overlook the simple fact that the president, as chief executive, is himself one of the three horses.

It is the American people themselves who are in the driver's seat.

It is the American people themselves who want the furrow plowed.

It is the American people themselves who expect the third horse to pull in unison with the other two.

I hope that you have re-read the Constitution of the United States in these past few weeks. Like the Bible, it ought to be read again and again.

It is an easy document to understand when you remember that it was called into being because the Articles of Confederation under which the original thirteen states tried to operate after the Revolution showed the need of a national government with power enough to handle national problems. In its Preamble, the Constitution states that it was intended to form a more perfect union and promote the general welfare; and the powers given to the Congress to carry out those purposes can best be described by saying that they were all the powers needed to meet each and every problem which then had a national character and which could not be met by merely local action.

But the framers of the Constitution went further. Having in mind that in succeeding generations many other problems then un-dreamed of would become national problems, they gave to the Congress the ample broad powers "to levy taxes ... and provide for the common defense and general welfare of the United States."

That, my friends, is what I honestly believe to have been the clear and underlying purpose of the patriots who wrote a federal Constitution to create a national government with national power, intended as they said, "to form a more perfect union ... for ourselves and our posterity."

For nearly twenty years there was no conflict between the Congress and the Court. Then in 1803 Congress passed a statute which the Court said violated an express provision of the Constitution.[4] The Court claimed the power to declare it unconstitutional and did so declare it. But a little later the Court itself admitted that it was an extraordinary power to exercise and through Mr. Justice Washington[5] laid down this limitation upon it: he said, "It is but a decent respect due to the wisdom, the integrity and the patriotism of the legislative body, by which any law is passed, to presume in favor of its validity until its violation of the Constitution is proved beyond all reasonable doubt."

[4] This was the landmark case of *Marbury v. Madison*, 1 Cranch 137 (1803).

[5] Justice Bushrod Washington (1762–1829), a Virginian, had been nominated to the Supreme Court by John Adams and served from 1798 until his death.

But since the rise of the modern movement for social and economic progress through legislation, the Court has more and more often and more and more boldly asserted a power to veto laws passed by the Congress and by state legislatures in complete disregard of this original limitation which I have just read.

In the last four years the sound rule of giving statutes the benefit of all reasonable doubt has been cast aside. The Court has been acting not as a judicial body, but as a policymaking body.

When the Congress has sought to stabilize national agriculture, to improve the conditions of labor, to safeguard business against unfair competition, to protect our national resources, and in many other ways, to serve our clearly national needs, the majority of the Court has been assuming the power to pass on the wisdom of these acts of the Congress—and to approve or disapprove the public policy written into these laws.

That is not only my accusation. It is the accusation of most distinguished justices of the present Supreme Court. I have not the time to quote to you all the language used by dissenting justices in many of these cases. But in the case holding the Railroad Retirement Act unconstitutional, for instance, Chief Justice Hughes said in a dissenting opinion that the majority opinion was "a departure from sound principles," and placed "an unwarranted limitation upon the commerce clause." And three other justices agreed with him.[6]

In the case of holding the AAA unconstitutional, Justice Stone said of the majority opinion that it was a "tortured construction of the Constitution." And two other justices agreed with him.[7]

In the case holding the New York minimum wage law unconstitutional, Justice Stone said that the majority were actually reading into the Constitution their own "personal economic predilections," and that if the legislative power is not left free to choose the methods of solving the problems of poverty, subsistence, and health of

[6] Charles Evans Hughes (1862–1948) climaxed a distinguished career in public service as chief justice of the Supreme Court from 1930 to 1941. The dissent came in *Retirement Board v. Alton Railroad Co.*, 295 U.S. 330 (1935). In this case, Justice Roberts joined the conservatives on the Court, giving them the narrow majority.

[7] The Supreme Court overturned the Agricultural Administration Act in *U.S. v. Butler*, 297 U.S. 1 (1936). The dissent to which Roosevelt refers was delivered by Justice Harlan Fiske Stone (1872–1946). In 1925 he was appointed by President Calvin Coolidge, whom he was serving as attorney general, to the Court; but Roosevelt elevated him to be chief justice, upon Hughes's retirement in 1941. In the *Butler* case, Stone's dissent was joined by Justices Brandeis and Cardozo.

large numbers in the community, then "government is to be rendered impotent." And two other justices agreed with him.[8]

In the face of these dissenting opinions, there is no basis for the claim made by some members of the Court that something in the Constitution has compelled them regretfully to thwart the will of the people.

In the face of such dissenting opinions, it is perfectly clear that, as Chief Justice Hughes has said, "We are under a Constitution, but the Constitution is what the judges say it is."

The Court in addition to the proper use of its judicial functions has improperly set itself up as a third house of the Congress—a super-legislature, as one of the justices has called it—reading into the Constitution words and implications which are not there, and which were never intended to be there.

We have, therefore, reached the point as a nation where we must take action to save the Constitution from the Court and the Court from itself. We must find a way to take an appeal from the Supreme Court to the Constitution itself. We want a Supreme Court which will do justice under the Constitution and not over it. In our courts we want a government of laws and not of men.

I want—as all Americans want—an independent judiciary as proposed by the framers of the Constitution. That means a Supreme Court that will enforce the Constitution as written, that will refuse to amend the Constitution by the arbitrary exercise of judicial power—in other words by judicial say-so. It does not mean a judiciary so independent that it can deny the existence of facts which are universally recognized.

How then could we proceed to perform the mandate given us? It was said in last year's Democratic platform, and here are the words, "If these problems cannot be effectively solved within the Constitution, we shall seek such clarifying amendments as will assure the power to enact those laws, adequately to regulate commerce, protect public health and safety, and safeguard economic security." In other words, we said we would seek an amendment only if every other possible means by legislation were to fail.

When I commenced to review the situation with the problem

[8] The New York minimum wage law was struck down in *Morehead v. Tipaldo*, 298 U.S. 587 (1936), Justice Roberts once again joining the conservative four.

squarely before me, I came by a process of elimination to the conclusion that, short of amendments, the only method which was
clearly constitutional, and would at the same time carry out other
much needed reforms, was to infuse new blood into all our courts.
We must have men worthy and equipped to carry out impartial justice. But, at the same time, we must have judges who will bring to
the courts a present-day sense of the Constitution—judges who will
retain in the courts the judicial functions of a court, and reject the
legislative powers which the courts have today assumed.

It is well for us to remember that in forty-five out of the forty-eight
states of the Union, judges are chosen not for life but for a period of
years. In many states judges must retire at the age of seventy. Congress has provided financial security by offering life pensions at full
pay for federal judges on all courts who are willing to retire at seventy. In the case of Supreme Court justices, that pension is $20,000
a year. But all federal judges, once appointed, can, if they choose,
hold office for life, no matter how old they may get to be.

What is my proposal? It is simply this: whenever a judge or justice
of any federal court has reached the age of seventy and does not
avail himself of the opportunity to retire on a pension, a new member shall be appointed by the president then in office, with the approval, as required by the Constitution, of the Senate of the United
States.

That plan has two chief purposes. By bringing into the judicial
system a steady and continuing stream of new and younger blood, I
hope, first, to make the administration of all federal justice, from the
bottom to the top,[9] speedier and, therefore, less costly; secondly, to
bring to the decision of social and economic problems younger men
who have had personal experience and contact with modern facts
and circumstances under which average men have to live and work.
This plan will save our national Constitution from hardening of the
judicial arteries.

The number of judges to be appointed would depend wholly on
the decision of present judges now over seventy, or those who
would subsequently reach the age of seventy.

If, for instance, any one of the six justices of the Supreme Court
now over the age of seventy should retire as provided under the
plan, no additional place would be created. Consequently, although

[9] Roosevelt added the phrase "from the bottom to the top" as he was reading the speech.

there never can be more than fifteen, there may be only fourteen, or thirteen, or twelve. And there may be only nine.

There is nothing novel or radical about this idea. It seeks to maintain the federal bench in full vigor. It has been discussed and approved by many persons of high authority ever since a similar proposal passed the House of Representatives in 1869.

Why was the age fixed at seventy? Because the laws of many states, and the practice of the civil service, the regulations of the Army and Navy, and the rules of many of our universities and of almost every great private business enterprise, commonly fix the retirement age at seventy years or less.

The statute would apply to all the courts in the federal system. There is general approval so far as the lower federal courts are concerned. The plan has met opposition only so far as the Supreme Court of the United States itself is concerned. But, my friends, if such a plan is good for the lower courts, it certainly ought to be equally good for the highest Court, from which there is no appeal.

Those opposing this plan have sought to arouse prejudice and fear by crying that I am seeking to "pack" the Supreme Court and that a baneful precedent will be established.

What do they mean by the words "packing the Supreme Court?"

Let me answer this question with a bluntness that will end all honest misunderstanding of my purposes.

If by that phrase "packing the Court" it is charged that I wish to place on the bench spineless puppets who would disregard the law and would decide specific cases as I wished them to be decided, I make this answer: that no president fit for his office would appoint, and no Senate of honorable men fit for their office would confirm, that kind of appointees to the Supreme Court.

But if by that phrase the charge is made that I would appoint and the Senate would confirm justices worthy to sit beside present members of the Court, who understand modern conditions, that I will appoint justices who will not undertake to override the judgment of the Congress on legislative policy, that I will appoint justices who will act as justices and not as legislators—if the appointment of such justices can be called "packing the Courts," then I say that I and with me the vast majority of the American people favor doing just that thing—now.

Is it a dangerous precedent for the Congress to change the number of the justices? The Congress has always had, and will have, that power. The number of justices has been changed several times before, in the administrations of John Adams and Thomas Jefferson—both of them signers of the Declaration of Independence—in the administrations of Andrew Jackson, Abraham Lincoln, and Ulysses S. Grant.[10]

I suggest only the addition of justices to the bench in accordance with a clearly defined principle relating to a clearly defined age limit. Fundamentally, if in the future, America cannot trust the Congress it elects to refrain from abuse of our constitutional usages, democracy will have failed far beyond the importance to democracy of any kind of precedent concerning the judiciary.

We think it so much in the public interest to maintain a vigorous judiciary that we encourage the retirement of elderly judges by offering them a life pension at full salary. Why then should we leave the fulfillment of this public policy to chance or make it dependent upon the desire or prejudice of any individual justice?

It is the clear intention of our public policy to provide for a constant flow of new and younger blood into the judiciary. Normally every president appoints a large number of district and circuit judges and a few members of the Supreme Court. Until my first term practically every president of the United States in our history had appointed at least one member of the Supreme Court. President Taft appointed five members and named a chief justice; President Wilson, three; President Harding, four, including a chief justice; President Coolidge, one; President Hoover, three including a chief justice.[11]

Such a succession of appointments should have provided a Court well balanced as to age. But chance and the disinclination of individuals to leave the Supreme bench have now given us a Court in which five justices will be over seventy-five years of age before next June and one over seventy.[12] Thus a sound public policy has been defeated.

---

[10] The Constitution does not stipulate the number of Supreme Court justices. At the start there were six; but the number was changed to five, to seven, to nine, to ten, to seven again, and then again to its current number of nine.

[11] Taft had named Justices Lurton, Hughes, Van Devanter, Lamar, and Pitney, as well as Chief Justice White; Wilson had named McReynolds, Brandeis, and Clarke; Harding had named Sutherland, Butler, Sanford, as well as Chief Justice Taft; Coolidge had named Stone; and Hoover had named Roberts, Cardozo, and Chief Justice Hughes.

[12] The "old men" on the Supreme Court were Justices Brandeis (b. 1856), Van Devanter (b. 1859), McReynolds (b. 1862), Sutherland (b. 1862), Hughes (b. 1862), and Butler (b. 1864).

So I now propose that we establish by law an assurance against any such ill-balanced Court in the future. I propose that hereafter, when a judge reaches the age of seventy, a new and younger judge shall be added to the Court automatically. In this way I propose to enforce a sound public policy by law instead of leaving the composition of our federal courts, including the highest, to be determined by chance or the personal decision of individuals.

If such a law as I propose is regarded as establishing a new precedent, is it not a most desirable precedent?

Like all lawyers, like all Americans, I regret the necessity of this controversy. But the welfare of the United States, and indeed of the Constitution itself, is what we all must think about first. Our difficulty with the Court today rises not from the Court as an institution but from human beings within it. But we cannot yield our constitutional destiny to the personal judgment of a few men who, being fearful of the future, would deny us the necessary means of dealing with the present.

This plan of mine is no attack on the Court; it seeks to restore the Court to its rightful and historic place in our system of constitutional government and to have it resume its high task of building anew on the Constitution "a system of living law." The Court itself can best undo what the Court has done.

I have thus explained to you the reasons that lie behind our efforts to secure results by legislation within the Constitution. I hope that thereby the difficult process of constitutional amendment may be rendered unnecessary. But let us examine that process.

There are many types of amendment proposed. Each one is radically different from the other. But there is no substantial group within the Congress or outside the Congress who are agreed on any single amendment.

I believe that it would take months or years to get substantial agreement upon the type and language of an amendment. It would take months and years thereafter to get a two-thirds majority in favor of that amendment in both houses of the Congress.

Then would come the long course of ratification by three-quarters of all the states. No amendment which any powerful economic interests or the leaders of any powerful political party have had reason to oppose has ever been ratified within anything like a reasonable time. And remember that thirteen states which contain only 5 percent of the voting population can block ratification even though the thirty-five states with 95 percent of the population are in favor of it.

A very large percentage of newspaper publishers and chambers of commerce and bar associations and manufacturers' associations, who are trying to give the impression today that they really do want a constitutional amendment, would be the very first to exclaim as soon as an amendment was proposed, "Oh! I was for an amendment all right, but this amendment that you've proposed is not the kind of an amendment that I was thinking about. And so, I am going to spend my time, my efforts, and my money to block this amendment, although I would be awfully glad to help to get some other kind of an amendment ratified."

Two groups oppose my plan on the ground that they favor a constitutional amendment. The first includes those who fundamentally object to social and economic legislation along modern lines. This is the same group who during the recent campaign tried to block the mandate of the people.

And the strategy of that last stand is to suggest the time-consuming process of amendment in order to kill off by delay the legislation demanded by the mandate.[13]

To those people I say, I do not think you will be able long to fool the American people as to your purposes.

The other group is composed of those who honestly believe the amendment process is the best and who would be willing to support a reasonable amendment if they could agree on one.

To them I say, we cannot rely on an amendment as the immediate or only answer to our present difficulties. When the time comes for action, you will find that many of those who pretend to support you will sabotage any constructive amendment which is proposed. Look at these strange bedfellows of yours. When before have you found them really at your side in your fights for progress?

And remember one thing more. Even if an amendment were passed, and even if in the years to come it were to be ratified, its meaning would depend upon the kind of justices who would be sitting on the Supreme Court bench. For an amendment, like the rest of the Constitution, is what the justices say it is rather than what its framers or you might hope it is.

---

[13]The original first sentence in this paragraph, "Now they are making a last stand," was skipped over by Roosevelt as he read.

This proposal of mine will not infringe in the slightest upon the civil or religious liberties so dear to every American.

My record as governor and as president proves my devotion to those liberties. You who know me can have no fear that I would tolerate the destruction by any branch of government of any part of our heritage of freedom.

The present attempt by those opposed to progress to play upon the fears of danger to personal liberty brings again to mind that crude and cruel strategy tried by the same opposition to frighten the workers of America in a pay-envelope propaganda against the Social Security law.[14] The workers were not fooled by that propaganda then. And the people of America will not be fooled by such propaganda now.

I am in favor of action through legislation:

First, because I believe it can be passed at this session of the Congress.

Second, because it will provide a reinvigorated, liberal-minded judiciary necessary to furnish quicker and cheaper justice from bottom to top.

Third, because it will provide a series of federal courts willing to enforce the Constitution as written, and unwilling to assert legislative powers by writing into it their own political and economic policies.

During the past half-century the balance of power between the three great branches of the federal government has been tipped out of balance by the courts in direct contradiction of the high purposes of the framers of the Constitution. It is my purpose to restore that balance. You who know me will accept my solemn assurance that in a world in which democracy is under attack,[15] I seek to make American democracy succeed. You and I will do our part.

---

[14] Republicans as well as Democrats favored at least the principle behind the Social Security Act of 1935; opponents, however, led by the National Association of Manufacturers, mounted an aggressive campaign against its adoption. Interestingly, some leaders of the American Federation of Labor also opposed the bill because it required payments from the workers.

[15] This is the first reference in the Fireside Chats to the rapidly worsening international situation, as Imperial Japan, Fascist Italy, and Nazi Germany stepped up their aggressive behavior.

NEW PROPOSALS AT HOME, FRIGHTENING STORM CLOUDS ABROAD

THE MAIN PURPOSE of this Fireside Chat was to outline to the American people the principal measures that Roosevelt intended to put before the Congress in a special session scheduled for the next month. At the end of the talk, however, the president also felt constrained to add a few words about the rapidly worsening international situation.

Roosevelt introduced the talk by contending that, while citizens were heartened by the substantial gains in prosperity, they were not yet fully satisfied. They wanted new legislation to make the prosperity more permanent. He suggested, moreover, that most of the American people had come to think of themselves as members of a single community and that they therefore would not resent laws which seemed to bestow benefits on particular segments or regions of the community. (This was the same appeal, of course, as when he had pushed for the TVA and relief to the dust-bowl states.) Having laid out this groundwork, he was ready to present his proposals.

In the first place, he sought some constitutional way to limit agricultural surpluses and resulting low prices for agricultural commodities—the conservation program of 1936 had failed to do the job. He also explored, in a rudimentary way, the possibility of leveling out the amount of agricultural produce between bumper years and scarce ones. Roosevelt then talked of an enhanced program of conservation, including new TVA-type projects. He also wanted Congress to consider a major governmental reorganization plan to bring order to the "higgledy-piggledy patchwork of duplicate responsibilities and overlapping powers." As far as industry was concerned, the president called for a bill stipulating a minimum wage and maximum number of work hours (now that the NRA codes, which had originally provided these things, were no longer legal), and he suggested a fresh look at the nation's antitrust policy, with an eye to breaking down monopolies and restoring free competition.

Congress reviewed Roosevelt's ambitious shopping list at its special session and decided to give him virtually nothing that he wanted. Republican conservatives were joined by southern Democrats to frustrate the president's hopes for further reform. On the other hand, the reluctance of Congress did not last very long. By the time the regular session convened in January 1938, it was obvious that the country was in the grasp of a very serious recession, a recession that had actually already begun at the time of this speech. That economic emergency could no longer be ignored by the time Congress met in January, and it was to result in one last flurry of New Deal reform.

Roosevelt's closing words, about the darkening foreign prospect and the growing threat of war, must be read in the context of the controversial and widely noticed address he had delivered exactly one week before. Returning from his western trip, Roosevelt stopped in Chicago where, in an unusually tough speech, he suggested that the aggressors be "quarantined" by the civilized nations of the world. Although the message seemed to fly in the face of predominant isolationist sentiment, initial reaction in the United States was favorable. This Fireside Chat was partly an attempt to head off mounting isolationist unease and to reassure and calm Americans concerned about the threat of war.

MY FRIENDS, this afternoon I have issued a proclamation calling a special session of the Congress to convene on Monday, November 15, 1937.

I do this in order to give to the Congress an opportunity to consider important legislation before the regular session in January, and to enable the Congress to avoid a lengthy session next year, extending through the summer.

I know that many enemies of democracy will say that it is bad for business,[1] bad for the tranquillity of the country, to have a special session—even one beginning only six weeks before the regular session. But I have never had sympathy with the point of view that a session of the Congress is an unfortunate intrusion of what they call

[1] Roosevelt added the words "bad for business" to his prepared text.

"politics" into our national affairs. Those who do not like democracy want to keep legislators at home. But the Congress is an essential instrument of democratic government; and democratic government can never be considered an intruder into the affairs of a democratic nation.

I shall ask this special session to consider immediately certain important legislation which on my recent trip through the nation convinces me the American people immediately need. This does not mean that other legislation, to which I am not referring tonight, is not an important part of our national well-being. But other legislation can be more readily discussed at the regular session.

Anyone charged with proposing or judging national policies should have firsthand knowledge of the nation as a whole.

That is why again this year I have taken trips to all parts of the country. Last spring I visited the Southwest. This summer I made several trips in the East. Now I am just back from a trip all the way across the continent, and later this autumn I hope to pay my annual visit to the Southeast.[2]

For a president especially it is a duty to think in national terms.

He must think not only of this year but of future years when someone else will be president.

He must look beyond the average of the prosperity and well-being of the country, because averages easily cover up danger spots of poverty and instability.

He must not let the country be deceived by a merely temporary prosperity which depends on wasteful exploitation of resources which cannot last.

He must think not only of keeping us out of war today, but also of keeping us out of war in generations to come.

The kind of prosperity we want is the sound and permanent kind which is not built up temporarily at the expense of any section or group. And the kind of peace we want is the sound and permanent kind, which is built on the cooperative search for peace by all the nations which want peace.

The other day I was asked to state my outstanding impression gained on this recent trip to the Pacific coast and back. And I said

[2] The president had been making regular visits to Warm Springs, Georgia, since the mid-1920s, believing that the region's waters were therapeutic for his polio. He also interested himself in developing Warm Springs as a retreat for other polio victims, especially children, from around the country.

that it seemed to me to be the general understanding on the part of the average citizen—understanding of the broad objectives and policies which I have just outlined.

Five years of fierce discussion and debate, five years of information through the radio and the moving picture, have taken the whole nation to school in the nation's business. Even those who have most attacked our objectives have, by their very criticism, encouraged the mass of our citizens to think about and understand the issues involved, and understanding, to approve.

Out of that process, we have learned to think as a nation. And out of that process we have learned to feel ourselves a nation. As never before in our history, each section of America says to every other section, "Thy people shall be my people."

For most of the country this has been a good year, better in dollars and cents than for many years and far better in the soundness of its prosperity. Everywhere I went, I found particular optimism about the good effect on business which is expected from the steady spending by farmers of the largest farm income in many years.

But we have not yet done all that must be done to make this prosperity stable. The people of the United States were checked in their efforts to prevent future piling up of huge agricultural surpluses and the tumbling prices which inevitably follow them. They were checked in their efforts to secure reasonable minimum wages and maximum hours and the end of child labor.[3] And because they were checked, many groups in many parts of the country still have less purchasing power and a lower standard of living than the nation as a whole can permanently allow.

Americans realize these facts. That is why they ask government not to stop governing simply because prosperity has come back a long way.

They do not look on government as an interloper in their affairs. On the contrary, they regard it as the most effective form of organized self-help.

Sometimes I get bored sitting in Washington hearing certain people talk and talk about all that government ought *not* to do, people who got all *they* wanted from government back in the days when the financial institutions and the railroads were being bailed

---

[3] Roosevelt refers here to the Supreme Court's decisions declaring both the AAA and the NRA unconstitutional.

out in 1933, bailed out by the government. It is refreshing to go out through the country and feel the common wisdom that the time to repair the roof is when the sun is shining.

They want the financial budget balanced, these American people. But they want the human budget balanced as well. They want to set up a national economy which balances itself with as little government subsidy as possible, for they realize that persistent subsidies ultimately bankrupt their government.

They are less concerned that every detail be immediately right than they are that the direction be right. They know that just so long as we are traveling on the right road, it does not make much difference if occasionally we hit a "thank you, marm."[4]

The overwhelming majority of our citizens who live by agriculture are thinking clearly how they want government to help them in connection with the production of crops. They want government help in two ways: first, in the control of surpluses, and, second, in the proper use of land.

The other day a reporter told me that he had never been able to understand why the government seeks to curtail crop production and, at the same time, to open up new irrigated areas.

He was confusing two totally separate objectives.

Crop surplus control relates to the total amount of any major crop grown in the whole nation on all cultivated land—good land or poor land—control by the cooperation of the crop growers themselves, and with the help of the government. Land use, however, is a policy of providing each farmer with the best quality and type of land we have, or can make available, for his part in that total production. Adding good new land for diversified crops is offset by abandoning poor land now uneconomically farmed.

The total amount of production largely determines the price of the crop, and, therefore, the difference between comfort and misery for the farmer.

Let me give you an example.[5] If we Americans were foolish enough to run every shoe factory twenty-four hours a day, seven days a week, we would soon have more shoes than the nation could possibly buy, a surplus of shoes so great that it would have to be destroyed, or given away, or sold at prices far below the cost of

[4]A "thank you, marm" is slang for a bump or a depression in the road that causes a passenger's head to nod.

[5]This sentence was added as Roosevelt delivered the talk.

production. That simple illustration, that simple law of supply and demand equally affects the price of all of our major crops.

You and I have heard big manufacturers talk about control of production by the farmer as an indefensible "economy of scarcity," as they call it. And yet these same manufacturers never hesitate to shut down their own huge plants, throw men out of work, and cut down the purchasing power of the whole community whenever they think that they must adjust their production to an oversupply of the goods they make. When it is their baby who has the measles, they call it not "an economy of scarcity" but "sound business judgment."

Of course, speaking seriously, what you and I want is such governmental rules of the game that labor and agriculture and industry will all produce a balanced abundance without waste.

So we intend this winter to find a way to prevent four-and-a-half-cent cotton and nine-cent corn and thirty-cent wheat—with all the disaster those prices mean for all of us—to prevent those prices from ever coming back again. To do that, the farmers themselves want to cooperate to build an all-weather farm program so that in the long run prices will be more stable. They believe this can be done, and the national budget kept out of the red.

And when we have found that way to protect the farmers' prices from the effects of alternating crop surpluses and crop scarcities, we shall also have found the way to protect the nation's food supply from the effects of the same fluctuation. We ought always to have enough food at prices within the reach of the consuming public. For the consumers in the cities of America, we must find a way to help the farmers to store up in years of plenty enough to avoid hardship in the years of scarcity.

Our land use policy is a different thing. I have just visited much of the work that the national government is doing to stop soil erosion, to save our forests, to prevent floods, to produce electric power for more general use, and to give people a chance to move from poor land to better land by irrigating thousands of acres that need only water to provide an opportunity to make a good living.

I saw bare and burned hillsides where only a few years ago great forests were growing. They are now being planted to young trees, not only to stop erosion, but to provide a lumber supply for the future.

I saw CCC boys and WPA workers building check dams and small ponds and terraces to raise the water table and make it possible for farms and villages to remain in safety where they now are. I saw the harnessing of the turbulent Missouri, a muddy stream with the top soil of many states. And I saw barges on new channels carrying produce and freight athwart the nation.

Let me give you two simple illustrations of why government projects of this type have a national importance for the whole country, and not merely a local importance.[6]

In the Boise Valley in Idaho I saw a district which had been recently irrigated to enormous fertility so that a family can now make a pretty good living from forty acres of its land. Many of the families, who are making good in that valley today, moved there from a thousand miles away. They came from the dust strip that runs through the middle of the nation all the way from the Canadian border to Texas, a strip which includes large portions of ten states. That valley in western Idaho, therefore, assumes at once a national importance as a second chance for willing farmers. And, year by year, we propose to add more valleys to take care of thousands of other families who need the same kind of a second chance in new green pastures.

The other illustration was at the Grand Coulee Dam in the state of Washington. The engineer in charge told me that almost half of the whole cost of that dam to date had been spent for materials that were manufactured east of the Mississippi River, giving employment and wages to thousands of industrial workers in the eastern third of the nation, two thousand miles away.

All of this work needs, of course, a more businesslike system of planning, a greater foresight than we use today.

And that is why I recommended to the last session of the Congress the creation of seven planning regions, in which local people will originate and coordinate recommendations as to the kind of this work to be done in their particular regions. The Congress, of course, will determine the projects to be selected within the budget limits.

To carry out any twentieth-century program, we must give to the executive branch of the government twentieth-century machinery to work with. I recognize that democratic processes are necessarily and I think rightly slower than dictatorial processes. But I refuse to believe that democratic processes need be dangerously slow.

For many years we have all known that the executive and administrative departments of the government in Washington are a

---

[6] The words "and not merely a local importance" were added by Roosevelt as he spoke.

higgledy-piggledy patchwork of duplicate responsibilities and over-lapping powers. The reorganization of this vast government machinery which I proposed to the Congress last winter does not conflict with the principle of the democratic process, as some people say. It only makes that process work more efficiently.

On my recent trip many people have talked to me about the millions of men and women and children who still work at insufficient wages and overlong hours.

American industry has searched the outside world to find new markets, but it can create on its very doorstep the biggest and most permanent market it has ever seen. It needs the reduction of trade barriers to improve its foreign markets, but it should not overlook the chance to reduce the domestic trade barrier right here, right away, without waiting for any treaty. A few more dollars a week in wages, a better distribution of jobs with a shorter working day will almost overnight make millions of our lowest-paid workers actual buyers of billions of dollars of industrial and farm products. That increased volume of sales ought to lessen other costs of production so much that even a considerable increase in labor costs can be absorbed without imposing higher prices on the consumer.

I am a firm believer in fully adequate pay for all labor. But right now I am most greatly concerned in increasing the pay of the lowest-paid labor, those who are our most numerous consuming group but who today do not make enough to maintain a decent standard of living or to buy the food and the clothes and the other articles necessary to keep our factories and farms fully running.

I think that farsighted businessmen already understand and agree with this policy. They agree also that no one section of the country can permanently benefit itself, or the rest of the country, by maintaining standards of wages and hours that are far inferior to other sections of the country.

Most businessmen, big and little, know that their government neither wants to put them out of business nor to prevent them from earning a decent profit. In spite of the alarms of a few who seek to regain control over American life, most businessmen, big and little, know that their government is trying to make property more secure than ever before by giving every family a real chance to have a property stake in the nation.

Whatever danger there may be to the property and profits of the many, if there be any danger, comes not from government's attitude toward business but from restraints now imposed upon business by private monopolies and financial oligarchies. The average businessman knows that a high cost of living is a great deterrent to business and that business prosperity depends much upon a low price policy which encourages the widest possible consumption. As one of the country's leading economists recently said, "The continuance of business recovery in the United States depends far more on business policies, business pricing policies, than it does on anything that may be done, or not done, in Washington."

Our competitive system is, of course, not altogether competitive. Anybody who buys any large quantity of manufactured goods knows this, whether it be the government or an individual buyer. We have antitrust laws, to be sure, but they have not been adequate to check the growth of many monopolies. Whether or not they might have been originally adequate, interpretation by the courts and the difficulties and delays of legal procedure have now definitely limited their effectiveness.

We are already studying how to strengthen our antitrust laws in order to end monopoly—not to hurt but to free the legitimate business of the nation.

I have touched briefly on these important subjects, which, taken together, make a program for the immediate future. And I know you will realize that to attain it, legislation is necessary.

As we plan today for the creation of ever higher standards of living for the people of the United States, we are aware that our plans may be most seriously affected by events in the world outside our borders.

By a series of trade agreements, we have been attempting to recreate the trade of the world, that trade of the world, that plays so important a part in our domestic prosperity;[7] but we know that if the world outside our borders falls into the chaos of war, world trade will be completely disrupted.

Nor can we view with indifference the destruction of civilized values throughout the world. We seek peace, not only for our generation but also for the generation of our children.

---

[7] Following upon the Reciprocal Trade Agreements Act of 1934, which authorized the president to reduce tariff rates up to 50 percent in conjunction with other governments, the Roosevelt administration set out to negotiate trade agreements with other nations. By the end of 1939, Secretary of State Cordell Hull had concluded trade agreements with twenty-one countries, lowering tariff rates almost 30 percent.

We seek for them, our children, the continuance of world civilization in order that their American civilization may continue to be invigorated, helped, by the achievements of civilized men and women in all the rest of the world.

I want our great democracy to be wise enough to realize that aloofness from war is not promoted by unawareness of war. In a world of mutual suspicions, peace must be affirmatively reached for. It cannot just be wished for. And it cannot just be waited for.

We have now made known our willingness to attend a conference of the parties to the Nine Power Treaty of 1922, the Treaty of Washington, of which we are one of the original signatories. The purpose of this conference will be to seek by agreement a solution of the present situation in China. In efforts to find that solution, it is our purpose to cooperate with the other signatories to this treaty, including China and Japan.[8]

Such cooperation would be an example of one of the possible paths to follow in our search for means toward peace throughout the whole world.

The development of civilization and of human welfare is based on the acceptance by individuals of certain fundamental decencies in their relations with each other. And equally the development of peace in the world is dependent similarly on the acceptance by nations of certain fundamental decencies in their relations with each other.

Ultimately, I hope *each* nation will accept the fact that violations of these rules of conduct are an injury to the well-being of *all* nations.

Meanwhile, remember that from 1913 to 1921, I personally was fairly close to world events, and in that period, while I learned much of what to do, I also learned much of what not to do.

The common sense, the intelligence of the people of America agree with my statement that "America hates war. America hopes for peace. Therefore, America actively engages in the search for peace."

[8] The Nine Power Treaty had been signed on February 6, 1922, along with the main business of the Washington Conference—the reduction of naval armaments among the great naval powers. The nine signatories agreed "to respect the sovereignty, the independence, and the territorial integrity of China." With the renewal of Japanese aggression in China, the League of Nations Assembly ruled that the Nine Power Treaty had been breached. A meeting was scheduled for Brussels three weeks after this speech, but since neither Germany nor Japan attended, it proved impossible to resolve the Chinese question.

SUPPORTING THE UNEMPLOYMENT CENSUS

GETTING AN ACCURATE COUNT of the number of unemployed Americans was not an easy thing to do, and estimates varied widely among the dozen counting agencies that published their findings. For example, in 1935 guesses about the number of the unemployed ranged everywhere from 9.09 million to 16.65 million, and in 1936, from 7.38 million to 14.75 million. Finally, Congress decided to conduct a National Unemployment Census in 1938, and the president (who was lukewarm, at best, about the undertaking) used this Fireside Chat to urge cooperation with the effort to obtain accurate statistics.

Not surprisingly, the effort appears not to have been terribly successful. The results were announced on January 18, 1938. Unemployment Report Cards, containing fourteen questions, were actually returned by 7,822,912 unemployed or partly unemployed Americans. But after authorities conducted a house-to-house survey in 1,864 randomly selected communities, they concluded that the mail survey was only around 70 percent accurate and calculated that 3,047,088 ought to be added to the original figure.

In any case, the figures were no sooner in than they were rendered obsolete by the recession that hit the American economy in late 1937 and early 1938. Suddenly (all the counting agencies agreed), the unemployment figures once again, discouragingly, skyrocketed.

I AM APPEALING to the people of America tonight to help in carrying out a task that is important to them and to their government.

It is a part, but an essential part, of the greater task of finding jobs for willing workers who are idle through no fault of their own; of finding more work for those who are insufficiently employed; and of surveying the needs of workers and industry to see if we can find the basis of a better long-range plan of reemployment than we have now.

Enforced idleness, embracing any considerable portion of our people, in a nation of such wealth and natural opportunity, is a paradox that challenges our ingenuity. Unemployment is one of the bitter and galling problems that now afflicts mankind. It has been with us, in a measure, since the beginning of our industrial era. It has been increased by the complexity of business and industry, and it has been made more acute by the depression. It has made necessary the expenditure of billions of dollars for relief and for publicly created work; it has delayed the balancing of our national budget, and increased the tax burden of all our people. And in addition to the problem faced by the national government, our states and local governments have been sorely pressed to meet the increased load resulting from unemployment.

It is a problem of every civilized nation, not ours alone. It has been solved in some countries by starting huge armament programs, but we Americans do not want to solve it that way.

Nevertheless, as a nation we adopted the policy that no unemployed man or woman can be permitted to starve for lack of aid. And that is still our policy. But the situation calls for a permanent cure and not just a temporary one.

Unemployment relief is, of course, not the permanent cure. The permanent cure lies in finding suitable jobs in industry and agriculture for all willing workers. It involves cooperative effort and planning which will lead to the absorption of this unused manpower in private industry. Such planning calls for facts—facts that we do not now possess.

Such planning applies not only to workers but to the employers in industry because it involves trying to get rid of what we call the peaks and valleys of employment and unemployment, trying with the help of industry to plan against producing more goods one year than people can or will consume, and cutting production drastically the following year with the resulting layoff of hundreds of thousands of workers.

That is a long and difficult problem to find the answer to, and it may take many efforts in the coming years to find the right answer. But in the meantime, we need more facts.

For several years varying estimates of the extent of unemployment in the United States have been made. Valuable as some of these estimates have been in providing us an approximation of the extent of unemployment, they have not provided us with sufficient factual data on which to base a comprehensive reemployment program. So during this coming week we are going to strive to get such facts. We are going to conduct a nationwide census of the unemployed and of the partly unemployed and we are going to conduct it in the genuinely democratic American way.

This is to be a wholly voluntary census. We are going to hold the mirror up to ourselves and try to get, not only a true and honest reflection of our present unemployment conditions, but facts that will help us to plan constructively for the future.

Only in a nation whose people are alert to their own self-interest and alive to the responsibilities of their citizenship could such a voluntary plan succeed. I am confident that this great American undertaking will succeed. Every effort is being put forth to make all of our people understand and fully appreciate its significance, and I am sure you will all give it your helpful aid as you have in previous efforts aimed at national improvement, efforts through which our people have shown their capacity for self-government.

On Tuesday next, November 16, the Post Office Department through its far-flung and highly efficient organization, will undertake to deliver to every abode in the United States an Unemployment Report Card, a card containing fourteen simple questions.

The report card which the postman will leave at your door on Tuesday is a double postcard, larger than the customary card. It is addressed especially to those who are unemployed or partly unemployed, and who are able to work and are seeking work. This card contains a message to you from me, a message carrying the assurance that if you will give me all the facts, it will help us in planning for the benefit of those who need and want work and do not now have it. This message calls upon the unemployed and everyone else throughout the land to help make this census complete, honest, and accurate.

If all the unemployed and partly employed persons, who are able to work and who are seeking work, will conscientiously fill out these cards and mail them just as they are, without a stamp, without an envelope, by or before midnight of November 20, our nation will have real facts upon which to base a sound reemployment program.

It is important for every unemployed person to understand that this report card is not an application for relief, nor a registration for a job. This is purely and simply a fact-seeking census. When you receive this card you will note that the fourteen questions are designed to give this nation a wider basis of knowledge of its unemployment conditions than it has ever had before.

If our unemployed and partly unemployed wholeheartedly give the information sought in these fourteen questions, we will know not only the extent of unemployment and partial unemployment, but we will know also the geographical location of unemployment by states and by communities. We will likewise be able to tell what age groups are most severely affected. But most important of all, we will know the work qualifications of the unemployed; we will know in what industries they are suited to function, and we will be equipped to determine what future industrial trends are most likely to absorb these idle workers.

I think it is necessary to emphasize that only those unemployed, or partly unemployed, who are able to work, and who are seeking work, should fill out these cards. All others may disregard them.

But I appeal also to all of you who are employed today, you who are employed, asking you to enlist as good neighbors to those who are unemployed in your communities and who may need help in filling out their·cards properly and promptly. They need the stimulus of your cooperation, to recognize the importance of this national effort to help them.

I think this neighborly cooperation will be very helpful in dispelling from the minds of the unemployed all fear that the information sought in this census is to be used for any purpose other than helpfulness. I repeat the assurance to the unemployed that the information which you give on these report cards will in no sense be used against you, but so far as lies within my power, will be employed for your own good and for the welfare of the nation.

When we have ascertained the full facts of unemployment, we can extend the voluntary and neighborly character of this effort to the task of finding the solution to the perplexing problem. Its importance justifies a national approach, free from prejudice or partisanship and warrants the cooperative endeavors of business, of labor, of agriculture, and of government.

I am confident that this nation of ours has the genius to reorder its affairs, and possesses the physical resources to make it possible for everyone, young or old, to enjoy the opportunity to work and earn. There is neither logic nor necessity for one-third of our population to have less of the needs of modern life than make for decent living.

Our national purchasing power is the soil from which comes all our prosperity. The steady flow of wages to our millions of workers is essential if the products of our industry and of our farmers are to be consumed.

Our farsighted industrial leaders now recognize that a very substantial share of corporate earnings must be paid out in wages, or the soil from which these industries grow will soon become impoverished. Our farmers recognize that their largest consumers are the workers for wages, and that farm markets cannot be maintained except through widespread purchasing power.

This unemployment problem is, therefore, one in which every individual and every economic group has a direct interest. It is a problem whose discussion must be removed from the field of prejudice to the field of logic. We shall find the solution only when we have the facts, and having the facts, accept our mutual responsibilities.

The inherent right to work is one of the elemental privileges of a free people. Continued failure to achieve that right, that privilege, by anyone who wants to work and needs work is a challenge to our civilization and to our security. Endowed, as our nation is, with abundant physical resources, and inspired as it should be with the high purpose to make those resources and opportunities available for the enjoyment of all, we approach this problem of reemployment with the real hope of finding a better answer than we have now.

The Unemployment Census, as a sensible first step to a constructive reemployment program, ought to be a successful bit of national teamwork from which will come again that feeling of national solidarity which is the strength and the glory of the American people.

COMBATTING THE 1937–1938 RECESSION

THE RECOVERY EXPERIENCED by the American economy until the end of the summer of 1937—while it did not restore the levels of 1929—was nevertheless substantial and gratifying to Roosevelt. Industrial productivity, for example, was nearly 80 percent greater than it had been in 1932 (even though it was still 7 percent below 1929 levels). Prices rose dramatically in early 1937. Agricultural income was almost back to 1929 totals, and workers were making 10 percent more than in 1929 and working fewer hours. Perhaps the time had come to turn a greater share of the workings of the economy back again to the private sector.

In fact, Roosevelt was so encouraged by these developments that he dared to recall an old dream and an old promise: actually to balance the federal budget. In the first seven months of 1937, he directed that the rolls of the WPA be cut about in half. Farm subsidies were reduced, some agencies were to be phased out, and the Reconstruction Finance Corporation was to make no new commitments. As a consequence of this belt-tightening, the federal deficit dropped from $4.36 billion in 1936 to $2.70 billion in 1937. Indeed, the economic news was so good that some of the president's advisers actually feared the reappearance of boom times, inflation, and another wave of irresponsible speculation like that of the late 1920s. The president responded by urging the Federal Reserve Board to tighten credit and by "sterilizing" new gold purchases by placing them into an "inactive" fund.

As it happened, the recovery of the early 1930s was still much too fragile to sustain these sudden cutbacks. The resulting downturn began in August 1937 and continued through the winter and spring of 1938. It was nothing short of catastrophic. Perhaps an additional 4 million workers were thrown out of work. Both the industrial index and the stock market fell disastrously. After some wavering, Roosevelt abandoned the plan of balancing the budget. He sent a message

111

to Congress on April 14, 1938, requesting a massive new infusion of public spending to lift the economy out of the recession. That same evening he delivered this Fireside Chat to the American people.

Congress—facing the dismal prospect of a fall campaign in the midst of a faltering economy—complied gladly with the president's requests. Farm subsidies were quadrupled, the WPA was restored, credit was relaxed; and by mid-summer of 1938, the economy began to rise painfully again—although the problem of unemployment would not be solved until the wartime economy made a place for everyone who wanted work. The principal permanent results of the "Roosevelt recession" of 1937–38 were—in addition to the countless projects contributed by the renewal of work relief programs—the Agricultural Adjustment Act of February 1938 (which, this time, met with the approval of the Supreme Court) and the Fair Labor Standards Act of June.

MY FRIENDS, five months have gone by since I last spoke to the people of the nation about the state of the nation.

I had hoped to be able to defer this talk until next week because, as we all know, this is Holy Week. But what I want to say to you, the people of the country, is of such immediate need and relates so closely to the lives of human beings and the prevention of human suffering that I have felt that there should be no delay. In this decision I have been strengthened by the thought that by speaking tonight there may be greater peace of mind and that the hope of Easter may be more real at firesides everywhere, and therefore that it is not inappropriate to encourage peace when so many of us are thinking of the Prince of Peace.

Five years ago we faced a very serious problem of economic and social recovery. For four and a half years that recovery proceeded apace. It is only in the past seven months that it has received a visible setback.

And it is only within the past two months, as we have waited patiently to see whether the forces of business itself would counteract it, that it has become apparent that government itself can no longer safely fail to take aggressive government steps to meet it.

This recession has not returned us to the disasters and the suffering of the beginning of 1933. Your money in the bank is safe; farmers are no longer in deep distress and have greater purchasing power; dangers of security speculation have been minimized; national income is almost 50 percent higher than it was in 1932; and government has an established and accepted responsibility for relief.

But I know that many of you have lost your jobs or have seen your friends or members of your families lose their jobs, and I do not propose that the government shall pretend not to see these things. I know that the effect of our present difficulties has been uneven; that they have affected some groups and some localities seriously, but that they have been scarcely felt in others. But I conceive the first duty of government is to protect the economic welfare of all the people in all sections and in all groups. I said in my message opening the last session of the Congress that if private enterprise did not provide jobs this spring, government would take up the slack—that I would not let the people down. We have all learned the lesson that government cannot afford to wait until it has lost the power to act.

Therefore, my friends, I have sent a message of far-reaching importance to the Congress. I want to read to you tonight certain passages from that message, and to talk with you about them.

In that message I analyzed the causes of the collapse of 1929 in these words: "overspeculation in and overproduction of practically every article or instrument used by man . . . millions of people to be sure had been put to work, but the products of their hands had exceeded the purchasing power of their pocketbooks. . . . Under the inexorable law of supply and demand, supplies so overran demand that production was compelled to stop. Unemployment and closed factories resulted. Hence the tragic years from 1929 to 1933."

Today I pointed out to the Congress that the national income—not the government's income, but the total of the income of all the individual citizens and families of the United States—every farmer, every worker, every banker, every professional man and every person who lived on income derived from investments—that national income had amounted, in the year 1929, to $81 billion. By 1932 this had fallen to $38 billion. Gradually, and up to a few months ago, it had risen to an annual[1] total of $68 billion—a pretty good comeback from the low point.

---

[1] Roosevelt added the words "an annual" to the prepared text.

I then said this to the Congress:

"But the very vigor of the recovery in both durable goods and consumers' goods brought into the picture early in 1937, a year ago, certain highly undesirable practices, which were in large part responsible for the economic decline which began in the later months of that year. Again production had outrun the ability to buy.

"There were many reasons for this overproduction. One of them was fear—fear of war abroad, fear of inflation, fear of nationwide strikes. None of these fears have been borne out.

"... Production in many important lines of goods outran the ability of the public to purchase them, as I have said. For example, through the winter and spring of 1937, cotton factories in hundreds of cases were running on a three-shift basis, piling up cotton goods in the factory, piling them up in the hands of middlemen and retailers. For example, also, automobile manufacturers not only turned out a normal increase of finished cars, but encouraged the normal increase to run into abnormal figures, using every known method to push their sales. This meant, of course, that the steel mills of the nation ran on a twenty-four-hour basis, and the tire companies and cotton factories and glass factories and others[2] speeded up to meet the same type of abnormally stimulated demand. Yet the buying power of the nation lagged behind.

"Thus by the autumn of 1937, last autumn, the nation again had stocks on hand which the consuming public could not buy because the purchasing power of the consuming public had not kept pace with the production.

"During the same period ... the prices of many vital products had risen faster than was warranted. For example, copper, which undoubtedly can be produced at a profit in this country for from ten to twelve cents a pound, was pushed up and up to over seventeen cents a pound. The price of steel products of many kinds was increased far more than was justified by the increased wages of the steelworkers.[3] In the case of many commodities the price to the consumer was actually raised well above the inflationary boom prices of 1929. In many lines of goods and materials, prices got so

---

[2] Roosevelt also added the words "and glass factories and others" to the prepared text.

[3] These lines, giving the examples of the copper and the steel industries, were not in the prepared text as published in the Rosenman edition.

high in the summer of 1937 that buyers and builders ceased to buy or to build.

"... The economic process of getting out the raw materials, putting them through the manufacturing and finishing processes, selling them to the retailers, selling them to the consumer, and finally using them, got completely out of balance.

"... The laying off of workers came upon us last autumn and has been continuing at such a pace ever since that all of us, government and banking and business and workers, and those faced with destitution, recognize the need for action."

All of this I said to the Congress today, and I repeat it to you, the people of the country, tonight.

I went on to point out to the Senate and the House of Representatives that all the energies of government and business must be directed to increasing the national income, to putting more people into private jobs, to giving security and a feeling of security to all people in all walks of life.

I am constantly thinking of all our people—unemployed and employed alike—of their human problems, their human problems of food and clothing and homes and education and health and old age. You and I agree that security is our greatest need; the chance to work, the opportunity of making a reasonable profit in our business—whether it be a very small business or a larger one—the possibility of selling our farm products for enough money for our families to live on decently. I know these are the things that decide the well-being of all our people.

Therefore, I am determined to do all in my power to help you attain that security; and because I know that the people themselves have a deep conviction that secure prosperity of that kind cannot be a lasting one except on a basis of fair business dealing and a basis where all from the top to the bottom share in the prosperity, I repeated to the Congress today that neither it nor the chief executive can afford "to weaken or destroy great reforms which, during the past five years, have been effected on behalf of the American people. In our rehabilitation of the banking structure and of agriculture, in our provisions for adequate and cheaper credit for all types of business, in our acceptance of national responsibility for unemployment relief, in our strengthening of the credit of state and local government, in our encouragement of housing, and slum clearance and home ownership, in our supervision of stock exchanges and public utility holding companies and the issuance of new securities, in our provision for social security itself, the electorate of America wants no backward steps taken.

"We have recognized the right of labor to free organization, to collective bargaining; and machinery for the handling of labor relations is now in existence.[4] The principles are established even though we can all admit that, through the evolution of time, administration and practices can be much improved. Such improvement can come about most quickly and most peacefully through sincere efforts to understand and assist on the part of labor leaders and employers alike.

"The never-ceasing evolution of human society will doubtless bring forth new problems which will require new adjustments. Our immediate task is to consolidate and maintain the gains we have achieved.

"In this situation there is no reason, there is no occasion for any American to allow his fears to be aroused or his energy and enterprise to be paralyzed by doubt or uncertainty."

I came to the conclusion that the present-day problem calls for action both by the government and by the people, that we suffer primarily from a failure of consumer demand because of lack of buying power. Therefore it is up to us to create an economic upturn.

"How and where can and should the government help to start an economic upturn?"

I went on in my message today to propose three groups of measures and I will summarize the recommendations.

First, I asked for certain appropriations which are intended to keep the government expenditures for work relief and similar purposes—during the coming fiscal year that begins on the first of July—keep them going at the same rate of expenditure as at present. That includes additional money for the Works Progress Administration; additional funds for the Farm Security Administration; additional allotments for the National Youth Administration; and more money for the Civilian Conservation Corps, in order that it can maintain the existing number of camps now in operation.

These appropriations, made necessary by increased unemploy-

[4] Roosevelt refers here to the Wagner National Labor Relations Act of July 1935, which established the National Labor Relations Board to guarantee labor's right to unionize and to bargain collectively.

ment, will cost about a billion and a quarter dollars more than the estimates which I sent to the Congress on the third of January last.

Second, I told the Congress that the administration proposes to make additional bank reserves available for the credit needs of the country. About $1,400,000,000 of gold now in the Treasury will be used to pay these additional expenses of the government, and three-quarters of a billion dollars of additional credit will be made available to the banks by reducing the reserves now required by the Federal Reserve Board.

These two steps, taking care of relief needs and adding to bank credits, are in our best judgment insufficient by themselves to start the nation on a sustained upward movement.

Therefore, I came to the third kind of government action which I consider to be vital. I said to the Congress:

"You and I cannot afford to equip ourselves with two rounds of ammunition where three rounds are necessary. If we stop at relief and credit, we may find ourselves without ammunition before the enemy is routed. If we are fully equipped with the third round of ammunition, we stand to win the battle against adversity."

This third proposal is to make definite additions to the purchasing power of the nation by providing new work over and above the continuing of the old work.

First, to enable the United States Housing Authority to undertake the immediate construction of about $300 million worth of additional slum clearance projects.

Second, to renew a pubic works program by starting as quickly as possible about $1 billion worth of needed permanent public improvements in our states and their counties and cities.

Third, to add $100 million to the estimate for federal aid highways in excess of the amount that I recommended in January.

Fourth, to add $37 million over and above the former estimate of $63 million for flood control and reclamation.

Fifth, to add $25 million additional for federal buildings in various parts of the country.[5]

In recommending this program I am thinking not only of the immediate economic needs of the people of the nation, but also of their personal liberties—the most precious possession of all Ameri-

---

[5] Congress, thoroughly frightened by the recession, responded to these requests in the Emergency Relief Appropriations Act, which Roosevelt signed into law on June 21.

cans. I am thinking of our democracy. I am thinking of the recent trend in other parts of the world away from the democratic ideal.

Democracy has disappeared in several other great nations—disappeared not because the people of those nations disliked democracy, but because they had grown tired of unemployment and insecurity, of seeing their children hungry while they sat helpless in the face of government confusion, government weakness, weakness through lack of leadership in government. Finally, in desperation, they chose to sacrifice liberty in the hope of getting something to eat. We in America know that our own democratic institutions can be preserved and made to work. But in order to preserve them we need to act together, to meet the problems of the nation boldly, and to prove that the practical operation of democratic government is equal to the task of protecting the security of the people.

Not only our future economic soundness but the very soundness of our democratic institutions depends on the determination of our government to give employment to idle men. The people of America are in agreement in defending their liberties at any cost, and the first line of that defense lies in the protection of economic security. Your government, seeking to protect democracy, must prove that government is stronger than the forces of business depression.

History proves that dictatorships do not grow out of strong and successful governments, but out of weak and helpless governments. If by democratic methods people get a government strong enough to protect them from fear and starvation, their democracy succeeds; but if they do not, they grow impatient. Therefore, the only sure bulwark of continuing liberty is a government strong enough to protect the interests of the people, and a people strong enough and well enough informed to maintain its sovereign control over its government.

We are a rich nation; we can afford to pay for security and prosperity without having to sacrifice our liberties into the bargain.

In the first century of our republic we were short of capital, short of workers, and short of industrial production; but we were rich, very rich, in free land, and free timber and free mineral wealth. The federal government of those days rightly assumed the duty of promoting business and relieving depression by giving subsidies of land and other resources.

Thus, from our earliest days we have had a tradition of substantial government help to our system of private enterprise. But today the government no longer has vast tracts of rich land to give away, and we have discovered too that we must spend large sums of money to conserve our land from further erosion and our forests from further depletion. The situation is also very different from the old days, because now we have plenty of capital, banks and insurance companies loaded with idle money; plenty of industrial productive capacity and many millions of workers looking for jobs. It is following tradition as well as necessity if government strives to put idle money and idle men to work, to increase our public wealth and to build up the health and strength of the people—to help our system of private enterprise to function again.

It is going to cost something to get out of this recession this way, but the profit of getting out of it will pay for the cost several times over. Lost working time is lost money. Every day that a workman is unemployed, or a machine is unused, or a business organization is marking time, it is a loss to the nation. Because of the idle men and idle machines this nation lost $100 billion between 1929 and the spring of 1933, in less than four years. This year you, the people of this country, are making about $12 billion less than you were last year.

If you think back to the experiences of the early years of this administration you will remember the doubts and fears expressed about the rising expenses of government. But to the surprise of the doubters, as we proceeded to carry on the program which included public works and work relief, the country grew richer instead of poorer.

It is worthwhile to remember that the annual national people's income was $30 billion more last year, in 1937, than it was in 1932. It is true that the national debt increased $16 billion; but remember that in that increase must be included several billion dollars worth of assets which eventually will reduce the debt, and that many billion dollars of permanent public improvements—schools, roads, bridges, tunnels, public buildings, parks, and a host of other things—meet your eye in every one of the 3,100 counties in the United States.

No doubt you will be told that the government spending program of the past five years did not cause the increase in our national income. They will tell you that business revived because of private spending and investment. That is true in part, for the government spent only a small part of the total. But that government spending acted as a trigger, a trigger to set off private activity. That is why the total addition to our national production and national income has been so much greater than the contribution of the government itself.

In pursuance of that thought I said to the Congress today: "I want to make it clear that we do not believe that we can get an adequate rise in national income merely by investing and lending or spending public funds. It is essential in our economy that private funds must be put to work, and all of us recognize that such funds are entitled to a fair profit."

As national income rises, "let us not forget that government expenditures will go down and government tax receipts will go up."

The government contribution of land that we once made to business was the land of all the people. And the government contribution of money which we now make to business ultimately comes out of the labor of all the people. It is, therefore, only sound morality, as well as a sound distribution of buying power, that the benefits of the prosperity coming from this use of the money of all the people ought to be distributed among all the people, the people at the bottom as well as the people at the top. Consequently I am again expressing my hope that the Congress will enact at this session a wage and hour bill putting a floor under industrial wages and a limit on working hours—to ensure a better distribution of our prosperity, a better distribution of available work, and a sounder distribution of buying power.[6]

You may get all kinds of impressions in regard to the total cost of this new program, or in regard to the amount that will be added to the net national debt.

It is a big program. Last autumn, in a sincere effort to bring government expenditures and government income into closer balance, the budget I worked out called for sharp decreases in government spending during the coming year.

But in the light of present conditions, the conditions of today, those estimates turn out to have been far too low. This new program adds $2,062,000,000 to direct Treasury expenditures and another $950,000,000 to government loans—and the later sum, because they are loans, will come back to the Treasury in the future.

---

[6] Congress finally granted Roosevelt's request for a wages and hours bill in the Fair Labor Standards Act. The act established a minimum hourly wage of twenty-five cents, scheduled to rise gradually to forty cents by 1945; it also fixed forty hours per week as the maximum, also to be gradually achieved. In addition the act abolished labor by children under sixteen years of age.

The net effect on the debt of the government is this: between now and July 1, 1939—fifteen months away—the Treasury will have to raise less than a billion and a half dollars of new money.

Such an addition to the net debt of the United States need not give concern to any citizen, for it will return to the people of the United States many times over in increased buying power and eventually in much greater government tax receipts because of the increase in the citizen income.

What I said to the Congress today in the close of my message I repeat to you now.

"Let us unanimously recognize the fact that the federal debt, whether it be 25 billions or 40 billions, can only be paid if the nation obtains a vastly increased citizen income. I repeat that if this citizen income can be raised to $80 billion a year the national government and the overwhelming majority of state and local governments will be definitely 'out of the red.' The higher the national income goes, the faster will we be able to reduce the total of federal and state and local debts. Viewed from every angle, today's purchasing power— the citizens' income of today—is not at this time sufficient to drive the economic system of America at higher speed. Responsibility of government requires us at this time to supplement the normal processes and in so supplementing them to make sure that the addition is adequate. We must start again on a long steady upward incline in national income.

"... And in that process, which I believe is ready to start, let us avoid the pitfalls of the past—the overproduction, the overspeculation, and indeed all the extremes which we did not succeed in avoiding in 1929. In all of this, government cannot and should not act alone. Business must help, and I am sure that business will help.

"We need more than the materials of recovery. We need a united national will.

"We need to recognize nationally that the demands of no group, however just, can be satisfied unless that group is prepared to share in finding a way to produce the income from which they[7] and all other groups can be paid.... You, as the Congress, I, as the president, must, by virtue of our offices, seek the national good by preserving the balance between all groups and all sections.

---

[7] Perhaps in fairness to his speech writers, it should be noted that Roosevelt's grammatical error was ad libbed, as he substituted "they" for the proper "it" that was in the printed text.

"We have at our disposal the national resources, the money, the skill of hand and head to raise our economic level—our citizens' income. Our capacity is limited only by our ability to work together. What is needed is the will.

"The time has come to bring that will into action with every driving force at our command. And I am determined to do my share.

"... Certain positive requirements seem to me to accompany the will—if we have that will.

"There is placed on all of us the duty of self-restraint .... That is the discipline of a democracy. Every patriotic citizen must say to himself or herself, that immoderate statement, appeals to prejudice, the creation of unkindness, are offenses not against an individual or individuals, but offenses against the whole population of the United States. Use of power by any group, however situated, to force its interests or to use its strategic position in order to receive more from the common fund than its contribution to the common fund justifies, is an attack against and not an aid to our national life.[8]

"Self-restraint implies restraint by articulate public opinion, trained to distinguish fact from falsehood, trained to believe that bitterness is never a useful instrument in public affairs. There can be no dictatorship by an individual or by a group in this nation, save through division fostered by hate. Such division there must never be."

And finally I should like to say a personal word to you.

I never forget that I live in a house owned by all the American people and that I have been given their trust.

I try always to remember that their deepest problems are human. I constantly talk with those who come to tell me their own points of view; with those who manage the great industries and financial institutions of the country; with those who represent the farmer and the worker; and often, very often, with average citizens without high position who come to this house. And constantly I seek to look beyond the doors of the White House, beyond the officialdom of the national capital, into the hopes and fears of men and women in their homes. I have traveled the country over many times. My friends, my enemies, my daily mail, bring to me reports of what you are thinking and hoping. I want to be sure that neither battles nor burdens of

[8] At some point, it was decided also to quote this long sentence from Roosevelt's speech to the Congress. It does not appear, however, in the published text.

office shall ever blind me to an intimate knowledge of the way the American people want to live and the simple purposes for which they put me here.

In these great problems of government I try not to forget that what really counts at the bottom of it all, is that the men and women willing to work can have a decent job, a decent job to take care of themselves and their homes and their children adequately; that the farmer, the factory worker, the storekeeper, the gas station man, the manufacturer, the merchant—big and small—the banker who takes pride in the help that he can give to the building of his community, that all of these can be sure of a reasonable profit and safety for the earnings that they make—not today or tomorrow alone, but as far ahead as they can see.

I can hear your unspoken wonder as to where we are headed in this troubled world. I cannot expect all of the people to understand all of the people's problems; but it is my job to try to understand all of the problems.

I always try to remember that reconciling differences cannot satisfy everyone completely. Because I do not expect too much, I am not disappointed. But I know that I must never give up—that I must never let the greater interest of all the people down, merely because that might be for the moment the easiest personal way out.

I believe that we have been right in the course we have charted. To abandon our purpose of building a greater, a more stable, and a more tolerant America, would be to miss the tide and perhaps to miss the port. I propose to sail ahead. I feel sure that your hopes, I feel sure that your help is with me. For to reach a port, we must sail—sail, not lie at anchor—sail, not drift.

PURGING THE DEMOCRATIC PARTY

THIS FIRESIDE CHAT would have been noteworthy for any number of reasons, but none of them received very careful attention because of the explosive announcement that Roosevelt made near the very end of his talk.

In addition to giving a somewhat predictable "report card" on the failures and achievements of the Seventy-fifth Congress, Roosevelt also made three other observations that might have aroused interest and comment in homes around the nation. He delivered his own definitions of the terms "liberal" and "conservative" and made a ringing defense of moderate liberalism. He declared that, despite what seemed like a clear defeat the year before, the battle against the Supreme Court might actually have been won. On the basis of some minor administrative and procedural reforms and on the basis of some new decisions handed down by the high Court, the president felt ready to declare victory. And he compared opponents of the New Deal to the shrill and unpatriotic Copperheads who criticized government policy during the early 1860s—in the process, of course, few could miss the implication that he, the assailed one, was a lot like Abraham Lincoln.

All these matters were pushed into the background, however, by Roosevelt's announcement that he intended to play an active part in the upcoming Democratic party primary elections. Many editors and opponents called the whole idea a "purge." He concentrated on the Senate, rather than the House, and he targeted nine conservative Democrats, mostly southerners and chairs of powerful committees. Roosevelt wanted them defeated by southern progressives not only because they obstructed New Deal legislation and challenged his ideological control of the Democratic party, but also because he saw them as great obstacles to better social relations in the American South. They, however, saw him as a liberal meddler in the carpetbag tradition and a man who—with that wife of his—might even go so far as to tamper with race relations and segregation. The president made some speeches endorsing the opponents of conservative Democrats, but he went after, with particular force, three of the conservatives: Walter George of Georgia, Millard Tydings of Maryland, and Ellison ("Cotton Ed") Smith of South Carolina. He even went so far as to endorse Walter George's opponent while George was sitting on the official speakers' platform.

Roosevelt was successful in a few electoral races, but the purge was more notable as a failure and an embarrassment. The three southerners he opposed all won—because they had entrenched and effective organizations, because they were willing to raise the race issue, because the administration was caught benefitting some of its favorites with WPA spending, and because, in general, even very popular presidents seem unable to transfer their popularity to other people. (There is convincing evidence that Roosevelt himself continued to command overwhelming approval in the South.)

Roosevelt's defeat in the primaries was a prelude to the gain in conservative strength in the November election. The Republicans gained eight seats in the Senate and eighty in the House of Representatives. If these joined with conservative Democrats, the president of the United States could count on a very rough time as far as any reform legislation was concerned. Congress's new complexion combined with the rapidly deteriorating international scene to bring about the end of the New Deal.

MY FRIENDS, the American public and the American newspapers are certainly creatures of habit. This is one of the warmest evenings that I have ever felt in Washington, D.C., and yet, this talk tonight will be referred to as a fireside talk.[1]

Our government, happily, is a democracy. As part of the democratic process, your president is again taking an opportunity to report on the progress of national affairs—to report to the real rulers of this country: the voting public.

The Seventy-fifth Congress, elected in November 1936 on a plat-

---

[1] This opening paragraph was not in the prepared text.

form uncompromisingly liberal, has adjourned. Barring unforeseen events, there will be no session until the new Congress, to be elected in November, assembles next January.

On the one hand, the Seventy-fifth Congress has left many things undone.

For example, it refused to provide more businesslike machinery for running the executive branch of the government.[2] The Congress also failed to meet my suggestion that it take the far-reaching steps necessary to put the railroads of the country back on their feet.[3]

But, on the other hand, the Congress, striving to carry out the platform on which most of them were elected,[4] achieved more for the future good of the country than any congress did between the end of the World War and the spring of 1933.

I mention tonight only the more important of these achievements.

The Congress improved still further our agricultural laws to give the farmer a fairer share of the national income, to preserve our soil, to provide an all-weather granary, to help the farm tenant towards independence, to find new uses for farm products, and to begin crop insurance.[5]

After many requests on my part the Congress passed a Fair Labor Standards Act, what we called the Wages and Hours Bill. That act—applying to products in interstate commerce—ends child labor, sets a floor below wages and a ceiling over the hours of labor.[6]

Except perhaps for the Social Security Act, it is the most far-reaching program, the most farsighted program for the benefit of

[2] Roosevelt introduced a sweeping plan for administrative reorganization of the government in January 1937. The measure, which critics claimed was designed to enhance the president's powers and enable him to become a "dictator," got mixed-up in the Supreme Court fight of the next month. The proposal bounced around the two Houses of Congress and finally went down to defeat in March 1938. A much watered down version became law in April 1939 as the Administrative Reorganization Act of 1939.

[3] Responding to the revenue crisis facing railroads at the beginning of 1938, Roosevelt delivered a message to Congress on April 11 asking for action. He was not specific about the sort of action he desired—except to say that he could not support a nationalization of the railroad system. The most commonly debated solutions included authorizing greater loans from the Reconstruction Finance Corporation (RFC) without requiring Interstate Commerce Commission (ICC) approval, making the elimination of waste and consolidation easier, and reforming the ICC itself. In the end, the Congress adjourned a month later without taking any action.

[4] The prepared text read, "on which most of its members were elected." Thus the president introduced this grammatical error spontaneously.

[5] Most of these benefits to farmers came in the Agricultural Adjustment Act of 1938, which was signed into law on February 16, 1938. The reference to tenants, however, was to the Bankhead-Jones Farm Tenant Act, which established the Farm Security Administration. It was signed by the president on July 22, 1937.

[6] The Fair Labor Standards Act was signed on June 25.

workers that has ever been adopted here or in any other country. Without question it starts us towards a better standard of living and increases purchasing power to buy the products of farm and of factory.

Do not let any calamity-howling executive with an income of $1,000 a day, who has been turning his employees over to the government relief rolls in order to preserve his company's undistributed reserves, tell you—using his stockholders' money to pay the postage for his personal opinions—tell you that a wage of $11 a week is going to have a disastrous effect on all American industry. Fortunately for business as a whole, and therefore, fortunately for the nation, that type of executive is a rarity with whom most business executives most heartily disagree.

The Congress has provided a fact-finding commission to find a path through the jungle of contradictory theories about the wise business practices—to find the necessary facts for any intelligent legislation on monopoly, on price-fixing, and on the relationship between big business and medium-sized business and little business.[7] Different from a great part of the world, we in America persist in our belief in individual enterprise and in the profit motive; but we realize we must continually seek improved practices to ensure the continuance of reasonable profits, together with scientific progress, individual initiative, opportunities for the little fellow, fair prices, decent wages, and continuing employment.

The Congress has coordinated the supervision of commercial aviation and air mail by establishing a new Civil Aeronautics Authority;[8] and it has placed all postmasters under the civil service for the first time in our national history.[9]

The Congress has set up the United States Housing Authority to help finance large-scale slum clearance and provide low-rent hous-

[7] The Temporary National Economic Committee (TNEC) was authorized by the Congress on June 16, 1938. After a year and a half of hearings, the TNEC made a number of recommendations designed to tighten the nation's antitrust laws and in other ways to combat the growth of monopolies. The testimony of the 552 witnesses ran to thirty-one published volumes, and the TNEC staff wrote dozens of additional monographs on aspects of American economic life. But by the time the TNEC's work was completed, the nation was absorbed by World War II, and nothing was ever done to implement the committee's recommendations.

[8] The Civil Aeronautics Act became law on June 23, 1938. It established the Civil Aeronautics Authority.

[9] At the suggestion of the president as well as many others, bills were introduced into both houses on January 6, 1937, to place most postmasters in the United States under civil service protection. Many in Congress, however, were reluctant to abandon this traditional source of patronage. The proposal languished and was declared dead by the end of the summer.

ing for the low-income groups in our cities.[10] And by improving the Federal Housing Act, the Congress has made it easier for private capital to build modest homes and low-rental dwellings.

The Congress has properly reduced taxes on small corporate enterprises, and has made it easier for the Reconstruction Finance Corporation to make credit available to all business. I think the bankers of the country can fairly be expected to participate in loans where the government, through the RFC, offers to take a fair portion of the risk.[11]

So too, the Congress has provided additional funds for the Works Progress Administration, the Public Works Administration, the Rural Electrification Administration, the Civilian Conservation Corps, and other agencies, in order to take care of what we hope is a temporary additional number of unemployed at this time and to encourage production of every kind by private enterprise.

All of these things together I call our program for the national defense of our economic system. It is a program of balanced action—of moving on all fronts at once in intelligent recognition that all of our economic problems, of every group, and of every section of the country are essentially one problem.

Finally, because of increasing armaments in other nations and an international situation which is definitely disturbing to all of us, the Congress has authorized important additions to the national armed defense of our shores and our people.[12]

On one other important subject, the net result of a struggle in the Congress, has been an important victory for the people of the United States—what might well be called a lost battle which won a war.

You will remember that a year and a half ago nearly, on February 5, 1937, I sent a message to the Congress dealing with the real need of federal court reforms of several kinds. In one way or another, during the sessions of this Congress, the ends I spoke of—the real objectives—sought in that message, have been substantially attained.

The attitude of the Supreme Court toward constitutional ques-

[10] The United States Housing Authority was established by the Wagner-Steagall National Housing Act, signed by Roosevelt on September 1, 1937.

[11] The Revenue Act of 1938 passed without Roosevelt's signature on May 11. He objected to the large reduction in taxes for large corporations. The RFC loans were part of his way of combatting the recession of 1937–38 and were embodied in the Emergency Relief Appropriation Act, signed on June 21.

[12] Congress had just passed the Vinson Naval Expansion Act of 1938, which among other things, appropriated money to create a "two ocean navy." Roosevelt signed the bill on May 17.

tions is entirely changed. Its recent decisions are eloquent testimony of a willingness to collaborate with the two other branches of government to make democracy work. The government has been granted the right to protect its interests in litigation between private parties when the constitutionality of federal statutes is involved, and to appeal directly to the Supreme Court in all cases involving the constitutionality of federal statutes; and no single judge is any longer empowered to suspend a federal statute on his sole judgment as to its constitutionality. Justices of the Supreme Court may now retire at the age of seventy after ten years of service, and a substantial number of additional judgeships have been created in order to expedite the trial of cases; and finally greater flexibility has been added to the federal judicial system by allowing judges to be assigned to congested districts.

Another indirect accomplishment of this Congress has been, I think, its response to the devotion of the American people to a course of sane and consistent liberalism. The Congress has understood that under modern conditions government has a continuing responsibility to meet continuing problems, and that government cannot take a holiday of a year or a month or even a day, just because a few people are tired or frightened by the inescapable pace, fast pace of this modern world in which we live.

Some of my opponents and some of my associates have considered that I have a mistakenly sentimental judgment as to the tenacity of purpose and the general level of intelligence of the American people.

I am still convinced that the American people, since 1932, continue to insist on two requisites of private enterprise, and the relationship of government to it. The first is a complete honesty, a complete honesty at the top in looking after the use of other people's money, and in apportioning and paying individual and corporate taxes in accordance with ability to pay. And the second is sincere respect for the need of all people who are at the bottom, all people at the bottom who need to get work—and through work to get a really fair share of the good things of life, and a chance to save and a chance to rise.

After the election of 1936 I was told, and the Congress was told, by an increasing number of politically and worldly wise people that I should coast along, enjoy an easy presidency for four years, and not take the Democratic platform too seriously. They told me that people were getting weary of reform through political effort and would no longer oppose that small minority which, in spite of its own disastrous leadership in 1929, is always eager to resume its control over the government of the United States.

Never in our lifetime has such a concerted campaign of defeatism been thrown at the heads of the president and senators and congressmen as in the case of this Seventy-fifth Congress. Never before have we had so many Copperheads—and you will remember that it was the Copperheads who, in the days of the War Between the States, tried their best to make Lincoln and his Congress give up the fight, let the nation remain split in two and return to peace—peace at any price.[13]

This Congress has ended on the side of the people. My faith in the American people and their faith in themselves have been justified. I congratulate the Congress and the leadership thereof and I congratulate the American people on their own staying power.

One word about our economic situation. It makes no difference to me whether you call it a recession or a depression. In 1932 the total national income of all the people in the country had reached the low point of $38 billion in that year. With each succeeding year it rose. Last year, 1937, it had risen to $70 billion—despite definitely worse business and agricultural prices in the last four months of last year. This year, in 1938, while it is too early to do more than give a mere estimate, we hope that the national income will not fall below $60 billion and that's a lot better than $38 billion.[14] We remember also that banking and business and farming are not falling apart like the one-hoss shay, as they did in the terrible winter of 1932 to 1933.

Last year mistakes were made by the leaders of private enterprise, by the leaders of labor and by the leaders of government—all three.

Last year the leaders of private enterprise pleaded for a sudden curtailment of public spending, and said they would take up the slack. But they made the mistake of increasing their inventories too fast and setting many of their prices too high for their goods to sell.

Some labor leaders, goaded by decades of oppression of labor, made the mistake of going too far. They were not wise in using

---

[13] The Copperheads were northerners who opposed the Civil War and Lincoln; they were often poor urban Irishmen or former southerners who had moved up into the Ohio Valley.

[14] Roosevelt added the phrase "and that's a lot better than $38 billion."

methods which frightened many well-wishing people.[15] They asked employers not only to bargain with them but to put up with jurisdictional disputes at the same time.

Government, too, made mistakes—mistakes of optimism in assuming that industry and labor would themselves make no mistakes—and government made a mistake of timing, in not passing a farm bill or a wage and hour bill last year.

As a result of the lessons of all these mistakes we hope that in the future private enterprise—capital and labor alike—will operate more intelligently together, operate in greater cooperation with their own government than they have in the past. Such cooperation on the part of both of them will be very welcome to me. Certainly at this stage there should be a united stand on the part of both of them to resist wage cuts which would further reduce purchasing power.

This afternoon, only a few hours ago, I am told that a great steel company announced a reduction in prices with a view to stimulating business recovery, and I was told and I am gratified to know that this reduction in prices has involved no wage cut.[16] Every encouragement ought to be given to industry which accepts a large-volume and high-wage policy.

If this is done throughout the nation it ought to result in conditions which will replace a great part of the government spending which the failure of cooperation has made necessary this year.

You will remember that from March 4, 1933, down to date, not a single week has passed without a cry from the opposition, a small opposition,[17] a cry "to do something, to say something, to restore confidence." There is a very articulate group of people in this country, with plenty of ability to procure publicity for their views, who have consistently refused to cooperate with the mass of the people, whether things were going well or going badly, on the ground that they required more concessions to their point of view before they would admit having what they called "confidence."

[15] Roosevelt refers here to two developments in labor-management relations. The notorious "sitdown strikes"—where workers seized their factories by refusing to leave them—seemed to many moderate Americans to be an attack on private property. The first major American sitdown strike was at General Motors' Flint, Michigan, factory in January 1937, but the tactic soon spread to other key industries. In addition, labor-management violence had increased dramatically. Particularly brutal were the incidents at Henry Ford's River Rouge plant and in the pitched battle during the Republic Steel strike in Chicago—both in May 1937.

[16] This was United States Steel.

[17] Roosevelt added the phrase "a small opposition" to the prepared text.

These people demanded "restoration of confidence" when the banks were closed—and demanded it again when the banks were reopened.

They demanded "restoration of confidence" when hungry people were thronging our streets—and demanded it again when the hungry people were fed and put to work.

They demanded "restoration of confidence" when droughts hit the country and demanded it again now when our fields are laden with bounteous yields and excessive crops.

They demanded "restoration of confidence" last year when the automobile industry was running three shifts day and night and turning out more cars than the country could buy—and they're demanding it again this year when the industry is trying to get rid of an automobile surplus and has shut down its factories as a result.

But, my friends, it is my belief that many of these people who have been crying aloud for "confidence" are beginning today to realize that that hand has been overplayed, and that they are now willing to talk cooperation instead. It is my belief that the mass of the American people do have confidence, do have confidence, in themselves, confidence in their ability, with the aid of their government, to solve their own problems.

It is because you are not satisfied, and I am not satisfied, with the progress that we have made in finally solving our business and agricultural and social problems that I believe the great majority of you want your own government to keep on trying to solve them. In simple frankness and in simple honesty, I need all the help I can get—and I see signs of getting more help in the future from many who have fought against progress with tooth and nail in the past.

And now, following out this line of thought, I want to say a few words about the coming political primaries.

Fifty years ago party nominations were generally made in conventions—a system typified in the public imagination by a little group in a smoke-filled room who made out the party slates.

The direct primary was invented to make the nominating process a more democratic one—to give the party voters themselves a chance to pick their party candidates.

What I am going to say to you tonight does not relate to the primaries of any particular political party, but to matters of principle in all parties—Democratic, Republican, Farmer-Labor, Progressive, Socialist, or any other. Let that be clearly understood.

It is my hope that everybody affiliated with any party will vote in the primaries, and that every such voter will consider the fundamental principles for which his or her party is on record. That makes for a healthy choice between the candidates of the opposing parties on election day in November.

An election cannot give a country a firm sense of direction if it has two or more national parties which merely have different names but are as alike in their principles and aims as peas in the same pod.

In the coming primaries in all parties, there will be many clashes between two schools of thought, generally classified as liberal and conservative. Roughly speaking, the liberal school of thought recognizes that the new conditions throughout the world call for new remedies.

Those of us in America who hold to this school of thought, insist that these new remedies can be adopted and successfully maintained in this country under our present form of government if we use government as an instrument of cooperation to provide these remedies. We believe that we can solve our problems through continuing effort, through democratic processes instead of Fascism or Communism. We are opposed to the kind of moratorium on reform which, in effect, means reaction itself.

Be it clearly understood, however, that when I use that word "liberal," I mean the believer in progressive principles of democratic, representative government and not the wild man who, in effect, leans in the direction of Communism, for that is just as dangerous to us as Fascism itself.

The opposing or conservative school of thought, as a general proposition, does not recognize the need for government itself to step in and take action to meet these new problems. It believes that individual initiative and private philanthropy will solve them—that we ought to repeal many of the things we have done and go back, for example, to the old gold standard, or stop all this business of old age pensions and unemployment insurance, or repeal the Securities and Exchange Act, or let monopolies thrive unchecked—return, in effect, to the kind of government that we had in the 1920s.

Assuming the mental capacity of all the candidates, the important question which it seems to me the primary voter must ask is this: "To which of these general schools of thought does the candidate belong?"

As president of the United States, I am not asking the voters of the country to vote for Democrats next November as opposed to Republicans or members of any other party. Nor am I, as president, taking part in Democratic primaries.

As the head of the Democratic party, however, charged with the responsibility of carrying out the definitely liberal declaration of principles set forth in the 1936 Democratic platform, I feel that I have every right to speak in those few instances where there may be a clear-cut issue between candidates for a Democratic nomination involving these principles, or involving a clear misuse of my own name.

Do not misunderstand me. I certainly would not indicate a preference in a state primary merely because a candidate, otherwise liberal in outlook, had conscientiously differed with me on any single issue. I should be far more concerned about the general attitude of a candidate toward present-day problems and his own inward desire to get practical needs attended to in a practical way. You and I all know that progress may be blocked by outspoken reactionaries but we also know that progress can be blocked by those who say yes to a progressive objective, but who always find some reason to oppose any special specific proposal to gain that objective. I call that type of candidate a "yes, but" fellow.

And I am concerned about the attitude of a candidate or his sponsors with respect to the rights of American citizens to assemble peaceably and to express publicly their views and opinions on important social and economic issues. There can be no constitutional democracy in any community which denies to the individual his freedom to speak and worship as he wishes.[18] The American people will not be deceived by anyone who attempts to suppress individual liberty under the pretense of patriotism.

This being a free country with freedom of expression—especially with freedom of the press, as is entirely proper—there will be a lot of mean blows struck between now and election day. By "blows" I mean misrepresentation and personal attack and appeals to prejudice. It would be a lot better, of course, if campaigns everywhere could be waged with arguments instead of with blows.

I hope the liberal candidates will confine themselves to argument and not resort to blows. For in nine cases out of ten, the speaker

[18] These remarks were generally thought to be a thinly veiled attack on Boss Frank Hague (1876–1956) of Jersey City, New Jersey, who was notorious for his political intimidation of city employees and others.

or the writer who, seeking to influence public opinion, descends from calm argument to unfair blows hurts himself more than his opponent.

The Chinese have a story on this—a story based on three or four thousand years of civilization: Two Chinese coolies were arguing heatedly in the middle of a crowd in the street. A stranger expressed surprise that no blows were being struck by them. His Chinese friend replied, "The man who strikes first admits that his ideas have given out."

I know that neither in the summer primaries nor in the November elections will the American voters fail to spot the candidates whose ideas have given out.

PART II

THE FOREIGN POLICY FIRESIDE CHATS

PART 4

THE GEOPOLICY FIRESIDE CHATS

THE CRISIS ABROAD

HAVING SPENT the better part of his first term attempting to ameliorate the effects of the Great Depression and reform the nation's economic system, President Roosevelt increasingly turned his attention, after the summer of 1937, to the international crisis developing in Europe and Asia. Between 1937 and 1941 the president's task became twofold: first, to fashion a policy for dealing with the breakdown of the post–World War I peace structure and with the threat to American interests posed by that breakdown; and second, to convince the American people of the rectitude of his approach. After 1941 his job was to lead the nation to victory in war and to prepare Americans for the new international responsibilities that would follow.

Roosevelt brought a peculiar blend of assets and weaknesses to these assignments. As much as any other president of the twentieth century he was cosmopolitan in experience and outlook. Beginning as a youth and continuing until adulthood he traveled frequently to England, France, and Germany—trips that brought him in contact with the governing classes and social elites in each of those countries. At Hyde Park his family subscribed to a number of foreign publications that enriched his knowledge of international cultures. He had extensive instruction in foreign language, both at home and in his formal schooling. His tenure as assistant secretary of the navy, during the Wilson administration, tended to reinforce his international outlook. This experience and knowledge of the world beyond America, combined with his other attributes—his immense popularity, his skill in appealing to the people, his practicality and energy—were formidable assets in grappling with the approaching crisis in foreign affairs.

Despite these assets, however, Roosevelt held no well-defined or sophisticated world view, although he believed, certainly by 1941, that the United States should abandon its isolationist tradition and play a more active global role. Furthermore, he thought that a by-product of greater involvement should be a brand of internationalism that he defined in quasi-Wilsonian–quasi-Lodgeian terms. If World War II seemed to vindicate Woodrow Wilson, it was largely because Roosevelt helped keep alive the idea that American participation in the League of Nations would have prevented war, though Roosevelt in the early 1930s had been unwilling to assume the political risks associated with even the limited step of taking the United States into the World Court.

He saw himself as a realistic Wilsonian, as one who would lead the nation forward through a war and into an international organization by avoiding Wilson's mistakes. His internationalism seems strikingly nationalistic and paternalistic, not far from that advocated by Henry Cabot Lodge after World War I. In rejecting Wilson's League of Nations, Lodge had suggested that an organization of the Allies would work just as well to keep the peace; the most efficient league was the "existing league of allies." Roosevelt thought that the British, Soviets, Americans, and Chinese—the "Four Policemen"—should dominate the new organization, with the United States assuming the role of moral leadership. In addition, Roosevelt believed that, because the USSR would play a powerful part in postwar European affairs, Soviet-American cooperation would be essential to world peace. Nothing should be allowed to interfere with good relations with the Russians. Moreover, he hoped to achieve an end to colonialism, although his plans for doing so were hopelessly ill-defined and vague.

Essentially Roosevelt's weltanschauung was a stew composed of lessons from his childhood, views he picked up at Harvard, faith in conventional Christianity, and a belief in progressive democracy— a mixture that he spiced generously with political expediency. To Roosevelt the Axis powers represented the truly reactionary forces in the world, while the British, as epitomized by Prime Minister Winston Churchill, were simply old-fashioned in their views. The Russians were crude and disagreeable but manageable, not unlike certain disagreeable American political bosses. The Axis had to be defeated, the British changed, and the Soviets accommodated. Beyond that Roosevelt knew only dimly what he wanted as the United States moved toward the Second World War.

Franklin Roosevelt gave his fourteenth Fireside Chat, and the first dealing mainly with foreign policy, two days after the German invasion of Poland—the beginning of the ultimate challenge to the peace structure. This invasion and the attending British and French declarations of war on Germany signaled the start of World War II and the end of the fragile interwar edifice erected to prevent international conflict. On the phone with William Bullitt, a longtime friend and then American ambassador to France, Roosevelt exclaimed, "Bill, this is it. It has come at last. God help us all!"

America would now have to face up to responsibilities that it had too long avoided. At the end of World War I, twenty years before, the United States had assumed only partial connection with the peace structure. The first part of that structure, the Treaty of Versailles and the League of Nations, it had refused to join at all. The second part, the World Court, it debated joining throughout the 1920s, only to decide against participation in the first year of the Roosevelt administration. In return for newspaper publisher William Randolph Hearst's support in the campaign of 1932, Roosevelt promised not to seek American membership. The other two parts of the structure, the Washington Conference treaties and the Kellogg-Briand Pact, the United States had taken the lead in developing. But both carried only moral obligations; neither required any political or military responses by the signatory powers.

Challenges to these arrangements began with the Japanese invasion of Manchuria in 1931, which violated the Nine Power Washington agreement as well as the Kellogg Pact. Since the United States saw no reason to do battle on behalf of the structure itself, and since it had only casual commercial and no security interests in Manchuria, it responded in a passive manner: The only measures the Hoover administration was prepared to take were the Stimson Doctrine (expressing U.S. "nonrecognition" of violations of American treaty rights in China, the "Open Door" policy, or the Kellogg-Briand pact) and Secretary of State Henry Stimson's letter to the Chairman of the Senate Foreign Relations Committee, William E. Borah, containing an implied American threat to disregard the Five Power Naval Treaty. Roosevelt's response to the Japanese aggression in China prior to 1937 amounted to even less than Hoover's: indeed Roosevelt's approach was to avoid protesting Japan's action unless and until the United States was prepared to do something concrete.

Meanwhile Germany and Italy were charting an aggressive course in Europe. On October 13, 1933, Hitler announced the withdrawal of Germany from the League of Nations and, more ominously, from the Geneva Disarmament Conference, thus effectively killing any hope of a disarmament agreement. In October 1935 Benito Mussolini sent Italian troops into Ethiopia in a vainglorious attempt to avenge the Italian defeat at Adowa in 1895 by the Abyssinians, who had fought with spears and bows and arrows, and to begin the creation of a new Roman Empire. In May 1936, Italy annexed Ethiopia and withdrew from the League. In a clear violation of the Treaty of Versailles, Hitler occupied the Rhineland in March 1936. He and Mussolini then threw their support to the forces of Francisco Franco, who began a rebellion against the liberal democratic government of Spain in 1936. The Spanish Civil War culminated in a Fascist victory in 1939.

To all these violations of the peace structure, President Roosevelt responded within the context of the isolationist mood in the United States—a mood that accurately reflected his own predilections in this period of his presidency. The reasons are not difficult to discern. World problems seemed remote and not terribly significant to the 25 percent of the American work force that found itself unemployed during these depression years. Nor did policymakers believe that using scarce American resources to project American power around the world was sound judgment. Then there was the American tradition in foreign policy. Noninvolvement and nonentanglement in political-military affairs outside the Western Hemisphere were the norm for the United States. Throughout its history (except for brief periods of war) the nation had followed a nonmilitarized foreign policy. In the 1930s, moreover, disillusionment about the Wilsonian crusade of the World War I era held sway, and a great many Americans in both private and public life came to believe that the country's involvement in the Great War had been a terrible mistake engineered by influential investment bankers, shipbuilders, and munitions-makers.

To guarantee that policymakers did not repeat this mistake, Congress drafted a series of "neutrality laws" in the period from 1935 through 1937. These laws—which, among other things, mandated an arms embargo and prevented loans to belligerents and travel on belligerent vessels—limited the president's latitude in regard to foreign crises, though little evidence exists to prove that Roosevelt had any desire prior to 1937 to pursue a more aggressive external policy. Challenges to the peace structure after 1937 led to President Roosevelt's change of heart about the proper American position toward world events.

In July 1937, an incident at the Marco Polo bridge, ten miles west of Peking (now Beijing), led to a Japanese occupation of the entire Peking area. This was followed by fighting in Shanghai and, soon, engagements throughout China. Coming back home from a speaking tour in the West, Roosevelt stopped in Chicago on October 5 to give a speech upon the occasion of the opening of a bridge along a section of new lakeshore highway. This address signaled a turning point: the president said "it seems to be unfortunately true that the epidemic of world lawlessness is spreading. When an epidemic of physical disease starts to spread, the community approves and joins in a quarantine of the patients in order to protect the health of the community against the spread of the disease." That Roosevelt almost immediately backed away from the statement given the isolationist outcry does not diminish the fact that he had begun to think in terms of greater responsibilities for the United States.

Absence of American assertiveness toward Axis aggression over the following year and a half tends to belie Roosevelt's interest. To Nazi annexation of Austria in violation of the Treaty of St. Germaine, there was barely a hint of action beyond the cancellation of a commercial treaty with Austria. Nor did the United States respond to Hitler's demands for the Sudetenland and the ultimate "solution" of the crisis at Munich, except for Roosevelt's announcement that "The government of the United States has no political involvement in Europe, and will assume no obligations in the conduct of present negotiations." When Germany annexed all of Czechoslovakia in March 1939, Roosevelt merely asked the Axis dictators not to invade thirty-one specified countries over a ten-year period, a request that Hitler and Mussolini lost no time in ridiculing. Worry that he not get too far ahead of public opinion, not lack of concern about events, governed the president's positions in these instances.

Conclusion of the unholy alliance between Stalin and Hitler in August 1939, and then the Nazi invasion of Poland on September 1, led to American support of the Western democracies. Unlike Wilson in 1914, Roosevelt made no commitment to neutrality in thought and deed. "Even a neutral has a right to take account of facts," he proclaimed; "even a neutral cannot be asked to close his mind or his conscience." In fact American policy between 1939 and December 7, 1941, is a record of support for the opponents of Germany, Japan, and Italy. As long as Axis action meant only challenges to the peace structure in the abstract, the United States did not respond. However, when it implied direct threats to American security—including threats to the nation's security in the greater-than-physical sense—and when it involved behavior deeply repugnant to American values, action became necessary.

Despite official neutrality, and strong isolationist sentiment around the country, the Roosevelt administration engineered Cash-and-Carry, the Destroyer-Bases deal, Lend-Lease, shoot-on-sight orders against German submarines in the Atlantic, and economic sanctions against the Japanese in the period from the beginning of the war down to the time of American entrance. Gaining approval of these measures and implementing them called for political dexterity and salesmanship on Roosevelt's part. He sold Cash-and-Carry to the public as a way to keep American ships out of war zones. He used his "garden hose" analogy in a Fireside Chat to convince the American people of the need for Lend-Lease. If a neighbor's house was on fire and the neighbor asked to borrow a hose, he said, one did not offer to sell the hose. The neighborly, as well as the self-interested, thing to do was to lend him the hose; otherwise the fire might spread to one's own house. Later, during the naval crisis in the North Atlantic, when he wanted to authorize American vessels convoying supplies to Great Britain to attack German submarines on sight, he evoked his "rattlesnake" analogy, telling the American people that German submarines were the rattlesnakes of the Atlantic and that one did not allow a rattlesnake to strike without taking preventive action.

Public opinion in the days prior to Pearl Harbor broke down into three broad groups: the isolationists, led by the America First Committee and such congressional luminaries as William E. Borah of Idaho and Hamilton Fish of New York, who opposed any involvement in the war; a group of indeterminate size that increasingly favored intervention; and the majority who feared direct involvement but wanted assistance for the Allies. Historians differ in assessing President Roosevelt's own attitude, though most would concede that as time passed his views coincided more and more with those of the second group.

During the war itself, Roosevelt affected a positive demeanor that did not always accord with military developments or with the state of U.S.-Allied relations. The first months of American participation in the conflict brought a series of German and Japanese successes. British and American relations with the Soviet Union, which had entered the war upon being attacked by Germany in June 1941, did not constitute an entente cordiale, but rather a marriage of convenience. Stalin, paranoid former ally of Hitler and master realpolitiker, believed that Roosevelt and, particularly Churchill, wanted the Soviet Union to carry the military burden while the Western Allies waited to pick up the spoils. A number of Americans, including then-Senator Harry Truman, had recommended allowing Germany and the Soviet Union to destroy one another; a great many saw Japan as the prime enemy of the United States and did not agree with the decision to give priority to the European conflict. In any event, the Western Allies' postponement of a second front until June 1944 remained a point of dispute, as did Stalin's secretiveness and general unwillingness to cooperate on a variety of military-diplomatic questions.

Nor were British-American relations always harmonious. Differences existed on the timing of a second front, which Churchill wanted to delay and Roosevelt and his chief of staff, General George Marshall, wished to hasten; over the level of American commitment to the Asian war and to the government of Chiang Kai-shek, which Churchill saw as tertiary to the task at hand and Roosevelt saw as central; and over the issue of colonial empire, which Churchill hoped to retain and Roosevelt wished to dissolve.

These issues, and a host of others pertaining to the fighting of the war and securing of the peace, the Allied leaders negotiated at a series of wartime conferences—at Casablanca, Moscow, Cairo, Teheran, and Yalta. Roosevelt saw himself not only as commander in chief of a major American military endeavor and as manager of the arsenal of democracy, but also as facilitator of accommodation among the Allies as they pursued disparate interests. That he did not succeed in creating a perfect world is of secondary importance in this account to the tone that he set in making the attempt.

At the time of his final Fireside Chat, his health had deteriorated severely. By the time he became sixty, in 1942, his heart was dangerously enlarged and his arteries had hardened like those of a man thirty years his senior. During the final year of the war he slept twelve to fourteen hours a day. Sometimes, as at the Quebec conference in September 1944, he dropped off in the middle of important conversations. By January 1945 he looked terrible. He could hardly sign his name; and he could not concentrate on lengthy documents, much less engage in strenuous bargaining as he might have done when he met with Churchill and Stalin at Yalta in February 1945. The imminence of his death had become evident to many observers.

REACTION TO WAR IN EUROPE: PREPARING FOR CASH-AND-CARRY

THE ISSUES that President Roosevelt addressed in his chats with the American people were nothing if not momentous. First it was the economic depression, the worst the world and the nation had ever faced; now it was war of a type the world had never before experienced. On September 1, Adolf Hitler, having concluded a nonaggression pact with Josef Stalin, sent his Panzer divisions hurtling into Poland. Germany would no longer accept the "terrible inequities" of the Versailles Treaty: the Polish Corridor carved out of German territory, the free port city of Danzig, which gave Poland access to the sea. Acting on their commitments of April 1939 to guarantee Polish territory, Great Britain and France declared war on Germany on September 3, only hours before the president's message. World War II had begun.

This Fireside Chat must be seen through the prism of Roosevelt's conception of American neutrality. He had been trying since May to secure congressional agreement to change the neutrality legislation: at a meeting in the White House in July he had pulled out all the stops in an effort to convince key senators of both parties of the need, when war finally came, to aid those countries resisting Axis aggression. Owing to the strength of the isolationist viewpoint, expressed most forcefully by Senator Borah of Idaho, he did not get very far prior to September 1. But Roosevelt persisted in his belief that "even a neutral cannot be asked to close his mind or his conscience." What he wanted was an amendment to the neutrality legislation that would end the arms embargo. The tactic he chose—transparent, as one reads the Fireside Chat—was to blend isolationism and intervention. He would assure Congress and the American people of his genuine desire for neutrality; and he would urge Congress to allow the sale of arms to Great Britain and France on a cash-and-carry basis. In return for repeal of the arms embargo, he would support legislation to keep

American ships out of particular danger zones. This would make American neutrality "a true neutrality."

True to his genius, Roosevelt had once again captured the national mood, which was both supportive of the Allies and fearful of American involvement in war. He submitted his proposal to Congress on September 21. It passed on November 3.

MY COUNTRYMEN and my friends. Tonight my single duty is to speak to the whole of America.

Until four-thirty o'clock this morning I had hoped against hope that some miracle would prevent a devastating war in Europe and bring to an end the invasion of Poland by Germany.

For four long years a succession of actual wars and constant crises have shaken the entire world and have threatened in each case to bring on the gigantic conflict which is today unhappily a fact.

It is right that I should recall to your minds the consistent and at times successful efforts of your government in these crises to throw the full weight of the United States into the cause of peace. In spite of spreading wars I think that we have every right and every reason to maintain as a national policy the fundamental moralities, the teachings of religion, the continuation of efforts to restore peace because some day, though the time may be distant, we can be of even greater help to a crippled humanity.

It is right, too, to point out that the unfortunate events of these recent years have, without question, been based on the use of force or the threat of force. And it seems to me clear, even at the outbreak of this great war, that the influence of America should be consistent in seeking for humanity a final peace which will eliminate, as far as it is possible to do so, the continued use of force between nations.

It is, of course, impossible to predict the future. I have my constant stream of information from American representatives and other sources throughout the world. You, the people of this country, are receiving news through your radios and your newspapers at every hour of the day.

You are, I believe, the most-enlightened and the best-informed people in all the world at this moment. You are subjected to no censorship of news, and I want to add that your government has no information which it withholds or which it has any thought of withholding from you.

At the same time, as I told my press conference on Friday, it is of the highest importance that the press and the radio use the utmost caution to discriminate between actual verified fact on the one hand, and mere rumor on the other.

I can add to that by saying that I hope the people of this country will also discriminate most carefully between news and rumor. Do not believe of necessity everything you hear or read. Check up on it first.

You must master at the outset a simple but unalterable fact in modern relations between nations. When peace has been broken anywhere, the peace of all countries everywhere is in danger.

It is easy for you and for me to shrug our shoulders and say that conflicts taking place thousands of miles from the continental United States, and, indeed thousands of miles from the whole American hemisphere, do not seriously affect the Americas—and that all the United States has to do is to ignore them and go about its own business. Passionately though we may desire detachment, we are forced to realize that every word that comes through the air, every ship that sails the sea, every battle that is fought, does affect the American future.

Let no man or woman thoughtlessly or falsely talk of America sending its armies to European fields. At this moment there is being prepared a proclamation of American neutrality. This would have been done even if there had been no neutrality statute on the books, for this proclamation is in accordance with international law and in accordance with American policy.

This will be followed by a proclamation required by the existing Neutrality Act. And I trust that in the days to come our neutrality can be made a true neutrality.

It is of the utmost importance that the people of this country, with the best information in the world, think things through. The most dangerous enemies of American peace are those who, without well-rounded information on the whole broad subject of the past, the present, and the future, undertake to speak with assumed authority, to talk in terms of glittering generalities, to give to the nation assurances or prophecies which are of little present or future value.

I myself cannot and do not prophesy the course of events abroad—

and the reason is that, because I have of necessity such a complete picture of what is going on in every part of the world, that I do not dare to do so. And the other reason is that I think it is honest for me to be honest with the people of the United States.

I cannot prophesy the immediate economic effect of this new war on our nation, but I do say that no American has the moral right to profiteer at the expense either of his fellow citizens or of the men, the women, and the children who are living and dying in the midst of war in Europe.

Some things we do know. Most of us in the United States believe in spiritual values. Most of us, regardless of what church we belong to, believe in the spirit of the New Testament—a great teaching which opposes itself to the use of force, of armed force, of marching armies and falling bombs. The overwhelming masses of our people seek peace—peace at home, and the kind of peace in other lands which will not jeopardize our peace at home.

We have certain ideas and certain ideals of national safety, and we must act to preserve that safety today, and to preserve the safety of our children in future years.

That safety is and will be bound up with the safety of the Western Hemisphere and of the seas adjacent thereto. We seek to keep war from our own firesides by keeping war from coming to the Americas. For that we have historic precedent that goes back to the days of the administration of President George Washington.[1] It is serious enough and tragic enough to every American family in every state in the Union to live in a world that is torn by wars on other continents. And those wars today affect every American home. It is our national duty to use every effort to keep those wars out of the Americas.

And at this time let me make the simple plea that partisanship and selfishness be adjourned; and that national unity be the thought that underlies all others.

This nation will remain a neutral nation, but I cannot ask that every American remain neutral in thought as well. Even a neutral

[1] The first "Neutrality Proclamation" in American history was issued by Washington on April 22, 1793; it reflected President Washington's desire to keep the new nation out of the general European war raging in the aftermath of the French Revolution. Perhaps, however, Roosevelt's reference here is an oblique one to the policy recommended by Washington in his Farewell Address of September 19, 1796, in which he urged that the nation remain free of foreign entanglements. The concern about the Western Hemisphere was most directly expressed by President James Monroe in the Monroe Doctrine of 1823.

has a right to take account of facts. Even a neutral cannot be asked to close his mind or close his conscience.

I have said not once, but many times, that I have seen war and that I hate war. I say that again and again.

I hope the United States will keep out of this war. I believe that it will. And I give you assurance and reassurance that every effort of your government will be directed toward that end.

As long as it remains within my power to prevent, there will be no blackout of peace in the United States.

DEEPENING CRISIS IN EUROPE AND AMERICAN MILITARY READINESS

THE GERMAN INVASION of Poland and the subsequent Soviet-German partition of that unhappy country was followed by a lull in the fighting. The Soviets, seeking territory from Finland that the Finns refused to give up, waged a winter war in 1939–40 against that tiny country, a costly conflict that eventually resulted in Soviet victory in March 1940. Meanwhile the absence of military activity in the West lent support to the contention of American isolationists that this was truly a "phony war." All that changed, however, in the period from April through June. Hitler in April unleashed a lightning blitz against Denmark and Norway that resulted in German occupations of those countries—action that led to heightened American anxiety about the Danish territories of Iceland and Greenland since the latter and part of the former lay within the Western Hemisphere. "Force and military aggression are once more on the march against small nations," the American president declared.

Hitler then attacked, in turn, the Netherlands, Belgium, Luxembourg, and France. In late May the British escaped from the continent, evacuating some 300,000 men from the beaches of Dunkirk to fight another day.

President Roosevelt's response to the French crisis was twofold: he hoped to prevent Italian intervention, and should France fall, the defeat of Great Britain. That he would fail in the first of these objectives soon became clear, and on June 10 in a speech at Charlottesville, Virginia, he condemned Mussolini: "the hand that held the dagger," he said, "has struck it into the back of its neighbor." The French succumbed to Nazi power on June 22. To provide the British with the requisite arms and equipment to withstand the Nazi onslaught would require opening the arsenals of the American government. Sales from private suppliers would not be sufficient: "We will extend to the opponents of force the material resources of this nation," he vowed in that same speech in Charlottesville. All of these things were swirling through his mind as he spoke to the American people on May 26. He hoped to prepare them for an expanded commitment to the British. He hoped also to reassure them both of the current state of American military readiness and of his determination to increase the nation's preparedness by increasing its military production.

MY FRIENDS, at this moment of sadness throughout most of the world, I want to talk with you about a number of subjects that directly affect the future of the United States. We are shocked by the almost incredible eyewitness stories that come to us, stories of what is happening at this moment to the civilian populations of Norway and Holland and Belgium and Luxembourg and France.

I think it is right on this Sabbath evening that I should say a word in behalf of women and children and old men who need help—immediate help in their present distress—help from us across the seas, help from us who are still free to give it.

Tonight over the once peaceful roads of Belgium and France millions are now moving, running from their homes to escape bombs and shells and fire and machine gunning, without shelter, and almost wholly without food. They stumble on, knowing not where the end of the road will be. I speak to you of these people because each one of you that is listening to me tonight has a way of helping them. The American Red Cross, that represents each of us, is rushing food and clothing and medical supplies to these destitute civilian millions. Please—I beg you—please give according to your means to your nearest Red Cross chapter, give as generously as you can. I ask this in the name of our common humanity.

Let us sit down together again, you and I, to consider our own pressing problems that confront us.

There are many among us who in the past closed their eyes to events abroad—because they believed in utter good faith what some of their fellow Americans told them—that what has taken place in Europe was none of our business; that no matter what happened over there, the United States could always pursue its peaceful and unique course in the world.

There are many among us that closed their eyes, from lack of interest or lack of knowledge; honestly and sincerely thinking that many hundreds of miles of salt water made the American hemisphere so remote that the people of North and Central and South America could go on living in the midst of their vast resources without reference to, or danger from, the other continents of the world.

There are some among us who were persuaded by minority groups that we could maintain our physical safety by retiring within our continental boundaries—the Atlantic on the east, the Pacific on the west, Canada on the north, and Mexico on the south. I illustrated the futility—the impossibility—of that idea in my message to the Congress last week. Obviously, a defense policy based on that is merely to invite future attack.

And, finally, there are a few among us who have deliberately and consciously closed their eyes because they were determined to be opposed to their government, its foreign policy and every other policy, to be partisan, and to believe that anything that the government did was wholly wrong.

To those who have closed their eyes for any of these many reasons, to those who would not admit the possibility of the approaching storm—to all of them the past two weeks have meant the shattering of many illusions.

They have lost the illusion that we are remote and isolated and, therefore, secure against the dangers from which no other land is free.

In some quarters, with this rude awakening has come fear, fear bordering on panic. It is said that we are defenseless. It is whispered by some that only by abandoning our freedom, our ideals, our way of life, can we build our defenses adequately, can we match the strength of the aggressors.

I did not share those illusions. I do not share these fears.

Today we are more realistic. But let us not be calamity-howlers and discount our strength. Let us have done with both fears and illusions. On this Sabbath evening, in our homes and in the midst of our American family,[1] let us calmly consider what we have done and what we must do.

In the past two or three weeks all kinds of stories have been handed out to the American public about our lack of preparedness. It has even been charged that the money we have spent on our mili-

---

[1] The printed version of the speech read, "in the midst of our American families."

tary and naval forces during the last few years has gone down the rathole. I think that it is a matter of fairness to the nation that you hear the facts.

Yes, we have spent large sums of money on the national defense. This money has been used to make our Army and Navy today the largest, the best-equipped, and the best-trained peacetime military establishment in the whole history of this country.

Let me tell you just a few of the many things accomplished during the past few years.

I do not propose, I could not go into every detail. It is a known fact, however, that in 1933, when this administration came into office, the United States Navy had fallen in standing among the navies of the world, in power of ships and in efficiency, to a relatively low ebb. The relative fighting power of the Navy had been greatly diminished by failure to replace ships and equipment, which had become out-of-date.

But between 1933 and this year, 1940—seven fiscal years—your government will have spent $1,487,000,000 more than it spent on the Navy during the seven years that preceded 1933.[2]

What did we get for this money? Money, incidentally, not included in the new defense appropriation—only money hitherto appropriated.[3]

The fighting personnel of the Navy rose from 79,000 to 145,000.

During this period 215 ships for the fighting fleet have been laid down or commissioned, practically seven times the number in the preceding seven-year period.

Of these 215 ships we have commissioned 12 cruisers; 63 destroyers; 26 submarines; 3 aircraft carriers; 2 gunboats; 7 auxiliaries; and many smaller craft. And among the many ships now being built and paid for as we build them are 8 new battleships.

Ship construction, of course, costs millions of dollars—more in the United States than anywhere else in the world; but it's a fact that we cannot have adequate naval defense for all American waters without ships, ships that sail the surface of the ocean, ships that move under the surface, and ships that move through the air. And, speaking of airplanes, airplanes that work with the Navy, in 1933 we had 1,127 of them—1,127 useful aircraft—and today we have 2,892

[2] It should be noted that the United States pursued a course of naval disarmament in the 1920s in accord with the Five Power Agreement of the Washington Conference.

[3] This sentence was added by Roosevelt to the printed version of the speech.

on hand and on order. Of course, nearly all of the old planes of 1933 have been replaced by new planes because they became obsolete or worn out.

Yes, the Navy is far stronger today than in any peacetime period in the whole long history of the nation. In hitting power and in efficiency, I would even make the assertion that it is stronger today than it was during the World War.[4]

The Army of the United States. In 1933, it consisted of 122,000 enlisted men. Now, in 1940, that number has been practically doubled. The Army of 1933 had been given few new implements of war since 1919, and it had been compelled to draw on old reserve stocks left over from the World War. The net result of this was that our Army by 1933 had very greatly declined in its ratio of strength with the armies of Europe and of the Far East.

That was the situation I found.

But, since then, great changes have taken place.

Between 1933 and 1940—this past seven fiscal years—your government will have spent $1,292,000,000 more than was spent on the Army in the previous seven years.

And what did we get for this money?

The personnel of the Army, as I have said, has been almost doubled, and by the end of this year every existing unit of the present regular Army will be equipped with its complete requirements of modern weapons. Existing units of the National Guard will also be largely equipped with similar items.

Here are some striking examples taken from a large number of them:

Since 1933, we have actually purchased 5,640 airplanes, including the most modern type of long-range bombers and fast pursuit planes, though, of course, many of these that were delivered four and five and six and seven years ago have worn out through use and been scrapped.

We must remember that these planes cost money—a lot of it. For example, one modern four-engine long-range bombing plane costs $350,000; one modern interceptor pursuit plane costs $133,000; one medium bomber costs $160,000.

To go on. In 1933 we had only 355 anti-aircraft guns. We now have

[4]The president's assertion on this point would have had special force since many of his listeners would have remembered that he had been an assistant secretary of the navy during World War I.

more than 1,700 modern anti-aircraft guns of all types on hand or on order, and we ought to know that a three-inch anti-aircraft gun costs $40,000 without any of the fire-control equipment that goes with it.

In 1933 there were only 24 modern infantry mortars in the entire Army. We now have on hand and on order more than 1,600.

In 1933 we had only 48 modern tanks and armored cars; today we have on hand and on order 1,700. Each one of our heavier tanks costs $46,000.

There are many other items in which our progress since 1933 has been rapid. And the great proportion of this advance consists of really modern equipment.

For instance, in 1933, on the personnel side we had 1,263 Army pilots. Today the Army alone has more than 3,200[5] of the best fighting fliers in the world, fliers who last year flew more than one million hours in combat training. And that figure does not include the hundreds of splendid pilots in the National Guard and in the organized reserves.

Within the past year the productive capacity of the aviation industry to produce modern planes[6] has been tremendously increased—in this past year more than doubled. But that capacity is still inadequate. The government, working with industry, is determined to increase that capacity to meet our needs. We intend to harness the efficient machinery of these manufacturers to the government's program of being able to get 50,000 planes a year.

One additional word about aircraft, about which we read so much. Recent wars, including the current war in Europe have demonstrated beyond doubt that fighting efficiency depends on unity of command, unity of control.

In sea operations the airplane is just as much an integral part of unity of operations as are the submarine, the destroyer, and the battleship; and in land warfare the airplane is just as much a part of military operations as are the tank corps, the engineers, the artillery, or the infantry itself. And therefore, air forces should continue to be a part of the Army and Navy.

In line with my request the Congress, this week, is voting the largest appropriations ever asked by the Army or the Navy in peacetime;

[5] According to the printed version of the speech, the number of Army pilots was 3,000.
[6] The printed version used the term "military" planes.

and the equipment and training provided for them will be in addition to the figures I have given you.

The world situation may so change that it will be necessary to reappraise our program at any time. And in such case I am confident that the Congress and the chief executive will work in harmony as a team, work in harmony as they are doing today.

I will not hesitate at any moment to ask for additional funds when they are required.

In this era of swift, mechanized warfare, we all have to remember that what is modern today and up-to-date, what is efficient and practical, becomes obsolete and outworn tomorrow.

Even while the production line turns out airplanes, new airplanes are being designed on the drafting table.

Even as a cruiser slides down the launching ways, plans for improvement, plans for increased efficiency in the next model, are taking shape in the blueprints of designers.

Every day's fighting in Europe, on land, on sea, and in the air, discloses constant changes in methods of warfare. We are constantly improving and redesigning, testing new weapons, learning the lessons of the moment,[7] and seeking to produce in accordance with the latest that the brains of science can conceive.

Yes, we are calling upon the resources, the efficiency and the ingenuity of American manufacturers of war material of all kinds—airplanes and tanks and guns and ships, and all the hundreds of products that go into this matériel. The government of the United States itself manufactures few of the implements of war. Private industry will continue to be the source of most of this matériel; and private industry will have to be speeded up to produce it at the rate and the efficiency called for by the needs of the times.

I know that private business cannot be expected to make all of the capital investments required for expansions of plants and factories and personnel which this program calls for at once. It would be unfair to expect industrial corporations or their investors to do this, when there is a chance that a change in international affairs may stop or curtail orders a year or two hence.

Therefore, the government of the United States stands ready to advance the necessary money to help provide for the enlargement

---

[7] The printed version read, "learning the lessons of the immediate war."

of factories, the establishment of new plants, the employment of thousands of necessary workers, the development of new sources of supply for the hundreds of raw materials required, the development of quick mass transportation of supplies. And the details of all of this are now being worked out in Washington, day and night.

We are calling on men now engaged in private industry to help us in carrying out this program, and you will hear more of this in detail in the next few days.

It does not mean that the men we call upon will be engaged in the actual production of this matériel. That will still have to be carried on in the plants and the factories throughout the land. Private industry will have the responsibility of providing the best, speediest, and most efficient mass production of which it is capable. The functions of the businessmen whose assistance we are calling upon will be to coordinate this program—to see to it that all of the plants continue to operate at maximum speed and efficiency.

Patriotic Americans of proven merit, of unquestioned ability in their special fields, are coming to Washington to help the government with their training, their experience, and their capability.

It is our purpose not only to speed up production but to increase the total facilities of the nation in such a way that they can be further enlarged to meet emergencies of the future.

But as this program proceeds there are several things we must continue to watch and to safeguard, things which are just as important to the sound defense of a nation as physical armament itself. While our Navy and our airplanes and our guns and our ships may be our first lines of defense, it is still clear that way down at the bottom, underlying them all, giving them their strength, sustenance, and power, are the spirit and the morale of a free people.

For that reason, we must make sure, in all that we do, that there be no breakdown or cancellation of any of the great social gains which we have made in these past years. We have carried on an offensive on a broad front against social and economic inequalities, against abuses which had made our society weak. That offensive should not now be broken down by the pincers movement of those who would use the present needs of physical military defense to destroy it.

There is nothing in our present emergency to justify making the workers of our nation toil for longer hours than those now limited by statute. As more orders come in and as more work has to be done, tens of thousands of people, who are now unemployed, will, I believe, receive employment.

There is nothing in our present emergency to justify a lowering of the standards of employment. Minimum wages should not be reduced. It is my hope, indeed, that the new speed-up of production will cause many businesses which now pay below the minimum standards to bring their wages up.

There is nothing in our present emergency to justify a breaking down of old-age pensions or of unemployment insurance. I would rather see the systems extended to other groups who do not now enjoy them.

There is nothing in our present emergency to justify a retreat—any retreat—from any of our social objectives—from conservation of natural resources, assistance to agriculture, housing, and help to the underprivileged.

Conversely, however, I am sure that responsible leaders will not permit some specialized group, which represents a minority of the total employees of a plant or an industry, to break up the continuity of employment of the majority of the employees. Let us remember that the policy and the laws that provide for collective bargaining are still in force. And, I can assure you that labor will be adequately represented in Washington in the carrying out of this program of defense.

And one more point on this.[8] Our present emergency and a common sense of decency make it imperative that no new group of war millionaires shall come into being in this nation as a result of the struggles abroad. The American people will not relish the idea of any American citizen growing rich and fat in an emergency of blood and slaughter and human suffering.

And, last of all, this emergency demands that the consumers of America be protected so that our general cost of living can be maintained at a reasonable level. We ought to avoid the spiral processes of the World War, the rising spiral of costs of all kinds. The soundest policy is for every employer in the country to help give useful employment to the millions who are unemployed. By giving to those millions an increased purchasing power, the prosperity of the whole nation will rise to a much higher level.

---

[8] This sentence was added spontaneously by the president.

Today's threat to our national security is not a matter of military weapons alone. We know of other methods, new methods of attack.

The Trojan horse. The fifth column that betrays a nation unprepared for treachery.[9]

Spies, saboteurs, and traitors are the actors in this new strategy. With all of these we must and will deal vigorously.

But there is an added technique for weakening a nation at its very roots, for disrupting the entire pattern of life of a people. And it's important that we understand it.

The method is simple. First, discord—the dissemination of discord. A group—not too large, a group that may be sectional or racial or political—is encouraged to exploit its prejudices through false slogans and emotional appeals. The aim of those who deliberately egg on these groups is to create confusion of counsel, public indecision, political paralysis, and, eventually, a state of panic.

Sound national policies come to be viewed with a new and unreasoning skepticism, not through the wholesome political debates of honest and free men, but through the clever schemes of foreign agents.

As a result of these new techniques, armament programs may be dangerously delayed. Singleness of national purpose may be undermined. Men can lose confidence in each other, and therefore lose confidence in the efficacy of their own united action. Faith and courage can yield to doubt and fear. The unity of the state can be so sapped that its strength is destroyed.

All this is no idle dream. It has happened time after time, in nation after nation, during the last two years. Fortunately, American men and women are not yet[10] easy dupes. Campaigns of group hatred or class struggle have never made much headway among us, and are not making headway now. But new forces are being unleashed, deliberately planned propagandas to divide and weaken us in the face of danger as other nations have been weakened before.

These dividing forces I do not hesitate to call undiluted poison. They must not be allowed to spread in the New World as they have in the Old. Our moral, our mental defenses[11] must be raised up as

[9]During the Spanish Civil War, the Fascist forces attacking Madrid claimed that, in addition to the four columns of troops closing in upon the city, there was a "fifth column" of citizens within the city itself who were working for the victory of the rebels. The term came to mean any disloyal citizens engaged on behalf of an enemy.

[10]Roosevelt added the word "yet" to the prepared text.

[11]The prepared text read, "Our morale and our mental defenses."

never before against those who would cast a smokescreen across our vision.

The development of our defense program makes it essential that each and every one of us, men and women, feel that we have some contribution to make toward the security of our nation.

At this time, when the world—and the world includes our own American hemisphere—when the world is threatened by forces of destruction, it is my resolve and yours to build up our armed defenses.

We shall build them to whatever heights the future may require.

We shall rebuild them swiftly, as the methods of warfare swiftly change.

For more than three centuries we Americans have been building on this continent a free society, a society in which the promise of the human spirit may find fulfillment. Commingled here are the blood and genius of all the peoples of the world who have sought this promise.

We have built well. We are continuing our efforts to bring the blessings of a free society, of a free and productive economic system, to every family in the land. And that is the promise of America.

It is this that we must continue to build—this that we must continue to defend.

It is the task of our generation, yours and mine. But we build and defend not for our generation alone. We defend the foundations laid down by our fathers. We build a life for generations yet unborn. We defend and we build a way of life, not for America alone, but for all mankind. Ours is a high duty, a noble task.

Day and night I pray for the restoration of peace in this mad world of ours. It is not necessary that I, the president, ask the American people to pray in behalf of such a cause—for I know you are praying with me.

I am certain that out of the heart of every man, woman and child in this land, in every waking minute, a supplication goes up to Almighty God; that all of us beg that suffering and starving, that death and destruction may end—and that peace may return to the world. In common affection for all mankind, your prayers join with mine— that God will heal the wounds and the hearts of humanity.

DECEMBER 29, 1940

THE ARSENAL OF DEMOCRACY: INTRODUCING LEND-LEASE

ABOUT 10:20 on the evening of December 29, Franklin Roosevelt was wheeled into the diplomatic reception room at the White House to deliver his first Fireside Chat since being elected to an unprecedented third term as president. It was to be one of the most important of his radio addresses to the American people. As he moved up to the desk supporting the microphones of the Columbia, National, and Mutual Broadcasting networks he surveyed an audience that included his mother, Sara Roosevelt, movie actor Clark Gable and his wife Carole Lombard, Secretary of State Cordell Hull, and a number of other cabinet officers.

His purpose in this address was to convey a sense of urgency about American security and about the need to provide war matériel to the British. Responding to their inability to gain control over British airspace, the Germans, in August 1940, had begun attacking airfields and Royal Air Force (RAF) fighters, then, shortly thereafter, British cities, hoping thereby to destroy the morale of the civilian population. The Battle of Britain led to desperate pleas for help by Prime Minister Winston Churchill, who had come to power in May. In November, he and Roosevelt had concluded a deal that involved sending fifty over-age American destroyers to the British in return for a string of bases in the Atlantic. The agreement was significant not only because the president, in concluding an executive agreement, had bypassed Congress, but because it constituted a virtual act of war—a total abandonment of any pretense of neutrality.

But given the state of Britain's defenses and the paucity of its dollar reserves, the Destroyers-Bases deal would prove to be little more than a palliative. And owing to the neutrality legislation's ban on loans to belligerents, the British could not borrow from American banks as they had done during the First World War. On a cruise in the Caribbean, Roosevelt hit upon a solution: the United States would produce

163

the implements of war and "lend" them in massive amounts to the British.

This "arsenal of democracy" Fireside Chat issued from the president's desire to prepare the American people for his Lend-Lease proposal. In its rhetoric of noninvolvement, the speech also represented an extension, from the 1940 election campaign, of Roosevelt's disingenuous approach toward the question of American participation in the actual fighting. He continued to imply that the way to stay out of the war was to draw closer to it.

MY FRIENDS, this is not a Fireside Chat on war. It is a talk on national security; because the nub of the whole purpose of your president is to keep you now, and your children later, and your grandchildren much later, out of a last-ditch war for the preservation of American independence and all of the things that American independence means to you and to me and to ours.

Tonight, in the presence of a world crisis, my mind goes back eight years to a night in the midst of a domestic crisis. It was a time when the wheels of American industry were grinding to a full stop, when the whole banking system of our country had ceased to function.

I well remember that while I sat in my study in the White House, preparing to talk with the people of the United States, I had before my eyes the picture of all those Americans with whom I was talking. I saw the workmen in the mills, the mines, the factories; the girl behind the counter; the small shopkeeper; the farmer doing his spring plowing; the widows and the old men wondering about their life's savings. I tried to convey to the great mass of American people what the banking crisis meant to them in their daily lives.

Tonight, I want to do the same thing, with the same people, in this new crisis which faces America.

We met the issue of 1933 with courage and realism.

We face this new crisis—this new threat to the security of our nation—with the same courage and realism.

Never before since Jamestown and Plymouth Rock has our American civilization been in such danger as now.

For on September 27, 1940, this year, by an agreement signed in Berlin, three powerful nations, two in Europe and one in Asia, joined themselves together in the threat that if the United States of America interfered with or blocked the expansion program of these three nations—a program aimed at world control—they would unite in ultimate action against the United States.[1]

The Nazi masters of Germany have made it clear that they intend not only to dominate all life and thought in their own country, but also to enslave the whole of Europe, and then to use the resources of Europe to dominate the rest of the world.

It was only three weeks ago that their leader stated this: "There are two worlds that stand opposed to each other." And then in defiant reply to his opponents, he said this: "Others are correct when they say: With this world we cannot ever reconcile ourselves ... I can beat any other power in the world." So said the leader of the Nazis.

In other words, the Axis not merely admits, but the Axis *proclaims*, that there can be no ultimate peace between their philosophy, their philosophy of government, and our philosophy of government.

In view of the nature of this undeniable threat, it can be asserted, properly and categorically, that the United States has no right or reason to encourage talk of peace, until the day shall come when there is a clear intention on the part of the aggressor nations to abandon all thought of dominating or conquering the world.

At this moment, the forces of the states that are leagued against all peoples who live in freedom, are being held away from our shores. The Germans and the Italians are being blocked on the other side of the Atlantic by the British, and by the Greeks, and by thousands of soldiers and sailors who were able to escape from subjugated countries. In Asia, the Japanese are being engaged by the Chinese nation in another great defense.

In the Pacific Ocean is our fleet.

---

[1] This was the Tripartite Pact in which the Japanese agreed to German and Italian supremacy in Europe, while Germany and Italy acknowledged Japanese supremacy in Asia. The three signatories also agreed to come to the defense of one another if any of them was attacked by a country not then engaged in either the European or Sino-Japanese war. This defensive alliance was aimed at the United States; a separate codicil exempted the Soviet Union.

Some of our people like to believe that wars in Europe and in Asia are of no concern to us. But it is a matter of most vital concern to us that European and Asiatic war-makers should not gain control of the oceans which lead to this hemisphere.

One hundred and seventeen years ago the Monroe Doctrine was conceived by our government as a measure of defense in the face of a threat against this hemisphere by an alliance in continental Europe.[2] Thereafter, we stood guard in the Atlantic, with the British as neighbors. There was no treaty. There was no "unwritten agreement."

And yet, there was the feeling, proven correct by history, that we as neighbors could settle any disputes in peaceful fashion. And the fact is that during the whole of this time the Western Hemisphere has remained free from aggression from Europe or from Asia.

Does anyone seriously believe that we need to fear attack anywhere in the Americas while a free Britain remains our most powerful naval neighbor in the Atlantic? And does anyone seriously believe, on the other hand, that we could rest easy if the Axis powers were our neighbors there?

If Great Britain goes down, the Axis powers will control the continents of Europe, Asia, Africa, Australasia, and the high seas—and they will be in a position to bring enormous military and naval resources against this hemisphere. It is no exaggeration to say that all of us, in all the Americas, would be living at the point of a gun—a gun loaded with explosive bullets, economic as well as military.

We should enter upon a new and terrible era in which the whole world, our hemisphere included, would be run by threats of brute force. And to survive in such a world, we would have to convert ourselves permanently into a militaristic power on the basis of war economy.

Some of us like to believe that even if Britain falls, we are still safe, because of the broad expanse of the Atlantic and of the Pacific.

But the width of those oceans is not what it was in the days of clipper ships. At one point between Africa and Brazil the distance is less than it is from Washington to Denver, Colorado—five hours for the latest type of bomber. And at the North end of the Pacific Ocean, America and Asia almost touch each other.

Why even today we have planes that could fly from the British

---

[2] The Monroe Doctrine of 1823 was issued, in part, as a response to the Quadruple Alliance that had defeated Napoleon—Great Britain, Russia, Prussia, and Austria.

Isles to New England and back again without refueling. And remember that the range of the modern bomber is ever being increased.

During the past week many people in all parts of the nation have told me what they wanted me to say tonight. Almost all of them expressed a courageous desire to hear the plain truth about the gravity of the situation. One telegram, however, expressed the attitude of the small minority who want to see no evil and hear no evil, even though they know in their hearts that evil exists. That telegram begged me not to tell again of the ease with which our American cities could be bombed by any hostile power which had gained bases in this Western Hemisphere. The gist of that telegram was, "Please, Mr. President, don't frighten us by telling us the facts."

Frankly and definitely there is danger ahead—danger against which we must prepare. But we well know that we cannot escape danger, or the fear of danger, by crawling into bed and pulling the covers over our heads.

Some nations of Europe were bound by solemn nonintervention pacts with Germany. Other nations were assured by Germany that they need *never* fear invasion. Nonintervention pact or not, the fact remains that they *were* attacked, overrun, thrown into modern slavery at an hour's notice, or even without any notice at all. As an exiled leader of one of these nations said to me the other day—"The notice was a minus quantity. It was given to my government two hours after German troops had poured into my country in a hundred places."

The fate of these nations tells us what it means to live at the point of a Nazi gun.

The Nazis have justified such actions by various pious frauds. One of these frauds is the claim that they are occupying a nation for the purpose of "restoring order." Another is that they are occupying or controlling a nation on the excuse that they are "protecting it" against the aggression of somebody else.

For example, Germany has said that she was occupying Belgium to save the Belgians from the British. Would she then hesitate to say to any South American country, "We are occupying you to protect you from aggression by the United States"?

Belgium today is being used as an invasion base against Britain, now fighting for its life. And any South American country, in Nazi hands, would always constitute a jumping-off place for German attack on any one of the other republics of this hemisphere.

Analyze for yourselves the future of two other places even nearer to Germany if the Nazis won. Could Ireland hold out? Would Irish freedom be permitted as an amazing pet exception in an unfree world? Or the Islands of the Azores, which still fly the flag of Portugal after five centuries? You and I think of Hawaii as an outpost of defense in the Pacific. And yet, the Azores are closer to our shores in the Atlantic than Hawaii is on the other side.

There are those who say that the Axis powers would never have any desire to attack the Western Hemisphere. That is the same dangerous form of wishful thinking which has destroyed the powers of resistance of so many conquered peoples. The plain facts are that the Nazis have proclaimed, time and again, that all other races are their inferiors and therefore subject to their orders. And most important of all, the vast resources and wealth of this American hemisphere constitute the most tempting loot in all of the round world.

Let us no longer blind ourselves to the undeniable fact that the evil forces which have crushed and undermined and corrupted so many others are already within our own gates. Your government knows much about them and every day is ferreting them out.

Their secret emissaries are active in our own and in neighboring countries. They seek to stir up suspicion and dissension to cause internal strife. They try to turn capital against labor, and vice versa. They try to reawaken long-slumbering racial and religious enmities which should have no place in this country. They are active in every group that promotes intolerance. They exploit for their own ends our own natural abhorrence of war. These trouble-breeders have but one purpose. It is to divide our people, to divide them into hostile groups and to destroy our unity and shatter our will to defend ourselves.

There are also American citizens, many of them in high places, who, unwittingly in most cases, are aiding and abetting the work of these agents. I do not charge these American citizens with being foreign agents. But I do charge them with doing exactly the kind of work that the dictators want done in the United States.

These people not only believe that we can save our own skins by shutting our eyes to the fate of other nations. Some of them go much further than that. They say that we can and should become the friends and even the partners of the Axis powers. Some of them even suggest that we should imitate the methods of the dictatorships. But Americans never can and never will do that.

The experience of the past two years has proven beyond doubt that no nation can appease the Nazis. No man can tame a tiger into a kitten by stroking it. There can be no appeasement with ruthlessness. There can be no reasoning with an incendiary bomb. We know now that a nation can have peace with the Nazis only at the price of total surrender.

Even the people of Italy have been forced to become accomplices of the Nazis; but at this moment they do not know how soon they will be embraced to death by their allies.

The American appeasers ignore the warning to be found in the fate of Austria, Czechoslovakia, Poland, Norway, Belgium, the Netherlands, Denmark, and France. They tell you that the Axis powers are going to win anyway; that all of this bloodshed in the world could be saved; that the United States might just as well throw its influence into the scale of a dictated peace, and get the best out of it that we can.

They call it a "negotiated peace." Nonsense! Is it a negotiated peace if a gang of outlaws surrounds your community and on threat of extermination makes you pay tribute to save your own skins?

For such a dictated peace would be no peace at all. It would be only another armistice, leading to the most gigantic armament race and the most devastating trade wars in all history. And in these contests the Americas would offer the only real resistance to the Axis powers.

With all their vaunted efficiency, with all their parade of pious purpose in this war, there are still in their background the concentration camp and the servants of God in chains.

The history of recent years proves that the shootings and the chains and the concentration camps are not simply the transient tools but the very altars of modern dictatorships. They may talk of a "new order" in the world, but what they have in mind is only a revival of the oldest and the worst tyranny. In that there is no liberty, no religion, no hope.

The proposed "new order" is the very opposite of a United States of Europe or a United States of Asia. It is not a government based upon the consent of the governed. It is not a union of ordinary, self-respecting men and women to protect themselves and their freedom and their dignity from oppression. It is an unholy alliance of power and pelf to dominate and to enslave the human race.

The British people and their allies today are conducting an active war against this unholy alliance. Our own future security is greatly dependent on the outcome of that fight. Our ability to keep out of war is going to be affected by that outcome.

Thinking in terms of today and tomorrow, I make the direct statement to the American people that there is far less chance of the United States getting into war if we do all we can now to support the nations defending themselves against attack by the Axis than if we acquiesce in their defeat, submit tamely to an Axis victory, and wait our turn to be the object of attack in another war later on.

If we are to be completely honest with ourselves, we must admit that there is risk in any course we may take. But I deeply believe that the great majority of our people agree that the course that I advocate involves the least risk now and the greatest hope for world peace in the future.

The people of Europe who are defending themselves do not ask us to do their fighting. They ask us for the implements of war, the planes, the tanks, the guns, the freighters which will enable them to fight for their liberty and for our security. Emphatically we must get these weapons to them, get them to them in sufficient volume and quickly enough, so that we and our children will be saved the agony and suffering of war which others have had to endure.

Let not the defeatists tell us that it is too late. It will never be earlier. Tomorrow will be later than today.

Certain facts are self-evident.

In a military sense Great Britain and the British Empire are today the spearhead of resistance to world conquest. And they are putting up a fight which will live forever in the story of human gallantry.

There is no demand for sending an American Expeditionary Force outside our own borders. There is no intention by any member of your government to send such a force. You can, therefore, nail, nail any talk about sending armies to Europe as deliberate untruth.

Our national policy is not directed toward war. Its sole purpose is to keep war away from our country and away from our people.

Democracy's fight against world conquest is being greatly aided, and must be more greatly aided, by the rearmament of the United States and by sending every ounce and every ton of munitions and supplies that we can possibly spare to help the defenders who are in the front lines. And it is no more unneutral for us to do that than it is for Sweden, Russia, and other nations near Germany, to send steel and ore and oil and other war materials into Germany every day in the week.

We are planning our own defense with the utmost urgency and in its vast scale we must integrate the war needs of Britain and the other free nations which are resisting aggression.

This is not a matter of sentiment or of controversial personal opinion. It is a matter of realistic, practical military policy, based on the advice of our military experts who are in close touch with existing warfare. These military and naval experts and the members of the Congress and the administration have a single-minded purpose—the defense of the United States.

This nation is making a great effort to produce everything that is necessary in this emergency—and with all possible speed. And this great effort requires great sacrifice.

I would ask no one to defend a democracy which in turn would not defend everyone in the nation against want and privation. The strength of this nation shall not be diluted by the failure of the government to protect the economic well-being of its citizens.

If our capacity to produce is limited by machines, it must ever be remembered that these machines are operated by the skill and the stamina of the worker. As the government is determined to protect the rights of the workers, so the nation has a right to expect that the men who man the machines will discharge their full responsibilities to the urgent needs of defense.

The worker possesses the same human dignity and is entitled to the same security of position as the engineer or the manager or the owner. For the workers provide the human power that turns out the destroyers, and the planes and the tanks.

The nation expects our defense industries to continue operation without interruption by strikes or lockouts. It expects and insists that management and workers will reconcile their differences by voluntary or legal means, to continue to produce the supplies that are so sorely needed.

And on the economic side of our great defense program, we are, as you know, bending every effort to maintain stability of prices and with that the stability of the cost of living.

Nine days ago I announced the setting up of a more effective organization to direct our gigantic efforts to increase the production of munitions. The appropriation of vast sums of money and a well-coordinated executive direction of our defense efforts are not in themselves enough. Guns, planes, ships, and many other things have to be built in the factories and the arsenals of America. They have to be produced by workers and managers and engineers with the aid of machines which in turn have to be built by hundreds of thousands of workers throughout the land.

In this great work there has been splendid cooperation between the government and industry and labor; and I am very thankful.

American industrial genius, unmatched throughout all the world in the solution of production problems, has been called upon to bring its resources and its talents into action. Manufacturers of watches, of farm implements, of linotypes and cash registers and automobiles and sewing machines and lawn mowers and locomotives are now making fuses and bomb packing crates and telescope mounts and shells and pistols and tanks.

But all of our present efforts are not enough. We must have more ships, more guns, more planes—more of everything. And this can be accomplished only if we discard the notion of "business as usual." This job cannot be done merely by superimposing on the existing productive facilities the added requirements of the nation for defense.

Our defense efforts must not be blocked by those who fear the future consequences of surplus plant capacity. The possible consequences of failure of our defense efforts now are much more to be feared.

And after the present needs of our defense are past, a proper handling of the country's peacetime needs will require all of the new productive capacity—if not still more.

No pessimistic policy about the future of America shall delay the immediate expansion of those industries essential to defense. We need them.

I want to make it clear that it is the purpose of the nation to build now with all possible speed every machine, every arsenal, every factory that we need to manufacture our defense material. We have the men, the skill, the wealth, and above all, the will.

I am confident that if and when production of consumer or luxury goods in certain industries requires the use of machines and raw materials that are essential for defense purposes, then such production must yield, and will gladly yield, to our primary and compelling purpose.

So I appeal to the owners of plants—to the managers, to the workers, to our own government employees—to put every ounce of effort into producing these munitions swiftly and without stint. With this appeal I give you the pledge that all of us who are officers of your government will devote ourselves to the same wholehearted extent to the great task that lies ahead.

As planes and ships and guns and shells are produced, your government, with its defense experts, can then determine how best to use them to defend this hemisphere. The decision as to how much shall be sent abroad and how much shall remain at home must be made on the basis of our overall military necessities.

We must be the great arsenal of democracy. For us this is an emergency as serious as war itself. We must apply ourselves to our task with the same resolution, the same sense of urgency, the same spirit of patriotism and sacrifice as we would show were we at war.

We have furnished the British great material support and we will furnish far more in the future.

There will be no bottlenecks in our determination to aid Great Britain. No dictator, no combination of dictators, will weaken that determination by threats of how they will construe that determination.

The British have received invaluable military support from the heroic Greek army, and from the forces of all the governments in exile. Their strength is growing. It is the strength of men and women who value their freedom more highly than they value their lives.

I believe that the Axis powers are not going to win this war. I base that belief on the latest and best of information.

We have no excuse for defeatism. We have every good reason for hope—hope for peace, yes, and hope for the defense of our civilization and for the building of a better civilization in the future.

I have the profound conviction that the American people are now determined to put forth a mightier effort than they have ever yet made to increase our production of all the implements of defense, to meet the threat to our democratic faith.

As president of the United States I call for that national effort. I call for it in the name of this nation which we love and honor and which we are privileged and proud to serve. I call upon our people with absolute confidence that our common cause will greatly succeed.

PROCLAIMING NATIONAL EMERGENCY

AS NAZI FORCES in April 1941 struck crushing blows in Greece, Yugoslavia, and North Africa, President Roosevelt seemed to be hoist with his own petard. He had talked a lot—perhaps too much—about nonintervention, about how aid for the democracies would keep the United States out of the war. But now, in the ominous world of the spring of 1941, what would America do? How would the president lead, given the deepening international crisis? Would, or could, he act on his belief that the country should not permit a German defeat of Great Britain?

Many of his advisers—Secretary of War Henry L. Stimson, Secretary of the Treasury Henry Morgenthau, Secretary of the Navy Frank Knox, Chief of Naval Operations Admiral Harold Stark, White House adviser Harry Hopkins—recommended aggressive American action against the German navy. To some, like Morgenthau, this should extend to an American declaration of war. Others, most particularly Stimson, thought the minimum step should be to begin escorting convoys across the North Atlantic, especially as reports arrived of heavy losses to German submarines of Lend-Lease supplies. Several advisers, at one time or another, urged the president to announce a national emergency.

Roosevelt himself seemed inert, unable to lead. He wanted—or so he said on several occasions—an incident of some sort, presumably a Nazi attack on an American vessel or the loss of American life, to rally public opinion. He refused, through May, to order the escorting of convoys. He spoke only of stepping up patrols in the Atlantic.

To a greater extent than most, the Fireside Chat of May 27, 1941, lacked firm direction. Roosevelt spoke eloquently of the danger of Nazi domination, of Hitler's intentions of world conquest, of what German ambitions would mean to American workers and farmers, of how dreadful it would be to live in a closed world under German control, of the need for hemispheric unity. He issued a proclamation of unlimited national emergency. He came close to recommending preventive war: "anyone with a reasonable knowledge of the sudden striking force of modern war, knows that it is stupid to wait until a probable enemy has gained a foothold from which to attack." Yet he did not recommend transferring a portion of the Pacific Fleet to the Atlantic, and he said nothing about escorting convoys. He still did not have a plan. His strategy, in the words of biographer James MacGregor Burns, was "a strategy of no strategy."

This Fireside Chat was delivered from the White House's East Room and was the only one which the president delivered before a rather large, invited audience.

MY FELLOW AMERICANS of all the Americas, my friends. I am speaking tonight from the White House in the presence of the governing board of the Pan-American Union, the Canadian minister, and their families. The members of this board are the ambassadors and ministers of the American republics in Washington. It is appropriate that I do this for now, as never before, the unity of the American republics is of supreme importance to each and every one of us and to the cause of freedom throughout the world. Our future, our future independence is bound up with the future independence of all of our sister republics.

The pressing problems that confront us are military and naval problems. We cannot afford to approach them from the point of view of wishful thinkers or sentimentalists. What we face is cold, hard facts.

The first and fundamental fact is that what started as a European war has developed, as the Nazi always intended it should develop, into a war for world domination.

Adolf Hitler never considered the domination of Europe as an end in itself. European conquest was but a step toward ultimate goals in all the other continents. It is unmistakably apparent to all of us that, unless the advance of Hitlerism is forcibly checked now, the Western Hemisphere will be within range of the Nazi weapons of destruction.

For our own defense we have accordingly undertaken certain obvious necessary measures:

First, we have joined in concluding a series of agreements with all the other American republics. This further solidified our hemisphere against the common danger.

And then, a year ago, we launched, and are successfully carrying out, the largest armament production program we have ever undertaken.

We have added substantially to our splendid Navy, and we have mustered our manpower to build up a new Army, which is already worthy of the highest traditions of our military service.

We instituted a policy of aid for the democracies—the nations which have fought for the continuation of human liberties.

This policy had its origin in the first month of the war, when I urged upon the Congress repeal of the arms embargo provisions in the old Neutrality law, and in that message of September 1939,[1] I said, "I should like to be able to offer the hope that the shadow over the world might swiftly pass. I cannot. The facts compel my stating, with candor, that darker periods may lie ahead."

In the subsequent months, the shadows did deepen and lengthen. And the night spread over Poland, Denmark, Norway, Holland, Belgium, Luxembourg, and France.

In June 1940, Britain stood alone, faced by the same machine of terror which had overwhelmed her allies. Our government rushed arms to meet her desperate needs.

In September 1940, an agreement was completed with Great Britain for the trade of fifty destroyers for eight important offshore bases.[2]

And in March 1941, this year, the Congress passed the Lend-Lease bill and an appropriation of $7 billion to implement it. This law realistically provided for material aid "for the government of any country whose defense the President deems vital to the defense of the United States."

Our whole program of aid for the democracies has been based on

[1] The prepared text specified September 3, 1939.
[2] The Destroyers-Bases deal was an executive agreement, completed on September 2, 1940, in which the United States provided fifty destroyers of World War I–vintage to the British, in return for the right to establish American military bases in Newfoundland, Bermuda, the Bahamas, Jamaica, St. Lucia, Antigua, Trinidad, and British Guiana.

hard-headed concern for our own security and for the kind of safe and civilized world in which we wish to live. Every dollar of material that we send helps to keep the dictators away from our own hemisphere, and every day that they are held off gives us time to build more guns and tanks and planes and ships.

We have made no pretense about our own self-interest in this aid. Great Britain understands it—and so does Nazi Germany.

And now, after a year, Britain still fights gallantly, on a far-flung battle line. We have doubled and redoubled our vast production, increasing, month by month, our material supply of the tools of war for ourselves and for Britain and for China—and eventually for all the democracies.

The supply of these tools will not fail—it will increase.

With greatly augmented strength, the United States and the other American republics now chart their course in the situation of today.

Your government knows what terms Hitler, if victorious, would impose. They are, indeed, the only terms on which he would accept a so-called "negotiated" peace.

And, under those terms, Germany would literally parcel out the world—hoisting the swastika itself over vast territories and populations, and setting up puppet governments of its own choosing, wholly subject to the will and the policy of a conqueror.

To the people of the Americas, a triumphant Hitler would say, as he said after the seizure of Austria, and as he said after Munich, and as he said after the seizure of Czechoslovakia, "I am now completely satisfied. This is the last territorial readjustment I will seek." And he would of course add, "All we want is peace and friendship and profitable trade relations with you in the New World."

Were any of us in the Americas so incredibly simple and forgetful as to accept those honeyed words, what would then happen?

Those in the New World who were seeking profits would be urging that all that the dictatorships desired was "peace." They would oppose toil and taxes for more American armament. And meanwhile, the dictatorships would be forcing the enslaved peoples of their Old World conquests into a system they are even now organizing to build a naval and air force intended to gain and hold and be master of the Atlantic and the Pacific as well.

They would fasten an economic stranglehold upon our several

nations. Quislings[3] would be found to subvert the governments in our republics; and the Nazis would back their fifth columns with invasion, if necessary.

No, I am not speculating about all this. I merely repeat what is already in the Nazi book of world conquest. They plan to treat the Latin American nations as they are now treating the Balkans. They plan then to strangle the United States of America and the Dominion of Canada.

The American laborer would have to compete with slave labor in the rest of the world. Minimum wages, maximum hours? Nonsense! Wages and hours fixed by Hitler. The dignity and power and standard of living of the American worker and farmer would be gone. Trade unions would become historical relics, and collective bargaining a joke.

Farm income? What happens to all farm surpluses without any foreign trade? The American farmer would get for his products exactly what Hitler wanted to give. And the farmer would face obvious disaster and complete regimentation.

Tariff walls—Chinese walls of isolation—would be futile. Freedom to trade is essential to our economic life. We do not eat all the food we produce; and we do not burn all the oil we can pump; we do not use all the goods we can manufacture. It would not be an American wall to keep Nazi goods out; it would be a Nazi wall to keep us in.

The whole fabric of working life as we know it—business and manufacturing, mining and agriculture—all would be mangled and crippled under such a system. Yet to maintain even that crippled independence would require permanent conscription of our manpower; it would curtail the funds we could spend on education, on housing, on public works, on flood control, on health and, instead, we should be permanently pouring our resources into armaments; and, year in and year out, standing day and night watch against the destruction of our cities.

Yes, even our right of worship would be threatened. The Nazi world does not recognize any God except Hitler; for the Nazis are as ruthless as the Communists in the denial of God. What place has religion which preaches the dignity of the human being, the majesty

[3]Vidkun Quisling (1887–1945) was the Norwegian Fascist whom the Germans placed in control of Norway. His name quickly became synonymous with "traitor." Quisling was executed after the German surrender.

of the human soul, in a world where moral standards are measured by treachery and bribery and fifth columnists? Will our children, too, wander off, goose-stepping in search of new gods?

We do not accept, we will not permit, this Nazi "shape of things to come." It will never be forced upon us, if we act in this present crisis with the wisdom and the courage which have distinguished our country in all the crises of the past.

Today, the Nazis have taken military possession of the greater part of Europe. In Africa they have occupied Tripoli and Libya, and they are threatening Egypt, the Suez Canal, and the Near East. But their plans do not stop there, for the Indian Ocean is the gateway to the farther East.

They also have the armed power at any moment to occupy Spain and Portugal; and that threat extends not only to French North Africa and the western end of the Mediterranean Sea, it extends also to the Atlantic fortress of Dakar, and to the island outposts of the New World—the Azores and Cape Verde Islands. Yes, these Cape Verde Islands are only seven hours' distance from Brazil by bomber or troop-carrying planes. They dominate shipping routes to and from the South Atlantic.

The war is approaching the brink of the Western Hemisphere itself. It is coming very close to home.

Control or occupation by Nazi forces of any of the islands of the Atlantic would jeopardize the immediate safety of portions of North and South America, and of the island possessions of the United States, and, therefore, of the ultimate safety of the continental United States itself.

Hitler's plan of world domination would be near its accomplishment today, were it not for two factors: One is the epic resistance of Britain, her colonies, and the great dominions, fighting not only to maintain the existence of the Island of Britain, but also to hold the Near East and Africa. The other is the magnificent defense of China, which will, I have reason to believe, increase in strength. And all of these, together, are preventing the Axis from winning control of the seas by ships and aircraft.

The Axis powers can never achieve their objective of world domination unless they first obtain control of the seas. That is their supreme purpose today; and to achieve it, they must capture Great Britain.

They could then have the power to dictate to the Western Hemisphere. No spurious argument, no appeal to sentiment, no false pledges like those given by Hitler at Munich, can deceive the American people into believing that he and his Axis partners would not, with Britain defeated, close in relentlessly on this hemisphere of ours.

But if the Axis powers fail to gain control of the seas, then they are certainly defeated. Their dreams of world domination will then go by the board; and the criminal leaders who started this war will suffer inevitable disaster.

Both they and their people know this—and they and their people are afraid. That is why they are risking everything they have, conducting desperate attempts to break through to the command of the ocean. Once they are limited to a continuing land war, their cruel forces of occupation will be unable to keep their heel on the necks of the millions of innocent, oppressed peoples on the continent of Europe; and in the end, their whole structure will break into little pieces. And let us remember that the wider the Nazi land effort, the greater is their ultimate danger.

We do not forget the silenced peoples. The masters of Germany—those, at least, who have not been assassinated or escaped to free soil—have marked these silenced peoples and their children's children for slavery.[4] But those people—spiritually unconquered: Austrians, Czechs, Poles, Norwegians, Dutch, Belgians, Frenchmen, Greeks, Southern Slavs—yes, even those Italians and Germans who themselves have been enslaved—will prove to be a powerful force in the final disruption of the Nazi system.

All freedom—meaning freedom to live, and not freedom to conquer and subjugate other peoples—depends on freedom of the seas. All of American history—North, Central, and South American history—has been inevitably tied up with those words "freedom of the seas."

Since 1799, 142 years ago, when our infant Navy made the West Indies and the Caribbean and the Gulf of Mexico safe for American ships; since 1804 and 1805 when we made all peaceful commerce safe from the depredations of the Barbary pirates; since the War of 1812, which was fought for the preservation of sailors' rights; since

---

[4]The sentence, as given above, was the way Roosevelt spoke it over the radio. The printed version, however, makes more sense: "The masters of Germany have marked these silenced peoples and their children's children for slavery—those, at least, who have not been assassinated or escaped to free soil."

1867, when our sea power made it possible for the Mexicans to expel the French Army of Louis Napoleon, we have striven and fought in defense of freedom of the seas, freedom of the seas for our own shipping, for the commerce of our sister republics, for the right of all nations to use the highways of world trade—and for our own safety.[5]

During the First World War we were able to escort merchant ships by the use of small cruisers and gunboats and destroyers; and that type, called convoy, was effective against submarines. In this Second World War, however, the problem is greater. It is different because the attack on the freedom of the seas is now fourfold: first, the improved submarine; second, the much greater use of the heavily armed raiding cruiser or the hit-and-run battleship; third, the bombing airplane, which is capable of destroying merchant ships seven or eight hundred miles from its nearest base; and fourth, the destruction of merchant ships in those ports of the world that are accessible to bombing attack.

The Battle of the Atlantic now extends from the icy waters of the North Pole to the frozen continent of the Antarctic. Throughout this huge area, there have been sinkings of merchant ships in alarming and increasing numbers by Nazi raiders or submarines. There have been sinkings even of ships carrying neutral flags. There have been sinkings in the South Atlantic, off West Africa and the Cape Verde Islands; between the Azores and the islands off the American coast; and between Greenland and Iceland. Great numbers of these sinkings have been actually within the waters of the Western Hemisphere itself.

The blunt truth seems to be this—and I reveal this with the full knowledge of the British government: the present rate of Nazi sinkings of merchant ships is more than three times as high as the capacity of British shipyards to replace them; it is more than twice the combined British and American output of merchant ships today.

---

[5] President Roosevelt's history lesson for the American people lacked texture and sophistication. Commerce became safe from the Barbary pirates not through Jefferson's and Madison's use of force against them but only after the defeat of Napoleon, when the British decided they would no longer tolerate the pirates' behavior. In December 1861 the French sent troops to Mexico and in 1864 put the Archduke Maximilian of Austria in power as emperor there. French forces left in the spring of 1867 after the application of American pressure. But the cost of the venture and its unpopularity in both France and Mexico were more decisive factors in the French decision to leave.

We can answer this peril by two simultaneous measures: first, by speeding up and increasing our own great shipbuilding program; and second, by helping to cut down the losses on the high seas.

Attacks on shipping off the very shores of land which we are determined to protect present an actual military danger to the Americas. And that danger has recently been heavily underlined by the presence in Western Hemisphere waters of a Nazi battleship of great striking power.

You remember that most of the supplies for Britain go by a northerly route, which comes close to Greenland and the nearby island of Iceland. Germany's heaviest attack is on that route. Nazi occupation of Iceland or bases in Greenland would bring the war close to our own continental shores, because those places are stepping-stones to Labrador, to Newfoundland, to Nova Scotia, yes, to the northern United States itself, including the great industrial centers of the North, the East, and the Middle West.

Equally, the Azores and the Cape Verde Islands, if occupied or controlled by Germany, would directly endanger the freedom of the Atlantic and our own American physical safety. Under German domination those islands would become bases for submarines, warships, and airplanes raiding the waters that lie immediately off our own coasts and attacking the shipping in the South Atlantic. They would provide a springboard for actual attack against the integrity and the independence of Brazil and her neighboring republics.

I have said on many occasions that the United States is mustering its men and its resources only for purposes of defense—only to repel attack. I repeat that statement now. But we must be realistic when we use the word "attack"; we have to relate it to the lightning speed of modern warfare.

Some people seem to think that we are not attacked until bombs actually drop in the streets of New York or San Francisco or New Orleans or Chicago. But they are simply shutting their eyes to the lesson that we must learn from the fate of every nation that the Nazis have conquered.

The attack on Czechoslovakia began with the conquest of Austria. The attack on Norway began with the occupation of Denmark. The attack on Greece began with occupation of Albania and Bulgaria. The attack on the Suez Canal began with the invasion of the Balkans and North Africa, and the attack on the United States can begin with the domination of any base which menaces our security—north or south.

Nobody can foretell tonight just when the acts of the dictators will ripen into attack on this hemisphere and us. But we know enough by now to realize that it would be suicide to wait until they are in our front yard.

When your enemy comes at you in a tank or a bombing plane, if you hold your fire until you see the whites of his eyes, you will never know what hit you. Our Bunker Hill of tomorrow may be several thousand miles from Boston, Massachusetts.

Anyone with an atlas, anyone with a reasonable knowledge of the sudden striking force of modern war, knows that it is stupid to wait until a probable enemy has gained a foothold from which to attack. Old-fashioned common sense calls for the use of a strategy that will prevent such an enemy from gaining a foothold in the first place.

We have, accordingly, extended our patrol in North and South Atlantic waters. We are steadily adding more and more ships and planes to that patrol. It is well known that the strength of the Atlantic Fleet has been greatly increased during the past year, and that it is constantly being built up.

These ships and planes warn of the presence of attacking raiders, on the sea, under the sea, and above the sea. The danger from these raiders is, of course, greatly lessened if their location is definitely known. And we are thus being forewarned. We shall be on our guard against efforts to establish Nazi bases closer to our hemisphere.

The deadly facts of war compel nations, for simple preservation, to make stern choices. It does not make sense, for instance, to say, "I believe in the defense of all the Western Hemisphere," and in the next breath to say, "I will not fight for that defense until the enemy has landed on our shores." If we believe in the independence and the integrity of the Americas, we must be willing to fight, to fight to defend them just as much as we would fight for the safety of our own homes.

It is time for us to realize that the safety of American homes even in the center of this our own country has a very definite relationship to the continued safety of homes in Nova Scotia or Trinidad or Brazil.

Our national policy today, therefore is this:

First, we shall actively resist wherever necessary, and with all our resources, every attempt by Hitler to extend his Nazi domination to the Western Hemisphere, or to threaten it. We shall actively resist his every attempt to gain control of the seas. We insist upon the vital importance of keeping Hitlerism away from any point in the world which could be used or would be used as a base of attack against the Americas.

Secondly, from the point of view of strict naval and military necessity, we shall give every possible assistance to Britain and to all who, with Britain, are resisting Hitlerism or its equivalent with force of arms. Our patrols are helping now to ensure delivery of the needed supplies to Britain. All additional measures necessary to deliver the goods will be taken. Any and all further methods or combination of methods, which can or should be utilized, are being devised by our military and naval technicians, who, with me, will work out and put into effect such new and additional safeguards as may be needed.

I say that the delivery of needed supplies to Britain is imperative. I say this can be done; it must be done; and it will be done.

To the other American nations—twenty republics and the Dominion of Canada—I say this: the United States does not merely propose these purposes, but is actively engaged today in carrying them out.

And I say to them further: you may disregard those few citizens of the United States who contend that we are disunited and cannot act.

There are some timid ones among us who say that we must preserve peace at any price—lest we lose our liberties forever. To them I say this: never in the history of the world has a nation lost its democracy by a successful struggle to defend its democracy. We must not be defeated by the fear of the very danger which we are preparing to resist. Our freedom has shown its ability to survive war, but our freedom would never survive surrender. "The only thing we have to fear is fear itself."

There is, of course, a small group of sincere, patriotic men and women whose real passion for peace has shut their eyes to the ugly realities of international banditry and to the need to resist it at all costs. I am sure they are embarrassed by the sinister support they are receiving from the enemies of democracy in our midst—the Bundists, the Fascists, and Communists, and every group devoted to bigotry and racial and religious intolerance. It is no mere coincidence that all the arguments put forward by these enemies of democracy—all their attempts to confuse and divide our people and to destroy public confidence in government, all their defeatist forebodings that Britain and democracy are already beaten, all their selfish promises that we can "do business" with Hitler—all of these are but echoes of the words that have been poured out from the Axis bureaus of propaganda. Those same words have been used before in other countries—to scare them, to divide them, to soften them up and invariably, those same words have formed the advance guard of physical attack.

Your government has the right to expect of all citizens that they take part in the common work of our common defense—take loyal part from this moment forward.

I have recently set up the machinery for civilian defense. It will rapidly organize, locality by locality. It will depend on the organized effort of men and women everywhere. All will have opportunities and responsibilities to fulfill.

Defense today means more than merely fighting. It means morale, civilian as well as military; it means using every available resource; it means enlarging every useful plant. It means the use of a greater American common sense in discarding rumor and distorted statement. It means recognizing, for what they are, racketeers and fifth columnists, the incendiary bombs in this country at the moment.

All of us know that we have made very great social progress in recent years. We propose to maintain that progress and strengthen it. When the nation is threatened from without, however, as it is today, the actual production and transportation of the machinery of defense must not be interrupted by disputes between capital and capital, labor and labor, or capital and labor. The future of all free enterprise—of capital and labor alike—is at stake.

This is no time for capital to make, or to be allowed to retain, excess profits. Articles of defense must have undisputed right of way in every industrial plant in the country.

A nationwide machinery for conciliation and mediation of industrial disputes has been set up. That machinery must be used promptly—and without stoppage of work. Collective bargaining will be retained, but the American people expect that impartial recommendations of our government conciliation and mediation services will be followed both by capital and by labor.

The overwhelming majority of our citizens expect their government to see that the tools of defense are built; and for the very purpose of preserving the democratic safeguards of both labor and management, this government is determined to use all of its powers to express the will of its people and to prevent interference with the production of materials essential to our nation's security.

Today the whole world is divided, divided between human slavery and human freedom—between the pagan brutality and the Christian ideal.

We choose human freedom—which is the Christian ideal.

No one of us can waver for a moment in his courage or his faith.

We will not accept a Hitler-dominated world. And we will not accept a world, like the postwar world of the 1920s, in which the seeds of Hitlerism can again be planted and allowed to grow.

We will accept only a world consecrated to freedom of speech and expression, freedom of every person to worship God in his own way, freedom from want, and freedom from terror.

Is such a world impossible of attainment?

Magna Carta, the Declaration of Independence, the Constitution of the United States, the Emancipation Proclamation, and every other milestone in human progress—all were ideals which seemed impossible of attainment, and yet they were attained.

As a military force, we were weak when we established our independence, but we successfully stood off tyrants, powerful in their day, tyrants who are now lost in the dust of history.

Odds meant nothing to us then. Shall we now, with all our potential strength, hesitate to take every single measure necessary to maintain our American liberties?

Our people and our government will not hesitate to meet that challenge.

As the president of a united and determined people, I say solemnly:

We reassert the ancient American doctrine of freedom of the seas.

We reassert the solidarity of the twenty-one American republics and the Dominion of Canada in the preservation of the independence of the hemisphere.

We have pledged material support to the other democracies of the world—and we will fulfill that pledge.

We in the Americas will decide for ourselves whether, and when, and where, our American interests are attacked or our security threatened.

We are placing our armed forces in strategic military position.

We will not hesitate to use our armed forces to repel attack.

We reassert our abiding faith in the vitality of our constitutional republic as a perpetual home of freedom, of tolerance, and of devotion to the word of God.

Therefore, with profound consciousness of my responsibilities to my countrymen and to my country's cause, I have tonight issued a proclamation that an unlimited national emergency exists and requires the strengthening of our defense to the extreme limit of our national power and authority.

The nation will expect all individuals and all groups to play their full parts, without stint, without selfishness, and without doubt that our democracy will triumphantly survive.

I repeat the words of the signers of the Declaration of Independence—that little band of patriots, fighting long ago against overwhelming odds, but certain, as we are now, of ultimate victory: "With a firm reliance on the protection of Divine Providence, we mutually pledge to each other our lives, our fortunes, and our sacred honor."

THE *GREER* INCIDENT: QUASI-WAR IN THE ATLANTIC

BY SEPTEMBER, President Roosevelt had become convinced of the need to provide escort protection for Lend-Lease convoys headed across the Atlantic. Indeed, at the end of August, he had quietly given the order to the American Navy to begin escorting as far as Iceland. Nevertheless, he remained concerned about isolationist opinion and still needed an incident on which to pin an appeal to the American people. The *Greer* episode gave him the excuse he needed, and he presented his case in this Fireside Chat.

That the president was not always precise or entirely candid is evident as one compares his account of the *Greer* incident with what actually happened. On September 4, the World War I–vintage destroyer *Greer* was completing a mail-carrying mission to Iceland. Some two hundred miles southwest of its destination a British spotter plane notified the ship that a German submarine lay ahead. The *Greer* pursued the sub and identified its location for a British plane, which dropped depth charges. The submarine fired torpedoes at the *Greer*, which then dropped some eight depth charges itself. The torpedoes missed the ship, the depth charges also missed their mark, and the *Greer* steamed on to Iceland, completing its mission.

Roosevelt chose to use the episode to his advantage. On September 11, only a few days after the death of his mother, the president, with a black armband on his sleeve, entered the diplomatic reception room of the White House to speak to the American people. His family, many of his advisers, and plenty of photographers were in attendance. Deceiving by omission—he omitted the part about the *Greer*'s having initiated action against the submarine—Roosevelt went on to tell his audience that the ship had been attacked by a submarine: "I tell you the blunt fact that the German submarine fired first upon this American destroyer without warning, and with deliberate design to sink her." These German subs, he said, were "the rattlesnakes of the Atlantic," and "when you see a rattlesnake poised to strike, you do not wait until he has struck before you crush him." When he had finished speaking, the playing of the national anthem brought all those in the room emotionally to their feet. The isolationists were helpless before Roosevelt's gambit; he went ahead with the convoy escorts, and he ordered the fleet to shoot on sight at German submarines. Eventually he secured the full repeal of the neutrality legislation.

MY FELLOW AMERICANS. The Navy Department of the United States has reported to me that on the morning of September 4, the United States destroyer *Greer*, proceeding in full daylight toward Iceland, had reached a point southeast of Greenland. She was carrying American mail to Iceland. She was flying the American flag. Her identity as an American ship was unmistakable.

She was then and there attacked by a submarine. Germany admits that it was a German submarine. The submarine deliberately fired a torpedo at the *Greer*, followed later by another torpedo attack. In spite of what Hitler's propaganda bureau has invented, and in spite of what any American obstructionist organization may prefer to believe, I tell you the blunt fact that the German submarine fired first upon this American destroyer without warning, and with deliberate design to sink her.

Our destroyer, at the time, was in waters which the government of the United States had declared to be waters of self-defense— surrounding outposts of American protection in the Atlantic.

In the north of the Atlantic, outposts have been established by us in Iceland, in Greenland, in Labrador, and in Newfoundland. Through these waters there pass many ships of many flags. They bear food and other supplies to civilians; and they bear matériel of war, for which the people of the United States are spending billions of dollars, and which, by congressional action, they have declared to be essential for the defense of our own land.

The United States destroyer, when attacked, was proceeding on a legitimate mission.

If the destroyer was visible to the submarine when the torpedo was fired, then the attack was a deliberate attempt by the Nazis to sink a clearly identified American warship. On the other hand, if the submarine was beneath the surface of the sea and, with the aid of its listening devices, fired in the direction of the sound of the American destroyer without even taking the trouble to learn its identity—as the official German communiqué would indicate—then the attack was even more outrageous. For it indicates a policy of indiscriminate violence against any vessel sailing the seas—belligerent or nonbelligerent.

This was piracy—piracy legally and morally. It was not the first nor the last act of piracy which the Nazi government has committed against the American flag in this war. For attack has followed attack.

A few months ago an American flag merchant ship, the *Robin Moor*, was sunk by a Nazi submarine in the middle of the South Atlantic, under circumstances violating long-established international law and violating every principle of humanity.[1] The passengers and the crew were forced into open boats hundreds of miles from land, in direct violation of international agreements signed by nearly all nations including the government of Germany. No apology, no allegation of mistake, no offer of reparations has come from the Nazi government.

In July 1941, nearly two months ago, an American battleship in North American waters was followed by a submarine which for a long time sought to maneuver itself into a position of attack upon the battleship. The periscope of the submarine was clearly seen. No British or American submarines were within hundreds of miles of this spot at the time, so the nationality of the submarine is clear.

Five days ago a United States Navy ship on patrol picked up three survivors of an American-owned ship operating under the flag of our sister Republic of Panama—the steamship *Sessa*. On August 17, she had been first torpedoed without warning, and then shelled, near Greenland, while carrying civilian supplies to Iceland. It is feared that the other members of the crew have been drowned. In view of the established presence of German submarines in this vicinity, there can be no reasonable doubt as to the identity of the flag of the attacker.

Five days ago, another United States merchant ship, the *Steel Sea-*

---

[1] The attack on the *Robin Moor*, a freighter headed for Capetown, occurred on June 12. No one was killed in the attack.

farer, was sunk by a German aircraft in the Red Sea 220 miles south of Suez. She was bound for an Egyptian port.

So four of the vessels sunk or attacked flew the American flag and were clearly identifiable. Two of these ships were warships of the American Navy. In the fifth case, the vessel sunk clearly carried the flag of our sister Republic of Panama.

In the face of all this, we Americans are keeping our feet on the ground. Our type of democratic civilization has outgrown the thought of feeling compelled to fight some other nation by reason of any single piratical attack on one of our ships. We are not becoming hysterical or losing our sense of proportion. Therefore, what I am thinking and saying tonight does not relate to any isolated episode.

Instead, we Americans are taking a long-range point of view in regard to certain fundamentals, a point of view in regard to a series of events on land and on sea which must be considered as a whole—as a part of a world pattern.

It would be unworthy of a great nation to exaggerate an isolated incident, or to become inflamed by some one act of violence. But it would be inexcusable folly to minimize such incidents in the face of evidence which makes it clear that the incident is not isolated, but is part of a general plan.

The important truth is that these acts of international lawlessness are a manifestation of a design, a design that has been made clear to the American people for a long time. It is the Nazi design to abolish the freedom of the seas, and to acquire absolute control and domination of these seas for themselves.

For with control of the seas in their own hands, the way can obviously become clear for their next step—domination of the United States, domination of the Western Hemisphere by force of arms. Under Nazi control of the seas, no merchant ship of the United States or of any other American republic would be free to carry on any peaceful commerce, except by the condescending grace of this foreign and tyrannical power. The Atlantic Ocean which has been, and which should always be, a free and friendly highway for us would then become a deadly menace to the commerce of the United States, to the coasts of the United States, and even to the inland cities of the United States.

The Hitler government, in defiance of the laws of the sea, in defiance of the recognized rights of all other nations, has presumed to declare, on paper, that great areas of the seas—even including a vast expanse lying in the Western Hemisphere—are to be closed, and that no ships may enter them for any purpose, except at peril of being sunk. Actually they are sinking ships at will and without warning in widely separated areas both within and far outside of these far-flung pretended zones.

This Nazi attempt to seize control of the oceans is but a counterpart of the Nazi plots now being carried on throughout the Western Hemisphere—all designed toward the same end. For Hitler's advance guards—not only his avowed agents but also, also his dupes among us—have sought to make ready for him footholds, bridgeheads in the New World, to be used as soon as he has gained control of the oceans.

His intrigues, his plots, his machinations, his sabotage in this New World are all known to the government of the United States. Conspiracy has followed conspiracy.

For example, last year a plot to seize the government of Uruguay was smashed by the prompt action of that country, which was supported in full by her American neighbors. A like plot was then hatching in Argentina, and that government has carefully and wisely blocked it at every point. More recently, an endeavor was made to subvert the government of Bolivia. And within the past few weeks the discovery was made of secret airlanding fields in Colombia, within easy range of the Panama Canal. I could multiply instance upon instance.

To be ultimately successful in world mastery, Hitler knows that he must get control of the seas. He must first destroy the bridge of ships which we are building across the Atlantic and over which we shall continue to roll the implements of war to help destroy him, to destroy all his works in the end. He must wipe out our patrol on sea and in the air if he is to do it. He must silence the British Navy.

I think it must be explained over and over again to people who like to think of the United States Navy as an invincible protection, that this can be true only if the British Navy survives. And that, my friends, is simple arithmetic.

For if the world outside of the Americas falls under Axis domination, the shipbuilding facilities which the Axis powers would then possess in all of Europe, in the British Isles, and in the Far East would be much greater than all the shipbuilding facilities and potentialities of all of the Americas—not only greater, but two or three times greater—enough to win. Even if the United States threw all its resources into such a situation, seeking to double and even re-double the size of our Navy, the Axis powers, in control of the rest of the world, would have the manpower and the physical resources to outbuild us several times over.

It is time for all Americans, Americans of all the Americas, to stop being deluded by the romantic notion that the Americas can go on living happily and peacefully in a Nazi-dominated world.

Generation after generation, America has battled for the general policy of the freedom of the seas. And that policy is a very simple one—but a basic, a fundamental one. It means that no nation has the right to make the broad oceans of the world at great distances from the actual theater of land war unsafe for the commerce of others.

That has been our policy, proved time and again, in all of our history.

Our policy has applied from the earliest days of the repub-lic—and still applies—not merely to the Atlantic but to the Pacific and to all other oceans as well.

Unrestricted submarine warfare in 1941 constitutes a defiance—an act of aggression—against that historic American policy.

It is now clear that Hitler has begun his campaign to control the seas by ruthless force and by wiping out every vestige of interna-tional law, every vestige of humanity.

His intention has been made clear. The American people can have no further illusions about it.

No tender whisperings of appeasers that Hitler is not interested in the Western Hemisphere, no soporific lullabies that a wide ocean protects us from him, can long have any effect on the hard-headed, farsighted, and realistic American people.

Because of these episodes, because of the movements and opera-tions of German warships, and because of the clear, repeated proof that the present government of Germany has no respect for treaties or for international law, that it has no decent attitude toward neutral nations or human life—we Americans are now face to face not with abstract theories but with cruel, relentless facts.

This attack on the *Greer* was no localized military operation in the North Atlantic. This was no mere episode in a struggle between two nations. This was one determined step toward creating a per-manent world system based on force, on terror, and on murder.

And I am sure that even now the Nazis are waiting, waiting to see whether the United States will by silence give them the green light to go ahead on this path of destruction.

The Nazi danger to our Western world has long ceased to be a mere possibility. The danger is here now—not only from a military enemy but from an enemy of all law, all liberty, all morality, all religion.

There has now come a time when you and I must see the cold, inexorable necessity of saying to these inhuman, unrestrained seekers of world conquest and permanent world domination by the sword: "You seek to throw our children and our children's children into your form of terrorism and slavery. You have now attacked our own safety. You shall go no further."

Normal practices of diplomacy—note writing—are of no possible use in dealing with international outlaws who sink our ships and kill our citizens.

One peaceful nation after another has met disaster because each refused to look the Nazi danger squarely in the eye until it had actually had them by the throat.

The United States will not make that fatal mistake.

No act of violence, no act of intimidation will keep us from maintaining intact two bulwarks of American defense: first, our line of supply of material to the enemies of Hitler; and second, the freedom of our shipping on the high seas.

No matter what it takes, no matter what it costs, we will keep open the line of legitimate commerce in these defensive waters of ours.

We have sought no shooting war with Hitler. We do not seek it now. But neither do we want peace so much that we are willing to pay for it by permitting him to attack our naval and merchant ships while they are on legitimate business.

I assume that the German leaders are not deeply concerned, tonight or any other time, by what we Americans or the American government says or publishes about them. We cannot bring about the downfall of Nazism by the use of long-range invective.

But when you see a rattlesnake poised to strike, you do not wait until he has struck before you crush him.

These Nazi submarines and raiders are the rattlesnakes of the Atlantic. They are a menace to the free pathways of the high seas. They are a challenge to our own sovereignty. They hammer at our most precious rights when they attack ships of the American flag—symbols of our independence, our freedom, our very life.

It is clear to all Americans that the time has come when the Americas themselves must now be defended. A continuation of attacks in our own waters, or in waters that could be used for further and greater attacks on us, will inevitably weaken our American ability to repel Hitlerism.

Do not let us be hair-splitters. Let us not ask ourselves whether the Americas should begin to defend themselves after the first attack, or the fifth attack, or the tenth attack, or the twentieth attack.

The time for active defense is now.

Do not let us split hairs. Let us not say; "We will only defend ourselves if the torpedo succeeds in getting home, or if the crew and the passengers are drowned."

This is the time for prevention of attack.

If submarines or raiders attack in distant waters, they can attack equally well within sight of our own shores. Their very presence in any waters which America deems vital to its defense constitutes an attack.

In the waters which we deem necessary for our defense, American naval vessels and American planes will no longer wait until Axis submarines lurking under the water, or Axis raiders on the surface of the sea, strike their deadly blow—first.

Upon our naval and air patrol—now operating in large number over a vast expanse of the Atlantic Ocean—falls the duty of maintaining the American policy of freedom of the seas—now. That means, very simply, very clearly, that our patrolling vessels and planes will protect all merchant ships—not only American ships but ships of any flag—engaged in commerce in our defensive waters. They will protect them from submarines; they will protect them from surface raiders.

This situation is not new. The second president of the United States, John Adams, ordered the United States Navy to clean out European privateers and European ships of war which were infesting the Caribbean and South American waters, destroying American commerce.[2]

---

[2] Roosevelt refers here to the "quasi-war" with France, 1798–1800. The tiny American Navy captured more than eighty French privateers.

The third president of the United States, Thomas Jefferson, ordered the United States Navy to end the attacks being made upon American and other ships by the corsairs of the nations of North Africa.[3]

My obligation as president is historic; it is clear. Yes, it is inescapable.

It is no act of war on our part when we decide to protect the seas that are vital to American defense. The aggression is not ours. Ours is solely defense.

But let this warning be clear. From now on, if German or Italian vessels of war enter the waters, the protection of which is necessary for American defense, they do so at their own peril.

The orders which I have given as commander in chief of the United States Army and Navy are to carry out that policy—at once.

The sole responsibility rests upon Germany. There will be no shooting unless Germany continues to seek it.

That is my obvious duty in this crisis. That is the clear right of this sovereign nation. This is the only step possible, if we would keep tight the wall of defense which we are pledged to maintain around this Western Hemisphere.

I have no illusions about the gravity of this step. I have not taken it hurriedly or lightly. It is the result of months and months of constant thought and anxiety and prayer. In the protection of your nation and mine it cannot be avoided.

The American people have faced other grave crises in their history—with American courage, with American resolution. They will do no less today.

They know the actualities of the attacks upon us. They know the necessities of a bold defense against these attacks. They know that the times call for clear heads and fearless hearts.

And with that inner strength that comes to a free people conscious of their duty, conscious of the righteousness of what they do, they will—with divine help and guidance—stand their ground against this latest assault upon their democracy, their sovereignty, and their freedom.

---

[3] This is another reference to the struggle against the Barbary pirates in the first years of the nineteenth century.

WAR WITH JAPAN

AS THE BATTLE of the Atlantic heated up in the late summer and fall of 1941, the United States found itself in a deepening diplomatic crisis with Japan. Although Japan had taken possession of a good part of China—the outlets of its major rivers, its railroads, chief cities, industrial areas, and raw materials—the issue was Southeast Asia. As Japan began to extend its reach beyond China into the resource-rich area to the south, the United States applied economic sanctions: first the restriction of certain key fuels and metals, then an embargo on oil, and, finally, the freezing of Japanese assets. Japan responded by trying to negotiate an empire-guaranteeing modus vivendi with the United States, and when that failed, planned and carried out a surprise attack on the American naval base at Pearl Harbor.

On December 8, Roosevelt went to Congress with a war resolution. "Yesterday, December 7, 1941—a date that will live in infamy—the United States of America was suddenly and deliberately attacked by naval and air forces of the Empire of Japan." Congress, with one dissent, voted a declaration of war thirty-three minutes after the conclusion of the president's speech.

The next day he spoke to the American people—in a press conference and, later in the evening, in this Fireside Chat. The press conference was not very edifying. In the radio chat he reviewed and condemned the Axis record of aggression and took pains to prepare the country for bad news. As he spoke, he was worried about what the Germans would do, because they had not yet declared war on the United States. Roosevelt had rejected advice that he ask Congress for a declaration of war on Germany when he presented his war resolution of December 8, on the assumption that Germany would soon come in of its own volition.

Although the American government had information at least a week before Pearl Harbor of a German pledge to join the Pacific war in the event Japan attacked the United States, everyone in policy

197

circles recognized that Hitler would act on the basis of his own interests and emotions. There was a possibility that he would insist on Japanese action against the Soviet Union as the price of his entering the war against the United States. But Hitler decided otherwise and on December 11, Germany declared war.

MY FELLOW AMERICANS. The sudden criminal attacks perpetrated by the Japanese in the Pacific provide the climax of a decade of international immorality.

Powerful and resourceful gangsters have banded together to make war upon the whole human race. Their challenge has now been flung at the United States of America. The Japanese have treacherously violated the long-standing peace between us. Many American soldiers and sailors have been killed by enemy action. American ships have been sunk; American airplanes have been destroyed.

The Congress and the people of the United States have accepted that challenge.

Together with other free peoples, we are now fighting to maintain our right to live among our world neighbors in freedom, in common decency, without fear of assault.

I have prepared the full record of our past relations with Japan, and it will be submitted to the Congress. It begins with the visit of Commodore Perry to Japan eighty-eight years ago.[1] It ends with the visit of two Japanese emissaries[2] to the secretary of state[3] last Sunday, an hour after Japanese forces had loosed their bombs and machine guns against our flag, our forces, and our citizens.

I can say with utmost confidence that no Americans, today or a thousand years hence, need feel anything but pride in our patience and in our efforts through all the years toward achieving a peace in

---

[1] Commodore Matthew C. Perry (1794–1858) led a naval expedition in 1853 to open Japan to American trade. He signed a treaty with the Japanese on March 31, 1854, after undertaking a second mission.

[2] Admiral Kichisaburo Nomura and Ambassador Saburo Kurusu.

[3] Cordell Hull.

the Pacific which would be fair and honorable to every nation, large or small. And no honest person, today or a thousand years hence, will be able to suppress a sense of indignation and horror at the treachery committed by the military dictators of Japan, under the very shadow of the flag of peace borne by their special envoys in our midst.

The course that Japan has followed for the past ten years in Asia has paralleled the course of Hitler and Mussolini in Europe and in Africa. Today, it has become far more than a parallel. It is collaboration, actual collaboration, so well calculated that all the continents of the world, and all the oceans, are now considered by the Axis strategists as one gigantic battlefield.

In 1931, ten years ago, Japan invaded Manchukuo[4]—without warning.

In 1935, Italy invaded Ethiopia—without warning.

In 1938, Hitler occupied Austria—without warning.

In 1939, Hitler invaded Czechoslovakia—without warning.

Later in '39, Hitler invaded Poland—without warning.

In 1940, Hitler invaded Norway, Denmark, the Netherlands, Belgium, and Luxembourg—without warning.

In 1940, Italy attacked France and later Greece—without warning.

And this year, in 1941, the Axis powers attacked Yugoslavia and Greece and they dominated the Balkans—without warning.

In 1941, also, Hitler invaded Russia—without warning.

And now Japan has attacked Malaya and Thailand—and the United States—without warning.

It is all of one pattern.

We are now in this war. We are all in it—all the way. Every single man, woman, and child is a partner in the most tremendous undertaking of our American history. We must share together the bad news and the good news, the defeats and the victories—the changing fortunes of war.

So far, the news has been all bad. We have suffered a serious setback in Hawaii. Our forces in the Philippines, which include the brave people of that commonwealth, are taking punishment, but are defending themselves vigorously. The reports from Guam and Wake

---

[4] Manchukuo was the name given by the Japanese in 1932 to the former Manchuria and the Jehol province of China. In theory an independent state, it was in fact a puppet of Japan.

and Midway islands are still confused, but we must be prepared for the announcement that all these three outposts have been seized.[5]

The casualty lists of these first few days will undoubtedly be large. I deeply feel the anxiety of all of the families of the men in our armed forces and the relatives of people in cities which have been bombed. I can only give them my solemn promise that they will get news just as quickly as possible.

This government will put its trust in the stamina of the American people, and will give the facts to the public just as soon as two conditions have been fulfilled: first, that the information has been definitely and officially confirmed; and, second, that the release of the information at the time it is received will not prove valuable to the enemy directly or indirectly.

Most earnestly I urge my countrymen to reject all rumors. These ugly little hints of complete disaster fly thick and fast in wartime. They have to be examined and appraised.

As an example, I can tell you frankly that until further surveys are made, I have not sufficient information to state the exact damage which has been done to our naval vessels at Pearl Harbor. Admittedly the damage is serious. But no one can say how serious, until we know how much of this damage can be repaired and how quickly the necessary repairs can be made.

I cite as another example a statement made on Sunday night that a Japanese carrier had been located and sunk off the canal zone. And when you hear statements that are attributed to what they call "an authoritative source," you can be reasonably sure from now on that under these war circumstances the "authoritative source" is not any person in authority.

Many rumors and reports which we now hear originate of course with enemy sources. For instance, today the Japanese are claiming that as a result of their one action against Hawaii they have gained naval supremacy in the Pacific. This is an old trick of propaganda which has been used innumerable times by the Nazis. The purposes of such fantastic claims are, of course, to spread fear and confusion among us, and to goad us into revealing military information which our enemies are desperately anxious to obtain.

[5] Guam fell to the Japanese on December 11, and Wake Island on December 23. The Americans managed to hold Midway, which was the site of a key naval and air battle in early June 1942.

Our government will not be caught in this obvious trap—and neither will the people of the United States.

It must be remembered by each and every one of us that our free and rapid communication these days must be greatly restricted in wartime. It is not possible to receive full and speedy and accurate reports from distant areas of combat. This is particularly true where naval operations are concerned. For in these days of the marvels of the radio it's often impossible for the commanders of various units to report their activities by radio at all, for the very simple reason that this information would become available to the enemy, and would disclose their position and their plan of defense or attack.

Of necessity there will be delays in officially confirming or denying reports of operations, but we will not hide facts from the country if we know the facts and if the enemy will not be aided by their disclosure.

To all newspapers and radio stations—all those who reach the eyes and ears of the American people—I say this: You have a most grave responsibility to the nation now and for the duration of this war.

If you feel that your government is not disclosing enough of the truth, you have every right to say so. But—in the absence of all the facts, as revealed by official sources—you have no right in the ethics of patriotism to deal out unconfirmed reports in such a way as to make people believe that they are gospel truth.

Every citizen, in every walk of life, shares this same responsibility. The lives of our soldiers and sailors—the whole future of this nation—depend upon the manner in which each and every one of us fulfills his obligation to our country.

Now a word about the recent past—and the future. A year and a half has elapsed since the fall of France, when the whole world first realized the mechanized might which the Axis nations had been building up for so many years. America has used that year and a half to great advantage. Knowing that the attack might reach us in all too short a time, we immediately began greatly to increase our industrial strength and our capacity to meet the demands of modern warfare.

Precious months were gained by sending vast quantities of our war material to the nations of the world still able to resist Axis aggression. Our policy rested on the fundamental truth that the defense of any country resisting Hitler or Japan was in the long run the defense of our own country. That policy has been justified. It has given us time, invaluable time, to build our American assembly lines of production.

Assembly lines are now in operation. Others are being rushed to completion. A steady stream of tanks and planes, of guns and ships and shells and equipment—that is what these eighteen months have given us.

But it is all only a beginning of what still has to be done. We must be set to face a long war against crafty and powerful bandits. The attack at Pearl Harbor can be repeated at any one of many points, points in both oceans and along both our coast lines and against all the rest of the hemisphere.

It will not only be a long war, it will be a hard war. That is the basis on which we now lay all our plans. That is the yardstick by which we measure what we shall need and demand; money, materials, doubled and quadrupled production—ever-increasing. The production must be not only for our own Army and Navy and Air Forces. It must reinforce the other armies and navies and air forces fighting the Nazis and the warlords of Japan throughout the Americas and throughout the world.

I have been working today on the subject of production. Your government has decided on two broad policies.

The first is to speed up all existing production by working on a seven-day-week basis in every war industry, including the production of essential raw materials.

The second policy, now being put into form, is to rush additions to the capacity of production by building more new plants, by adding to old plants, and by using the many smaller plants for war needs.

Over the hard road of the past months, we have at times met obstacles and difficulties, divisions and disputes, indifference and callousness. That is now all past—and, I am sure, forgotten.

The fact is that the country now has an organization in Washington built around men and women who are recognized experts in their own fields. I think the country knows that the people who are actually responsible in each and every one of these many fields are pulling together with a teamwork that has never before been excelled.

On the road ahead there lies hard work—grueling work—day and night, every hour and every minute.

I was about to add that ahead there lies sacrifice for all of us.

But it is not correct to use that word. The United States does not consider it a sacrifice to do all one can, to give one's best to our nation, when the nation is fighting for its existence and its future life.

It is not a sacrifice for any man, old or young, to be in the Army or the Navy of the United States. Rather is it a privilege.

It is not a sacrifice for the industrialist or the wage earner, the farmer or the shopkeeper, the trainman or the doctor, to pay more taxes, to buy more bonds, to forego extra profits, to work longer or harder at the task for which he is best fitted. Rather it is a privilege.

It is not a sacrifice to do without many things to which we are accustomed if the national defense calls for doing without it.[6]

A review this morning leads me to the conclusion that at present we shall not have to curtail the normal use of articles of food. There is enough food today for all of us and enough left over to send to those who are fighting on the same side with us.

But there will be a clear and definite shortage of metals for many kinds of civilian use, for the very good reason that in our increased program we shall need for war purposes more than half of that portion of the principal metals which during the past year have gone into articles for civilian use. Yes, we shall have to give up many things entirely.

And I am sure that the people in every part of the nation are prepared in their individual living to win this war. I am sure that they will cheerfully help to pay a large part of its financial cost while it goes on. I am sure they will cheerfully give up those material things that they are asked to give up.

And I am sure that they will retain all those great spiritual things without which we cannot win through.

I repeat that the United States can accept no result save victory, final, complete. Not only must the shame of Japanese treachery be wiped out, but the sources of international brutality, wherever they exist, must be absolutely and finally broken.

In my message to the Congress yesterday I said that we "will make

---

[6]The grammatical error was caused by President Roosevelt spontaneously adding the word "it" to the prepared text.

very certain that this form of treachery shall never endanger us again." In order to achieve that certainty, we must begin the great task that is before us by abandoning once and for all the illusion that we can ever again isolate ourselves from the rest of humanity.

In these past few years—and, most violently, in the past three days—we have learned a terrible lesson.

It is our obligation to our dead—it is our sacred obligation to their children and to our children—that we must never forget what we have learned.

And what we have learned is this:

There is no such thing as security for any nation—or any individual—in a world ruled by the principles of gangsterism.

There is no such thing as impregnable defense against powerful aggressors who sneak up in the dark and strike without warning.

We have learned that our ocean-girt hemisphere is not immune from severe attack—that we cannot measure our safety in terms of miles on any map anymore.

We may acknowledge that our enemies have performed a brilliant feat of deception, perfectly timed and executed with great skill. It was a thoroughly dishonorable deed, but we must face the fact that modern warfare as conducted in the Nazi manner is a dirty business. We don't like it—we didn't want to get in it—but we are in it and we're going to fight it with everything we've got.

I do not think any American has any doubt of our ability to administer proper punishment to the perpetrators of these crimes.

Your government knows that for weeks Germany has been telling Japan that if Japan did not attack the United States, Japan would not share in dividing the spoils with Germany when peace came. She was promised by Germany that if she came in she would receive the complete and perpetual control of the whole of the Pacific area—and that means not only the Far East, but also all of the islands in the Pacific, and also a stranglehold on the west coast of North and Central and South America.

We know also that Germany and Japan are conducting their military and naval operations in accordance with a joint plan. That plan considers all peoples and nations which are not helping the Axis powers as common enemies of each and every one of the Axis powers.

That is their simple and obvious grand strategy. The American people must realize that it can be matched only with similar grand strategy. We must realize for example that Japanese successes against the United States in the Pacific are helpful to German operations in Libya; that any German success against the Caucasus is inevitably an assistance to Japan in her operations against the Dutch East Indies; that a German attack against Algiers or Morocco opens the way to a German attack against South America and the Canal.

On the other side of the picture, we must learn also to know that guerrilla warfare against the Germans in, let us say, Serbia or Norway helps us; that a successful Russian offensive against the Germans helps us; and that British successes on land or sea in any part of the world strengthen our hands.

Remember always that Germany and Italy, regardless of any formal declaration of war, consider themselves at war with the United States at this moment just as much as they consider themselves at war with Britain or Russia. And Germany puts all the other republics of the Americas into the same category of enemies. The people of our sister republics of this hemisphere can be honored by that fact.

The true goal we seek is far above and beyond the ugly field of battle. When we resort to force, as now we must, we are determined that this force shall be directed toward ultimate good as well as against immediate evil. We Americans are not destroyers—we are builders.

We are now in the midst of a war, not for conquest, not for vengeance, but for a world in which this nation, and all that this nation represents, will be safe for our children. We expect to eliminate the danger from Japan, but it would serve us ill if we accomplished that and found that the rest of the world was dominated by Hitler and Mussolini.

So, we are going to win the war and we are going to win the peace that follows.

And in these difficult hours of this day—through the dark days that may be yet to come—we will know that the vast majority of the members of the human race are on our side. Many of them are fighting with us. All of them are praying for us. For in representing our cause, we represent theirs as well—our hope and their hope for liberty under God.

FIGHTING DEFEATISM

FROM DECEMBER 1941 through February 1942, the United States and its allies suffered a series of military defeats on battlefronts throughout the world. It was a bleak and difficult time for President Roosevelt and for the country as a whole. The early excitement, sense of purpose, and feeling of unity that had inspired the nation immediately after the Japanese attack, soon began giving way to selfishness and large-scale hoarding, to grumbling about the losses at Pearl Harbor, and to armchair strategists' proposals about the proper way to fight the war.

By February, Roosevelt did not like what he saw or heard. The old isolationists had become "Asia-firsters" and were attacking his approach to the war; they wanted all-out support for General Douglas MacArthur in the Philippines and for the focus to be on Japan. Harry Hopkins and Eleanor Roosevelt were under attack as "policymakers" who had never been elected by the people to any office. Roosevelt was criticized for not using prominent critics of his policies, such as Colonel Charles A. Lindbergh, the famous aviator and public idol. There was an odor of defeatism in the air. Optimism and confidence were being replaced by pessimism and self-doubt.

Roosevelt decided that Washington's Birthday would provide a fitting occasion to buoy the national spirit in a Fireside Chat. Washington and his army, he began, had experienced the very kind of hardship the nation was currently enduring—"every winter was a Valley Forge." But, he asserted, "Washington's conduct in those hard times has provided the model for all Americans since then—a model of moral stamina." He then asked his listeners to take out their maps and follow his comments so that they could understand the interdependence of the various parts of the world: a glance at the map, he said, makes it "obvious what would happen if all these great reservoirs of power were cut off from each other either by enemy action or by self-imposed isolation." His words were a ringing defense of the administration's strategy. They declared the need for sacrifice and determination in the face of adversity and set a tone of reassurance and confidence in the ultimate outcome.

MY FELLOW AMERICANS. Washington's Birthday is a most appropriate occasion for us to talk with each other about things as they are today and things as we know they shall be in the future.

For eight years, General Washington and his Continental army were faced continually with formidable odds and recurring defeats. Supplies and equipment were lacking. In a sense, every winter was a Valley Forge. Throughout the thirteen states there existed fifth columnists—and selfish men, jealous men, fearful men, who proclaimed that Washington's cause was hopeless, and that he should ask for a negotiated peace.

Washington's conduct in those hard times has provided the model for all Americans ever since—a model of moral stamina. He held to his course, as it had been charted in the Declaration of Independence. He and the brave men who served with him knew that no man's life or fortune was secure, without freedom and free institutions.

The present great struggle has taught us increasingly that freedom of person and security of property anywhere in the world depend upon the security of the rights and obligations of liberty and justice everywhere in the world.

This war is a new kind of war. It is different from all other wars of the past, not only in its methods and weapons but also in its geography. It is warfare in terms of every continent, every island, every sea, every air lane in the world.

That is the reason why I have asked you to take out and spread before you a map of the whole earth, and to follow me in the references which I shall make to the world-encircling battle lines of this war. Many questions will, I fear, remain unanswered tonight; but I know you will realize that I cannot cover everything in one short report to the people.

The broad oceans which have been heralded in the past as our protection from attack have become endless battlefields on which we are constantly being challenged by our enemies.

We must all understand and face the hard fact that our job now is to fight at distances which extend all the way around the globe.

We fight at these vast distances because that is where our enemies are. Until our flow of supplies gives us clear superiority we must keep on striking our enemies wherever and whenever we can meet them, even if, for a while, we have to yield ground. Actually, though, we are taking a heavy toll of the enemy every day that goes by.

We must fight at these vast distances to protect our supply lines and our lines of communication with our allies—protect these lines from the enemies who are bending every ounce of their strength, striving against time, to cut them. The object of the Nazis and the Japanese is, of course, to separate the United States, Britain, China, and Russia, and to isolate them one from another, so that each will be surrounded and cut off from sources of supplies and reinforcements. It's the old familiar Axis policy of "divide and conquer."

There are those who still think, however, in terms of the days of sailing ships. They advise us to pull our warships and our planes and our merchant ships into our own home waters and concentrate solely on last-ditch defense. But let me illustrate what would happen if we followed such foolish advice.

Look at your map. Look at the vast area of China, with its millions of fighting men. Look at the vast area of Russia, with its powerful armies and proven military might. Look at the islands of Britain, Australia, New Zealand, the Dutch Indies, India, the Near East and the continent of Africa, with their sources of raw materials, their resources of raw materials,[1] and of peoples determined to resist Axis domination. Look too at North America, Central America, and South America.

It is obvious what would happen if all of these great reservoirs of power were cut off from each other either by enemy action or by self-imposed isolation:

First, in such a case, we could no longer send aid of any kind to China—to the brave people who, for nearly five years, have withstood Japanese assault, destroyed hundreds of thousands of Japa-

[1] The printed text read simply, "with their resources of raw materials."

nese soldiers and vast quantities of Japanese war munitions. It is essential that we help China in her magnificent defense and in her inevitable counteroffensive—for that is one important element in the ultimate defeat of Japan.

Secondly, if we lost communication with the Southwest Pacific, all of that area, including Australia and New Zealand and the Dutch Indies, would fall under Japanese domination. Japan in such a case could release great numbers of ships and men to launch attacks on a large scale against the coasts of the Western Hemisphere—South America and Central America and North America—including Alaska. At the same time, she could immediately extend her conquests in the other direction toward India, through the Indian Ocean to Africa, to the Near East, and try to join forces with Germany and Italy.

Third, if we were to stop sending munitions to the British and the Russians in the Mediterranean area, in the Persian Gulf, and the Red Sea, we would be helping the Nazis to overrun Turkey, and Syria and Iraq, and Persia, that's now called Iran,[2] and Egypt and the Suez Canal, the whole coast of North Africa itself, and with that inevitably the whole coast of West Africa—putting Germany within easy striking distance of South America, fifteen hundred miles away.

Fourth, if by such a fatuous policy we ceased to protect the North Atlantic supply line to Britain and to Russia, we would help to cripple the splendid counteroffensive by Russia against the Nazis, and we would help to deprive Britain of essential food supplies and munitions.

Those Americans who believed that we could live under the illusion of isolationism wanted the American eagle to imitate the tactics of the ostrich. Now, many of those same people, afraid that we may be sticking our necks out, want our national bird to be turned into a turtle. But we prefer to retain the eagle as it is—flying high and striking hard.

I know I speak for the mass of the American people when I say that we reject the turtle policy and will continue increasingly the policy of carrying the war to the enemy in distant lands and distant waters—as far away as possible from our own home grounds.

There are four main lines of communication now being traveled by our ships: the North Atlantic, the South Atlantic, the Indian

[2] Roosevelt spontaneously added the words "that's now called Iran."

Ocean, and the South Pacific. These routes are not one-way streets, for the ships that carry our troops and munitions outbound bring back essential raw materials which we require for our own use.

The maintenance of these vital lines is a very tough job. It is a job which requires tremendous daring, tremendous resourcefulness, and, above all, tremendous production of planes and tanks and guns and also of the ships to carry them. And I speak again for the American people when I say that we can and will do that job.

The defense of the worldwide lines of communication demands compel[3] relatively safe use by us of the sea and of the air along the various routes; and this, in turn, depends upon control by the United Nations of many strategic bases along those routes.

Control of the air involves the simultaneous use of two types of planes—first, the long-range heavy bomber; and second, the light bombers, the dive bombers, the torpedo planes, the short-range pursuit planes, all of which are essential to cooperate with and[4] protect the bases and the bombers themselves.

Heavy bombers can fly under their own power from here to the Southwest Pacific, either way;[5] but the smaller planes cannot. Therefore, these lighter planes have to be packed in crates and sent on board cargo ships. Look at your map again; and you will see that the route is long—and at many places perilous—either across the South Atlantic all the way around South Africa and the Cape of Good Hope, or from California to the East Indies direct. A vessel can make a round trip by either route in about four months, or only three round trips in a whole year.

In spite of the length, in spite of the difficulties of this transportation, I can tell you that in two and a half months we already have a large number of bombers and pursuit planes, manned by American pilots and crews, which are now in daily contact with the enemy in the Southwest Pacific. And thousands of American troops are today in that area engaged in operations not only in the air but on the ground as well.

In this battle area, Japan has had an obvious initial advantage. For she could fly even her short-range planes to the points of attack by using many stepping stones open to her—bases in a multitude of

---

[3]It is not clear why Roosevelt added the confusing word "compel" as he read this portion of the prepared text.

[4]Roosevelt added the words "cooperate with and" to the prepared text.

[5]For some reason Roosevelt added the words "either way" to the prepared text.

Pacific islands and also bases on the China coast, the Indochina coast, and in Thailand and Malaya. Japanese troop transports could go south from Japan and from China through the narrow China Sea, which can be protected by Japanese planes throughout its whole length.

I ask you to look at your maps again, particularly at that portion of the Pacific Ocean lying west of Hawaii. Before this war even started, the Philippine Islands were already surrounded on three sides by Japanese power. On the west, the China side, the Japanese were in possession of the coast of China and the coast of Indochina, which had been yielded to them by the Vichy French.[6] On the north are the islands of Japan themselves, reaching down almost to northern Luzon. On the east are the Mandated Islands—which Japan had occupied exclusively, and had fortified in absolute violation of her written word.

The islands that lie between Hawaii and the Philippines—these islands, hundreds of them, appear only as dots on most maps, or do not appear at all, but they cover a large strategic area. Guam lies in the middle of them—a lone outpost which we have never fortified.

Under the Washington Treaty of 1921 we had solemnly agreed not to add to the fortification of the Philippines.[7] We had no safe naval base there, so we could not use the islands for extensive naval operations.

Immediately after this war started, the Japanese forces moved down on either side of the Philippines to numerous points south of them—thereby completely encircling the Philippines from north and south and east and west.

It is that complete encirclement, with control of the air by Japanese land-based aircraft, which has prevented us from sending substantial reinforcements of men and materials to the gallant defenders of the Philippines. For forty years it has always been our strategy— a strategy born of necessity—that in the event of a full-scale attack on the islands by Japan, we should fight a delaying action, attempting to retire slowly into Bataan Peninsula and Corregidor.

We knew that the war as a whole would have to be fought and

---

[6]The Vichy government was established after the German conquest of France to rule over unoccupied France and the colonies. It soon became only a tool of German administration and was never recognized by the Allies.

[7]Roosevelt refers here to Article 19 of the Five Power Naval Treaty, signed on February 5, 1922.

won by a process of attrition against Japan itself. We knew all along that, with our greater resources, we could ultimately outbuild Japan and overwhelm her on sea and on land, and in the air. We knew that, to obtain our objective, many varieties of operations would be necessary in areas other than the Philippines.

Now nothing that has occurred in the past two months has caused us to revise this basic strategy of necessity—except that the defense put up by General MacArthur[8] has magnificently exceeded the previous estimates of endurance; and he and his men are gaining eternal glory therefor.

MacArthur's army of Filipinos and Americans, and the forces of the United Nations in China, in Burma, and the Netherlands East Indies, are all together fulfilling the same essential task. They are making Japan pay an increasingly terrible price for her ambitious attempts to seize control of the whole Asiatic world. Every Japanese transport sunk off Java is one less transport that they can use to carry reinforcements to their army opposing General MacArthur in Luzon.

It has been said that Japanese gains in the Philippines were made possible only by the success of their surprise attack on Pearl Harbor. I tell you that this is not so.

Even if the attack had not been made your map will show that it would have been a hopeless operation for us to send the fleet to the Philippines through thousands of miles of ocean, while all those island bases were under the sole control of the Japanese.

The consequences of the attack on Pearl Harbor—serious as they were—have been wildly exaggerated in other ways. And these exaggerations come originally from Axis propagandists; but they have been repeated, I regret to say, by Americans in and out of public life.

You and I have the utmost contempt for Americans who, since Pearl Harbor, have whispered or announced "off the record" that there was no longer any Pacific Fleet—that the fleet was all sunk or destroyed on December 7—that more than a thousand of our planes were destroyed on the ground. They have suggested slyly that the government has withheld the truth about casualties—that eleven or

---

[8] General Douglas MacArthur (1880–1964) was a career officer, who emerged as one of the great popular heroes of World War II. Roosevelt had appointed him commander of U.S. forces in the Far East and he was currently supervising the defense of the Philippines. In March 1942 he left the islands for Australia, under Roosevelt's orders, vowing that he would return in victory. It was MacArthur who eventually accepted the Japanese surrender aboard the *Missouri* in 1945.

twelve thousand men were killed at Pearl Harbor instead of the figures as officially announced. They have even served the enemy propagandists by spreading the incredible story that shiploads of bodies of our honored American dead were about to arrive in New York Harbor to be put into a common grave.

Almost every Axis broadcast—Berlin, Rome, Tokyo—directly quotes Americans who, by speech or in the press, make damnable misstatements such as these.

The American people realize that in many cases details of military operations cannot be disclosed until we are absolutely certain that the announcement will not give to the enemy military information which he does not already possess.

Your government has unmistakable confidence in your ability to hear the worst, without flinching or losing heart. You must, in turn, have complete confidence that your government is keeping nothing from you except information that will help the enemy in his attempt to destroy us. In a democracy there is always a solemn pact of truth between government and the people; but there must also always be a full use of discretion—and that word "discretion" applies to the critics of government as well.

This is war. The American people want to know, and will be told, the general trend of how the war is going. But they do not wish to help the enemy any more than our fighting forces do; and they will pay little attention to the rumormongers and the poison-peddlers in our midst.

To pass from the realm of rumor and poison to the field of facts: The number of our officers and men killed in the attack on Pearl Harbor on December 7 was 2,340, and the number wounded was 946. Of all of the combatant ships based at Pearl Harbor—battleships, heavy cruisers, light cruisers, aircraft carriers, destroyers, and submarines—only three are permanently put out of commission.

Very many of the ships of the Pacific Fleet were not even in Pearl Harbor. Some of those that were there were hit very slightly; and others that were damaged have either rejoined the fleet by now or are still undergoing repairs. And when those repairs are completed, the ships will be more efficient fighting machines than they were before.

The report that we lost more than a thousand planes at Pearl Harbor is as baseless as the other weird rumors. The Japanese do not know just how many planes they destroyed that day, and I am not going to tell them.[9] But I can say that to date—and including Pearl Harbor—we have destroyed considerably more Japanese planes than they have destroyed of ours.

We have most certainly suffered losses—from Hitler's U-boats in the Atlantic as well as from the Japanese in the Pacific—and we shall suffer more of them before the turn of the tide. But, speaking for the United States of America, let me say once and for all to the people of the world: We Americans have been compelled to yield ground, but we will regain it. We and the other United Nations[10] are committed to the destruction of the militarism of Japan and Germany. We are daily increasing our strength. Soon, we and not our enemies will have the offensive; we, not they, will win the final battles; and we, not they, will make the final peace.

Conquered nations in Europe know what the yoke of the Nazis is like. And the people of Korea and of Manchuria know in their flesh the harsh despotism of Japan. All of the people of Asia know that if there is to be an honorable and decent future for any of them or any of us, that future depends on victory by the United Nations over the forces of Axis enslavement.

If a just and durable peace is to be attained, or even if all of us are merely to save our own skins, there is one thought for us here at home to keep uppermost—the fulfillment of our special task of production—uninterrupted production. I stress that word uninterrupted.[11]

Germany, Italy, and Japan are very close to their maximum output of planes and guns and tanks and ships. The United Nations are not—especially the United States of America.

Our first job then is to build up production—uninterrupted production—so that the Nations[12] can maintain control of the seas and attain control of the air—not merely a slight superiority, but an overwhelming superiority.

[9] The Japanese destroyed 188 American aircraft at Pearl Harbor. Roosevelt's figures for the number of American military killed and wounded are reasonably accurate, but on the low side. His comments about damage to ships are much too optimistic. Nineteen vessels were sunk or severely damaged—among them eight battleships.

[10] The term United Nations refers to the twenty-six countries at war with Axis powers. These nations constituted the nucleus of the world governance organization that began its work, with fifty-one nations, in October 1945.

[11] Roosevelt spontaneously added to the prepared text the words "uninterrupted production. I stress that word uninterrupted."

[12] Roosevelt skipped over the word "United," which preceded "Nations" in the prepared text.

On January 6 of this year, I set certain definite goals of production for airplanes, tanks, guns, and ships. The Axis propagandists called them fantastic. Tonight, nearly two months later, and after a careful survey of progress by Donald Nelson[13] and others charged with the responsibility for our production, I can tell you that those goals will be attained.

In every part of the country, experts in production and the men and women at work in the plants are giving loyal service. With few exceptions, labor, capital, and farming realize that this is no time either to make undue profits or to gain special advantages, one over the other.

We are calling for new plants and additions, additions to old plants. We are calling for plant conversion to war needs. We are seeking more men and more women to run them. We are working longer hours. We are coming to realize that one extra plane or extra tank or extra gun or extra ship completed tomorrow may, in a few months, turn the tide on some distant battlefield; it may make the difference between life and death for some of our own fighting men. We know now that if we lose this war it'll be generations or even centuries before our conception of democracy can live again. And we can lose this war only if we slow up our effort or if we waste our ammunition sniping at each other.

Here are three high purposes for every American:

1. We shall not stop work for a single day. If any dispute arises we shall keep on working while the dispute is solved by mediation or conciliation, or arbitration—until the war is won.

2. We shall not demand special gains or special privileges or special advantages for any one group or occupation.

3. We shall give up conveniences and modify the routine of our lives if our country asks us to do so. We will do it cheerfully, remembering that the common enemy seeks to destroy every home and every freedom in every part of our land.

This generation of Americans has come to realize, with a present and personal realization, that there is something larger and more important than the life of any individual or of any individual group— something for which a man will sacrifice, and gladly sacrifice, not

---

[13] Donald M. Nelson (1888–1959), former vice president of Sears, Roebuck, and Company, was head of the War Production Board.

only his pleasures, not only his goods, not only his associations with those he loves, but his life itself. In time of crisis when the future is in the balance, we come to understand, with full recognition and devotion, what this nation is, and what we owe to it.

The Axis propagandists have tried in various evil ways to destroy our determination and our morale. Failing in that, they are now trying to destroy our confidence in our own allies. They say that the British are finished, that the Russians and the Chinese are about to quit. Patriotic and sensible Americans will reject these absurdities. And instead of listening to any of this crude propaganda, they will recall some of the things that Nazis and Japanese have said and are still saying about us.

Ever since this nation became the arsenal of democracy—ever since enactment of Lend-Lease—there has been one persistent theme through all Axis propaganda. This theme has been that Americans are admittedly rich, that Americans have considerable industrial power—but that Americans are soft and decadent, that they cannot and will not unite and work and fight.

From Berlin, Rome, and Tokyo we have been described as a nation of weaklings—"playboys"—who would hire British soldiers, or Russian soldiers, or Chinese soldiers to do our fighting for us.

Let them repeat that now!

Let them tell that to General MacArthur and his men.

Let them tell that to the sailors who today are hitting hard in the far waters of the Pacific.

Let them tell that to the boys in the Flying Fortresses.

Let them tell that to the marines!

The United Nations constitute an association of independent peoples of equal dignity and equal importance. The United Nations are dedicated to a common cause. We share equally and with equal zeal the anguish and the awful sacrifices of war. In the partnership of our common enterprise, we must share in a unified plan in which all of us must play our several parts, each of us being equally indispensable and dependent one on the other.

We have unified command and cooperation and comradeship.

We Americans will contribute unified production and unified acceptance of sacrifice and of effort. That means a national unity that can know no limitations of race or creed or selfish politics. The American people expect that much from themselves. And the American people will find ways and means of expressing their determination to their enemies, including the Japanese admiral who has said that he will dictate the terms of peace here in the White House.

We of the United Nations are agreed on certain broad principles in the kind of peace we seek. The Atlantic Charter applies not only to the parts of the world that border the Atlantic but to the whole world; disarmament of aggressors, self-determination of nations and peoples, and the four freedoms—freedom of speech, freedom of religion, freedom from want, and freedom from fear.[14]

The British and the Russian people have known the full fury of Nazi onslaught. There have been times when the fate of London and Moscow was in serious doubt. But there was never the slightest question that either the British or the Russians would yield. And today all the United Nations salute the superb Russian army as it celebrates the twenty-fourth anniversary of its first assembly.

Though their homeland was overrun, the Dutch people are still fighting stubbornly and powerfully overseas.

The great Chinese people have suffered grievous losses; Chungking has been almost wiped out of existence—yet it remains the capital of an unbeatable China.

That is the conquering spirit which prevails throughout the United Nations in this war.

The task that we Americans now face will test us to the uttermost. Never before have we been called upon for such a prodigious effort. Never before have we had so little time in which to do so much.

"These are the times that try men's souls." Tom Paine wrote those words on a drumhead, by the light of a campfire. That was when Washington's little army of ragged, rugged men was retreating across New Jersey, having tasted naught but defeat.

And General Washington ordered that these great words written by Tom Paine be read to the men of every regiment in the Continental Army, and this was the assurance given to the first American armed forces:

"The summer soldier and the sunshine patriot will, in this crisis,

[14]The Atlantic Charter was an eight-point pronouncement issuing from a conference between Roosevelt and Churchill, held at Argentia, Newfoundland, in August 1941. It can be compared roughly to Woodrow Wilson's Fourteen Points in its idealistic objectives. In his annual Message to Congress of January 7, 1941, Roosevelt had enunciated "the four freedoms": freedom of speech, freedom of religion, freedom from want, freedom from fear. Two of these freedoms (from want and fear) were incorporated in the Atlantic Charter.

shrink from the service of their country; but he that stands it now, deserves the love and thanks of man and woman. Tyranny, like hell, is not easily conquered; yet we have this consolation with us, that the harder the sacrifice, the more glorious the triumph." [15]

So spoke Americans in the year 1776.

So speak Americans today!

[15] Roosevelt quotes the opening words from Paine's *The Crisis*, paper no. 1 (December 23, 1776).

A CALL FOR SACRIFICE

IN THE TWO MONTHS that had elapsed since the last Fireside Chat, the military picture had not brightened appreciably. Indeed, in almost every respect things seemed worse. American forces had fought valiantly against overwhelming odds in the Philippines. But as President Roosevelt spoke, Corregidor, the three-mile-long island in Manila Bay to which the American forces had retreated, was under siege. Japanese artillery was pounding the half-starved defenders of that distant outpost, softening it up for a landing that was to take place only a few days later. Referring to what had happened and was about to happen, the president said, "In the Far East we have passed through a phase of serious losses. We have inevitably lost control of a large portion of the Philippine Islands. But the whole nation pays tribute to the Filipino and American officers and men who held out so long on Bataan Peninsula, to those grim and gallant fighters who still hold Corregidor."

Meanwhile, British and American officials were debating the location and timing of a military offensive against Germany. Although Hitler's forces had bogged down in the Soviet Union and were suffering heavy casualties from both the Russian military and the Russian winter, western leaders understood the importance of relieving the pressure on the eastern front, where the bulk of the fighting was occurring in the European war. Roosevelt's advisers, particularly Generals George C. Marshall and Dwight D. Eisenhower and Secretary of War Stimson, strongly recommended an invasion of the European continent—a course of action that Churchill considered but stoutly resisted. Military strategy weighed heavily on the president's mind as he spoke to the American people.

So, too, did the matter of production of war material and the need to resist inflation in the United States. "There is one front and one battle where everyone in the United States . . . is in action, and will be privileged to remain in action throughout the war," the president said. "That front is right here at home, in our daily lives, in our daily tasks. Here at home everyone will have the privilege of making whatever self-denial is necessary, not only to supply our fighting men, but to keep the economic structure of our country fortified and secure during the war and after the war." To combat inflation he recommended a seven point program of taxation, price stabilization, rationing, and the sale of war bonds. This speech was a call for sacrifice and dedication in the context of military uncertainty.

MY FELLOW AMERICANS, it is nearly five months since we were attacked at Pearl Harbor. For the two years prior to that attack this country had been gearing itself up to a high level of production of munitions. And yet our war efforts had done little to dislocate the normal lives of most of us.

Since then we have dispatched strong forces of our Army and Navy, several hundred thousands of them, to bases and battlefronts thousands of miles from home. We have stepped up our war production on a scale that is testing our industrial power, our engineering genius, and our economic structure to the utmost. We have had no illusions about the fact that this is a tough job—and a long one.

American warships are now in combat in the North and South Atlantic, in the Arctic, in the Mediterranean, in the Indian Ocean, and in the North and South Pacific. American troops have taken stations in South America, Greenland, Iceland, the British Isles, the Near East, the Middle East and the Far East, the continent of Australia, and many islands of the Pacific. American war planes, manned by Americans, are flying in actual combat over all the continents and all the oceans.

On the European front the most important development of the past year has been without question the crushing counteroffensive on the part of the great armies of Russia against the powerful German army. These Russian forces have destroyed and are destroying more armed power of our enemies—troops, planes, tanks, and guns—than all the other United Nations put together.

In the Mediterranean area, matters remain on the surface much as they were. But the situation there is receiving very careful attention.

Recently, we've received news of a change in government in what we used to know as the Republic of France—a name dear to the hearts of all lovers of liberty, a name and an institution which we hope will soon be restored to full dignity.

Throughout the Nazi occupation of France, we have hoped for the maintenance of a French government which would strive to regain independence, to reestablish the principles of "Liberty, Equality, and Fraternity," and to restore the historic culture of France. Our policy has been consistent from the very beginning. However, we are now greatly concerned lest those who have recently come to power may seek to force the brave French people into submission to Nazi despotism.

The United Nations will take measures, if necessary, to prevent the use of French territory in any part of the world for military purposes by the Axis powers. The good people of France will readily understand that such action is essential for the United Nations to prevent assistance to the armies or navies or air forces of Germany or Italy or Japan. The overwhelming majority of the French people understand that the fight of the United Nations is fundamentally their fight, that our victory means the restoration of a free and independent France—and the saving of France from the slavery which would be imposed upon her by her external enemies and by her internal traitors.

We know how the French people really feel. We know that a deep-seated determination to obstruct every step in the Axis plan extends from occupied France through Vichy France all the way to the people of their colonies in every ocean and on every continent.

Our planes are helping in the defense of French colonies today, and soon American Flying Fortresses will be fighting for the liberation of the darkened continent of Europe itself.

In all the occupied countries there are men and women, and even little children, who have never stopped fighting, never stopped resisting, never stopped proving to the Nazis that their so-called new order will never be enforced upon free peoples.

In the German and Italian peoples themselves there's a growing conviction that the cause of Nazism and Fascism is hopeless—that their political and military leaders have led them along the bitter road which leads not to world conquest but to final defeat. They cannot fail to contrast the present frantic speeches of these leaders with their arrogant boastings of a year ago, and two years ago.

And on the other side of the world, in the Far East, we have passed through a phase of serious losses.

We have inevitably lost control of a large portion of the Philippine Islands. But this whole nation pays tribute to the Filipino and American officers and men who held out so long on Bataan Peninsula, to those grim and gallant fighters who still hold Corregidor, where the flag flies, and to the forces that are still striking effectively at the enemy on Mindanao and other islands.

The Malayan Peninsula and Singapore are in the hands of the enemy; the Netherlands East Indies are almost entirely occupied, though resistance there continues. Many other islands are in the possession of the Japanese. But there is good reason to believe that their southward advance has been checked. Australia, New Zealand, and much other territory will be bases for offensive action—and we are determined that the territory that has been lost will be regained.

The Japanese are pressing their northward advance against Burma with considerable power, driving toward India and China. They have been opposed with great bravery by small British and Chinese forces aided by American fliers.

The news in Burma tonight is not good. The Japanese may cut the Burma Road;[1] but I want to say to the gallant people of China that no matter what advances the Japanese may make, ways will be found to deliver airplanes and munitions of war to the armies of Generalissimo Chiang Kai-shek.[2]

We remember that the Chinese people were the first to stand up and fight against the aggressors in this war; and in the future a still unconquerable China will play its proper role in maintaining peace and prosperity, not only in eastern Asia but in the whole world.

For every advance that the Japanese have made since they started their frenzied career of conquest, they have had to pay a very heavy toll in warships, in transports, in planes, and in men. They are feeling the effects of those losses.

It is even reported from Japan that somebody has dropped bombs on Tokyo, and on other principal centers of Japanese war industries.

[1] The Burma Road ran seven hundred miles from a Burmese railhead, through very difficult mountain terrain, and into China's Yunnan province. It was a main supply route to the beleaguered Chinese, especially after the Japanese closed China's east-coast ports.

[2] Chiang Kai-shek (1887–1975) was the leader of the Chinese Nationalists, opposed both to the Japanese invaders and to the native Chinese Communists. During World War II his prestige was at its height as he and his wife were befriended by President Roosevelt, despite accusations in some quarters of incompetence and corruption.

If this be true, it is the first time in history that Japan has suffered such indignities.[3]

Although the treacherous attack on Pearl Harbor was the immediate cause of our entry into the war, that event found the American people spiritually prepared for war on a worldwide scale. We went into this war fighting. We know what we are fighting for. We realize that the war has become what Hitler originally proclaimed it to be—a total war.

Not all of us can have the privilege of fighting our enemies in distant parts of the world.

Not all of us can have the privilege of working in a munitions factory or a shipyard, or on the farms or in oil fields or mines, producing the weapons or the raw materials that are needed by our armed forces.

But there is one front and one battle where everyone in the United States—every man, woman, and child—is in action, and will be privileged to remain in action throughout this war. That front is right here at home, in our daily lives, in our daily tasks. Here at home everyone will have the privilege of making whatever self-denial is necessary, not only to supply our fighting men, but to keep the economic structure of our country fortified and secure during the war and after the war.

This will require, of course, the abandonment not only of luxuries but of many other creature comforts.

Every loyal American is aware of his individual responsibility. Whenever I hear anyone saying, "The American people are complacent—they need to be aroused," I feel like asking him to come to Washington to read the mail that floods into the White House and into all departments of this government. The one question that recurs through all these thousands of letters and messages is, "What more can I do to help my country in winning this war?"

To build the factories, to buy the materials, to pay the labor, to provide the transportation, to equip and feed and house the soldiers and sailors and marines, and to do all the thousands of things necessary in a war—all cost a lot of money, more money than has ever been spent by any nation at anytime in the long history of the world.

---

[3] This passage, delivered by Roosevelt with sly sarcasm in his voice, was a vague reference to the bombing raid by Army airmen under the command of Colonel James Doolittle only ten days before this speech. Sixteen B-25 bombers, taking off from the carrier *Hornet*, carried out attacks on Tokyo and other Japanese cities. Damage in Japan was negligible.

We are now spending, solely for war purposes, the sum of about $100 million every day in the week. But, before this year is over, that almost unbelievable rate of expenditure will be doubled.

All of this money has to be spent—and spent quickly—if we are to produce within the time now available the enormous quantities of weapons of war which we need. But the spending of these tremendous sums presents grave danger of disaster to our national economy.

When your government continues to spend these unprecedented sums for munitions month by month and year by year, that money goes into the pocketbooks and bank accounts of the people of the United States. At the same time raw materials and many manufactured goods are necessarily taken away from civilian use; and machinery and factories are being converted to war production.

You do not have to be a professor of mathematics or economics to see that if people with plenty of cash start bidding against each other for scarce goods, the price of those goods goes up.

Yesterday I submitted to the Congress of the United States a seven-point program, a program of general principles which taken together could be called the national economic policy for attaining the great objective of keeping the cost of living down.

I repeat them now to you in substance:

First, we must, through heavier taxes, keep personal and corporate profits at a low reasonable rate.

Second, we must fix ceilings on prices and rents.

Third, we must stabilize wages.

Fourth, we must stabilize farm prices.

Fifth, we must put more billions into war bonds.

Sixth, we must ration all essential commodities which are scarce.

And seventh, we must discourage installment buying, and encourage paying off debts and mortgages.

I do not think it is necessary to repeat what I said yesterday to the Congress in discussing these general principles.

The important thing to remember is that each one of these points is dependent on the others if the whole program is to work.

Some people are already taking the position that every one of the seven points is correct except the one point which steps on their own individual toes. A few seem very willing to approve self-denial—on the part of their neighbors. The only effective course of action is a simultaneous attack on all of the factors which increase the cost of living, in one comprehensive, all-embracing program covering prices and profits and wages and taxes and debts.

The blunt fact is that every single person in the United States is going to be affected by this program. Some of you will be affected more directly by one or two of these restrictive measures, but all of you will be affected indirectly by all of them.

Are you a businessman, or do you own stock in a business corporation? Well, your profits are going to be cut down to a reasonably low level by taxation. Your income will be subject to higher taxes. Indeed in these days, when every available dollar should go to the war effort, I do not think that any American citizen should have a net income in excess of $25,000 per year after payment of taxes.

Are you a retailer or a wholesaler or a manufacturer or a farmer or a landlord? Ceilings are being placed on the prices at which you can sell your goods or rent your property.

Do you work for wages? You will have to forgo higher wages for your particular job for the duration of the war.

All of us are used to spending money for things that we want, things, however, which are not absolutely essential. We will all have to forgo that kind of spending. Because we must put every dime and every dollar we can possibly spare out of our earnings into war bonds and stamps. Because the demands of the war effort require the rationing of goods of which there is not enough to go around. Because the stopping of purchases of nonessentials will release thousands of workers who are needed in the war effort.

As I told the Congress yesterday, "sacrifice" is not exactly the proper word with which to describe this program of self-denial. When, at the end of this great struggle, we shall have saved our free way of life, we shall have made no "sacrifice."

The price for civilization must be paid in hard work and sorrow and blood. The price is not too high. If you doubt it, ask those millions who live today under the tyranny of Hitlerism.

Ask the workers of France and Norway and the Netherlands, whipped to labor by the lash, whether the stabilization of wages is too great a "sacrifice."

Ask the farmers of Poland and Denmark and Czechoslovakia and France, looted of their livestock, starving while their own crops are stolen from their land, ask them whether parity prices are too great a "sacrifice."

Ask the businessmen of Europe, whose enterprises have been stolen from their owners, whether the limitation of profits and personal incomes is too great a "sacrifice."

Ask the women and children whom Hitler is starving whether the rationing of tires and gasoline and sugar is too great a "sacrifice."

We do not have to ask them. They have already given us their agonized answers.

This great war effort must be carried through to its victorious conclusion by the indomitable will and determination of the people as one great whole.

It must not be impeded by the faint of heart.

It must not be impeded by those who put their own selfish interests above the interests of the nation.

It must not be impeded by those who pervert honest criticism into falsification of fact.

It must not be impeded by self-styled experts either in economics or military problems who know neither true figures nor geography itself.

It must not be impeded by a few bogus patriots who use the sacred freedom of the press to echo the sentiments of the propagandists in Tokyo and Berlin.

And, above all, it shall not be imperiled by the handful of noisy traitors—betrayers of America, betrayers of Christianity itself—would-be dictators who in their hearts and souls have yielded to Hitlerism and would have this republic do likewise.

I shall use all of the executive power that I have to carry out the policy laid down. If it becomes necessary to ask for any additional legislation in order to attain our objective of preventing a spiral in the cost of living, I shall do so.

I know the American farmer, the American workman, and the American businessman. I know that they will gladly embrace this economy and equality of sacrifice—satisfied that it is necessary for the most vital and compelling motive in all their lives—winning through to victory.

Never in the memory of man has there been a war in which the courage, the endurance, and the loyalty of civilians played so vital a part.

Many thousands of civilians all over the world have been and are being killed or maimed by enemy action. Indeed, it is the fortitude of the common people of Britain under fire which enabled that island to stand and prevented Hitler from winning the war in 1940. The ruins of London and Coventry and other cities are today the proudest monuments to British heroism.

Our own American civilian population is now relatively safe from such disasters. And, to an ever increasing extent, our soldiers, sailors, and marines are fighting with great bravery and great skills on far distant fronts to make sure that we shall remain safe.

I should like to tell you one or two stories about the men we have in our armed forces:

There is, for example, Dr. Corydon M. Wassell. He was a missionary, well known for his good works in China. He is a simple, modest, retiring man, nearly sixty years old, but he entered the service of his country and was commissioned a lieutenant commander in the navy.

Dr. Wassell was assigned to duty in Java caring for wounded officers and men of the cruisers *Houston* and *Marblehead* which had been in heavy action in the Java seas.

When the Japanese advanced across the island, it was decided to evacuate as many as possible of the wounded to Australia. But about twelve of the men were so badly wounded that they couldn't be moved. Dr. Wassell remained with them, knowing that he would be captured by the enemy. But he decided to make a last desperate attempt to get the men out of Java. He asked each of them if he wished to take the chance, and every one agreed.

He first had to get the twelve men to the seacoast—fifty miles away. To do this, he had to improvise stretchers for the hazardous journey. The men were suffering severely, but Dr. Wassell kept them alive by his skill, inspired them by his own courage.

And as the official report said, Dr. Wassell was "almost like a Christ-like shepherd devoted to his flock."

On the seacoast, he embarked the men on a little Dutch ship. They were bombed, they were machine-gunned by waves of Japanese planes. Dr. Wassell took virtual command of the ship, and by great skill avoided destruction, hiding in little bays and little inlets.

A few days later, Dr. Wassell and his small flock of wounded men reached Australia safely.

And today Dr. Wassell wears the Navy Cross.

Another story concerns a ship, a ship rather than an individual man.

You may remember the tragic sinking of the submarine, the United States Ship *Squalus*, off the New England coast in the summer of 1939. Some of the crew were lost, but others were saved by the speed and the efficiency of the surface rescue crews. The *Squalus* itself was tediously raised from the bottom of the sea.

She was repaired, put back into commission, and eventually she sailed again under a new name, the United States Ship *Sailfish*. Today, she is a potent and effective unit of our submarine fleet in the Southwest Pacific.

The *Sailfish* has covered many thousands of miles in operations in those far waters.

She has sunk a Japanese destroyer.

She has torpedoed a Japanese cruiser.

She has made torpedo hits—two of them—on a Japanese aircraft carrier.

Three of the enlisted men of our Navy who went down with the *Squalus* in 1939 and were rescued are today serving on the same ship, the United States Ship *Sailfish*, in this war.

It seems to me that it is heartening to know that the *Squalus*, once given up as lost, rose from the depths to fight for our country in time of peril.

One more story that I heard only this morning.

This is a story of one of our Army Flying Fortresses operating in the western Pacific. The pilot of this plane is a modest young man, proud of his crew for one of the toughest fights a bomber has yet experienced.

The bomber departed from its base, as part of a flight of five bombers, to attack Japanese transports that were landing troops against us in the Philippines. When they had gone about halfway to their destination, one of the motors of this bomber went out of commission. The young pilot lost contact with the other bombers. The crew, however, got the motor working, got it going again and the plane proceeded on its mission alone.

By the time it arrived at its target the other four Flying Fortresses had already passed over, had dropped their bombs, and had stirred up the hornets' nest of Japanese "Zero" planes. Eighteen of these Zero fighters attacked our one Flying Fortress. Despite this mass attack, our plane proceeded on its mission, and dropped all of its bombs on six Japanese transports which were lined up along the docks.

As it turned back on its homeward journey a running fight between the bomber and the eighteen Japanese pursuit planes continued for seventy-five miles. Four pursuit planes of the Japs attacked simultaneously at each side. Four were shot down with the side guns. During this fight, the bomber's radio operator was killed, the engineer's right hand was shot off, and one gunner was crippled, leaving only one man available to operate both side guns. Although wounded in one hand, this gunner alternately manned both side guns, bringing down three more Japanese Zero planes. While this was going on, one engine on the American bomber was shot out, one gas tank was hit, the radio was shot off, and the oxygen system was entirely destroyed. Out of eleven control cables all but four were shot away. The rear landing wheel was blown off entirely, and the two front wheels were both shot flat.

The fight continued until the remaining Japanese pursuit ships exhausted their ammunition and turned back. With two engines gone and the plane practically out of control, the American bomber returned to its base after dark and made an emergency landing. The mission had been accomplished.

The name of that pilot is Captain Hewitt T. Wheless, of the United States Army. He comes from a place called Menard, Texas—with a population of 2,375. He has been awarded the Distinguished Service Cross. And I hope that he is listening.

These stories I have told you are not exceptional. They are typical examples of individual heroism and skill.

As we here at home contemplate our own duties, our own responsibilities, let us think and think hard of the example which is being set for us by our fighting men.

Our soldiers and sailors are members of well-disciplined units. But they're still and forever individuals—free individuals. They are farmers and workers, businessmen, professional men, artists, clerks.

They are the United States of America.

That is why they fight.

We too are the United States of America.

That is why we must work and sacrifice.

It is for them. It is for us. It is for victory.

STABILIZATION OF
THE PRICE OF FOOD

THROUGH THE SUMMER of 1942 the most pressing domestic problem facing Roosevelt was the rising cost of living. In a stabilization
measure passed in May, farm prices had been set at more than 100
percent of parity—due to the strength of farm bloc lobbying. The
result in practical terms was that food costs were spiraling upward at
a rate of roughly 3 percent a month for those foodstuffs exempt from
controls. If food prices could not be effectively controlled, neither
could wages; and indeed wage rates, given the fact that 1942 was an
election year, were allowed to increase simultaneously with food
prices. Inflation threatened to get out of hand unless the means necessary to stop it were quickly implemented: a tax law to drain away
private purchasing power, greater voluntary citizen investment in government bonds, tight control of the price of food.

A number of his advisers recommended that Roosevelt utilize his
war powers and implement stabilization with or without the approval
of Congress. They recommended that he act in accord with the tone
set in his first months in office in 1933, when he said he would seek
executive power "as great as the power that would be given to me if
we were in fact invaded by a foreign foe." Though sorely tempted, he
steadfastly refused to assume such power—at least directly.

On September 7, he went to Congress for legislation to stabilize
food prices and raise taxes. "We cannot hold the actual cost of food
and clothing down to approximately the present level beyond October 1," he said. If Congress did not take action by then, he would do
so: "Inaction on your part by that date will leave me with an inescapable responsibility to the people of this country to see to it that the
war effort is no longer imperiled by threat of economic chaos."

He then went to the people. In this Fireside Chat, delivered the
same evening, he began by arousing the emotions of his hearers with
a story about an American war hero in the battle of the Coral Sea, to
whom he was awarding the Medal of Honor. He then repeated much

of what he had just told the Congress. That body passed a stabilization bill on October 2 that encompassed most of the president's recommendations. The radio address is also notable for the "progress report," made by Roosevelt at the close of the speech, about Allied prospects on each of the four chief battlefronts of the war.

MY FRIENDS, I wish that all Americans could read all the citations for various medals recommended for our soldiers and sailors and marines. I am picking out one of these citations which tells of the accomplishments of Lieutenant John James Powers, United States Navy, during three days of the battles with Japanese forces in the Coral Sea.

During the first two days, Lieutenant Powers, flying a dive bomber in the face of blasting enemy anti-aircraft fire, demolished one large enemy gunboat, put another gunboat out of commission, severely damaged an aircraft tender and a 20,000-ton transport, and scored a direct hit on an aircraft carrier which burst into flames and sank soon after.

The official citation then describes the morning of the third day of battle. As the pilots of his squadron left the ready room to man their planes, Lieutenant Powers said to them, "Remember, the folks back home are counting on us. I am going to get a hit if I have to lay it on their flight deck."

He led his section down to the target from an altitude of 18,000 feet, through a wall of bursting anti-aircraft shells and swarms of enemy planes. He dived almost to the very deck of the enemy carrier, and did not release his bomb until he was sure of a direct hit. He was last seen attempting recovery from his dive at the extremely low altitude of 200 feet, amid a terrific barrage of shell and bomb fragments and smoke and flame and debris from the stricken vessel. His own plane was destroyed by the explosion of his own bomb. But he had made good his promise to "lay it on the flight deck."

I have received a recommendation from the secretary of the navy that Lieutenant John James Powers of New York City, missing in action, be awarded the Medal of Honor. I hereby and now make this award.

You and I are "the folks back home" for whose protection Lieutenant Powers fought and repeatedly risked his life. He said that we counted on him and his men. We did not count in vain. But have not those men a right to be counting on us? How are we playing our part "back home" in winning this war?

The answer is that we are not doing enough.

Today I sent a message to the Congress, pointing out the overwhelming urgency of the serious domestic economic crisis in which we are threatened. Some call it "inflation," which is a vague sort of term, and others call it a "rise in the cost of living," which is much more easily understood by most families.

That phrase, "the cost of living," means essentially what a dollar can buy.

From January 1, 1941, to May of this year—nearly a year and a half—the cost of living went up about 15 percent. And at that point last May we undertook to freeze the cost of living. But we could not do a complete job of it, because the congressional authority at the time exempted a large part of farm products used for food and for making clothing, although several weeks before, I had asked the Congress for legislation to stabilize all farm prices.

At that time I had told the Congress that there were seven elements in our national economy, all of which had to be controlled; and that if any one essential element remained exempt, the cost of living could not be held down.

On only two of these points—both of them vital, however—did I call for congressional action. These two vital points were, first, taxation; and second, the stabilization of all farm prices at parity.

"Parity" is a standard for the maintenance of good farm prices. It was established as our national policy way back in 1933.[1] It means that the farmer and the city worker are on the same relative ratio with each other in purchasing power as they were during a period some thirty years before—at a time when the farmer had a satisfactory purchasing power. One hundred percent of parity, therefore, has been accepted by farmers as the fair standard for the prices they receive.

Last January, however, the Congress passed a law forbidding ceilings on farm prices below 110 percent of parity on some commodi-

[1] The idea of parity was incorporated into the Agricultural Adjustment Act of 1933. Under the terms of the plan, farmers would receive cash payments for certain crops that would make their purchasing power equal to what it had been during the relatively prosperous years 1909–14.

ties. And on other commodities the ceiling was even higher, so that the average possible ceiling is now about 116 percent of parity for agricultural products as a whole.

This act of favoritism for one particular group in the community increased the cost of food to everybody—not only to the workers in the city or in the munitions plants, and their families, but also to the families of the farmers themselves.

Since last May, ceilings have been set on nearly all commodities, rents, services, except the exempted farm products. Installment buying, for example, has been effactually stabilized and controlled.

Wages in certain key industries have been stabilized on the basis of the present cost of living.

But it is obvious to all of us that if the cost of food continues to go up, as it is doing at present, the wage earner, particularly in the lower brackets, will have a right to an increase in his wages. I think that would be essential justice and a practical necessity.

Our experience with the control of other prices during the past few months has brought out one important fact—the rising cost of living can be controlled, providing that all elements making up the cost of living are controlled at the same time. I think that also is an essential justice and a practical necessity. We know that parity prices for farm products not now controlled will not put up the cost of living more than a very small amount; but we also know that if we must go up to an average of 116 percent of parity for food and other farm products—which is necessary at present under the Emergency Price Control Act before we can control all farm prices—the cost of living will get well out of hand. We are face to face with this danger today. Let us meet it and remove it.

I realize that it may seem to you to be overstressing these economic problems at a time like this, when we're all deeply concerned about the news from far distant fields of battle. But I give you the solemn assurance that failure to solve this problem here at home—and to solve it now—will make more difficult the winning of this war.

If the vicious spiral of inflation ever gets under way, the whole economic system will stagger. Prices and wages will go up so rapidly that the entire production program will be endangered. The cost of the war, paid by taxpayers, will jump beyond all present calculations. It will mean an uncontrollable rise in prices and in wages, which can result in raising the overall cost of living as high as another 20 percent soon. That would mean that the purchasing power of every dollar that you have in your pay envelope or in the bank or included in your insurance policy or your pension, would be reduced to about eighty cents' worth. I need not tell you that this would have a demoralizing effect on our people, soldiers and civilians alike.

Overall stabilization of prices and salaries and wages and profits is necessary to the continued increasing production of planes and tanks and ships and guns.

In my message to Congress today, I have said that this must be done quickly. If we wait for two or three or four or six months, it may well be too late.

I have told the Congress that the administration cannot hold the actual cost of food and clothing down to the present level beyond October 1.

Therefore, I have asked the Congress to pass legislation under which the president would be specifically authorized to stabilize the cost of living, including the price of all farm commodities. The purpose should be to hold farm prices at parity, or at levels of a recent date, whichever is higher. The purpose should also be to keep wages at a point stabilized with today's cost of living. Both must be regulated at the same time, and neither one of them can or should be regulated without the other.

At the same time that farm prices are stabilized, I will stabilize wages.

That is plain justice—and plain common sense.

And so I have asked the Congress to take this action by the first of October. We must now act with the dispatch which the stern necessities of war require.

I have told the Congress that inaction on their part by that date will leave me with an inescapable responsibility, a responsibility to the people of this country to see to it that the war effort is no longer imperiled by the threat of economic chaos.

As I said in my message to the Congress:

In the event that the Congress should fail to act, and act adequately, I shall accept the responsibility, and I will act.

The president has the powers, under the Constitution and under congressional acts, to take measures necessary to avert a disaster which would interfere with the winning of the war.

I have given the most careful and thoughtful consideration to meeting this issue without further reference to the Congress. I have determined, however, on this vital matter to consult with the Congress.

There may be those who will say that, if the situation is as grave as I have stated it to be, I should use my powers and act now. I can only say that I have approached this problem from every angle, and that I have decided that the course of conduct which I am following in this case is consistent with my sense of responsibility as president in time of war, and with my deep and unalterable devotion to the processes of democracy.

The responsibilities of the president in wartime to protect the nation are very grave. This total war, with our fighting fronts all over the world, makes the use of the executive power far more essential than in any previous war.

If we were invaded, the people of this country would expect the president to use any and all means to repel the invader.

Now the Revolution and the War Between the States were fought on our own soil, but today this war will be won or lost on other continents and in remote seas. I cannot tell what powers may have to be exercised in order to win this war.

The American people can be sure that I will use my powers with a full sense of responsibility to the Constitution and to my country. The American people can also be sure that I shall not hesitate to use every power vested in me to accomplish the defeat of our enemies in any part of the world where our own safety demands such defeat.

And when the war is won, the powers under which I act will automatically revert to the people of the United States—to the people to whom those powers belong.

I think I know the American farmers. I know that they're as wholehearted in their patriotism as any other group. They have suffered from the constant fluctuations of farm prices—occasionally too high, but more often too low. Nobody knows better than farmers the disastrous effects of wartime inflationary booms, and postwar deflationary panics.

So I have also suggested today that the Congress make our agricultural economy more stable. I have recommended that in addition to putting ceilings on all farm products now, we also place a definite floor under those prices for a period beginning now, continuing through the war, and for as long as necessary after the war. In this way we will be able to avoid the collapse of farm prices that happened after the last war. The farmers must be assured of a fair minimum price during the readjustment period which will follow the great, excessive world food demands that now prevail.

We must have some floor under farm prices, as we must have under wages, if we are to avoid the dangers of a postwar inflation, on the one hand, or the catastrophe of a crash in farm prices and wages, on the other.

Today I have also advised the Congress of the importance of speeding up the passage of the tax bill. The federal Treasury is losing millions of dollars each and every day because the bill has not yet been passed. Taxation is the only practical way of preventing the incomes and profits of individuals and corporations from getting too high.

I have told the Congress once more that all net individual incomes, after payment of all taxes, should be limited effectively by further taxation to a maximum net income of $25,000 a year. And it is equally important that corporate profits should not exceed a reasonable amount in any case.

The nation must have more money to run the war. People must stop spending for luxuries. Our country needs a far greater share of our incomes.

For this is a global war, and it will cost this nation nearly $100 billion in 1943.

In that global war there are now four main areas of combat; and I should like to speak briefly of them, not in the order of their importance, for all of them are vital and all of them are interrelated.

1. The Russian front. Here the Germans are still unable to gain the smashing victory which, almost a year ago, Hitler announced he had already achieved. Germany has been able to capture important Russian territory. Nevertheless, Hitler has been unable to destroy a single Russian army; and this, you may be sure, has been, and still is, his main objective. Millions of German troops seem doomed to spend another cruel and bitter winter on the Russian front. Yes, the Russians are killing more Nazis, and destroying more airplanes and tanks than are being smashed on any other front. They are fighting not only bravely but brilliantly. In spite of any setbacks Russia will hold out, and with the help of her allies will ultimately drive every Nazi from her soil.

2. The Pacific Ocean area. This area must be grouped together as a whole—every part of it, land and sea. We have stopped one major Japanese offensive; and we have inflicted heavy losses on their fleet. But they still possess great strength; they seek to keep the initiative; and they will undoubtedly strike hard again. We must not overrate the importance of our successes in the Solomon Islands, though we may be proud of the skill with which these local operations were conducted. At the same time, we need not underrate the significance of our victory at Midway. There we stopped the major Japanese offensive.

3. In the Mediterranean and the Middle East the British, together with the South Africans, Australians, New Zealanders, Indian troops, and others of the United Nations, including ourselves, are fighting a desperate battle with the Germans and Italians. The Axis powers are fighting to gain control of that area, dominate the Mediterranean and the Indian Ocean, and gain contact with the Japanese navy. The battle in the Middle East is now joined. We are well aware of our danger, but we are hopeful of the outcome.

4. The European area. Here the aim is an offensive against Germany. There are at least a dozen different points at which attacks can be launched. You, of course, do not expect me to give details of future plans, but you can rest assured that preparations are being made here and in Britain toward this purpose. The power of Germany must be broken on the battlefields of Europe.

Various people urge that we concentrate our forces on one or another of these four areas, although no one suggests that any one of the four areas should be abandoned. Certainly, it could not be seriously urged that we abandon aid to Russia, or that we surrender all of the Pacific to Japan, or the Mediterranean and Middle East to Germany, or give up an offensive against Germany. The American people may be sure that we shall neglect none of the four great theaters of war.

Certain vital military decisions have been made. In due time you will know what these decisions are—and so will our enemies. I can say now that all of these decisions are directed toward taking the offensive.

Today, exactly nine months after Pearl Harbor, we have sent overseas three times more men than we transported to France in the first nine months of the First World War. We have done this in spite of greater danger and fewer ships. And every week sees a gain in the actual number of American men and weapons in the fighting areas. These reinforcements in men and munitions are continuing, and will continue to go forward.

This war will finally be won by the coordination of all the armies and navies and air forces of all of the United Nations operating in unison against our enemies.

This will require vast assemblies of weapons and men at all the vital points of attack. We and our allies have worked for years to achieve superiority in weapons. We have no doubts about the superiority of our men. We glory in the individual exploits of our soldiers, our sailors, our marines, our merchant seamen. Lieutenant John James Powers was one of these—and there are thousands of others in the forces of the United Nations.

Several thousand Americans have met death in battle. Other thousands will lose their lives. But many millions stand ready to step into their places—to engage in a struggle to the very death. For they know that the enemy is determined to destroy us, our homes and our institutions—that in this war it is kill or be killed.

Battles are not won by soldiers or sailors who think first of their own personal safety. And wars are not won by peoples who are concerned primarily with their own comfort, their own convenience, their own pocketbooks.

We Americans of today bear the gravest of responsibilities. And all of the United Nations share them.

All of us here at home are being tested—for our fortitude, for our selfless devotion to our country and to our cause.

This is the toughest war of all time. We need not leave it to historians of the future to answer the question whether we are tough enough to meet this unprecedented challenge. We can give that answer now. The answer is yes.

OCTOBER 12, 1942

REPORT ON A TRIP ACROSS THE COUNTRY

THE FIRESIDE CHAT of October 12, 1942, derived from President Roosevelt's recent tour of the nation; it was a report on conditions as he had observed them during a two-week swing around the country. The trip had been nearly surreptitious—the president made few speeches and attracted little publicity.

He had left Washington on September 17 on the presidential train accompanied by his wife Eleanor, a few photographers, a handful of reporters, some Secret Service men, and members of the White House staff. His first stop was Detroit, where he paid a visit to a tank factory—his car actually drove through the assembly lines—and hobnobbed with automotive moguls Henry and Edsel Ford. From there he went to Chicago, then to Minneapolis–St. Paul, stopping at one war production factory after another, enjoying the excitement of surprising local citizens and engaging in good-natured banter with workers. The trip across the nation eventually took him to Seattle and to the Boeing aircraft plant, then to San Francisco, Los Angeles, San Diego, and eastward to Texas, New Orleans, and back home to Washington—a trip of more than 8,750 miles.

If this Fireside Chat accurately reflected his emotions, the journey across America left Roosevelt in high spirits and with an optimistic appraisal of his fellow citizens. The speech was rambling and unfocused, but filled with praise for the men and women of the nation: he was impressed with "the plain fact that the American people are united as never before in their determination to do a job and do it well." "If the leaders of Germany and Japan could have come along with me," he said, and "had seen what I saw, they would agree with my conclusions." He touched on a great many topics: the course of the war and the need to keep the peace after it had been won; the irritating "typewriter strategists" who second-guessed professional military men; the possibility of bringing to trial some of the Axis leaders; the splendid work of women in the defense plants; the need to draft eighteen-year-olds and, perhaps, to manage civilian employment by applying a Selective Service form of organization. In general, the president bobbed and weaved expertly, as he often did in giving a speech. Although impossible to measure, the chatty, upbeat nature of this particular address must have had vast appeal to the radio audience.

MY FELLOW AMERICANS. As you know, I have recently come back from a trip of inspection of camps and training stations and war factories.

The main thing that I observed on this trip is not exactly news. It is the plain fact that the American people are united as never before in their determination to do a job and to do it well.

This whole nation of 130 million free men and women and children is becoming one great fighting force. Some of us are soldiers or sailors, some of us are civilians. Some of us are fighting the war in airplanes five miles above the continent of Europe or the islands of the Pacific—and some of us are fighting it in mines deep down in the earth of Pennsylvania or Montana. A few of us are decorated with medals for heroic achievement, but all of us can have that deep and permanent inner satisfaction that comes from doing the best we know how—each of us playing an honorable part in the great struggle to save our democratic civilization.

Whatever our individual circumstances or opportunities, we are all in it, and our spirit is good, and we Americans and our allies are going to win—and don't let anyone tell you anything different.

That is the main thing that I saw on my trip around the country—unbeatable spirit. If the leaders of Germany and Japan could have come along with me, and had seen what I saw they would agree with my conclusions. Unfortunately, they were unable to make the trip with me. And that is one reason why we are carrying our war effort overseas—to them.

With every passing week the war increases in scope and intensity. That is true in Europe, in Africa, in Asia, and on all the seas.

The strength of the United Nations is on the upgrade in this war. The Axis leaders, on the other hand, know by now that they have already reached their full strength, and that their steadily mounting losses in men and material cannot be fully replaced. Germany and Japan are already realizing what the inevitable result will be when the total strength of the United Nations hits them—at additional places on the earth's surface.

One of the principal weapons of our enemies in the past has been their use of what is called the "war of nerves." They have spread falsehood and terror; they have started fifth columns everywhere; they have duped the innocent; they have fomented suspicion and hate between neighbors; they have aided and abetted those people in other nations—including our own—whose words and deeds are advertised from Berlin and Tokyo as proof of our disunity.

The greatest defense against all such propaganda, of course, is the common sense of the common people—and that defense is prevailing.

The war of nerves against the United Nations is now turning into a boomerang. For the first time, the Nazi propaganda machine is on the defensive. They begin to apologize to their own people for the repulse of their vast forces at Stalingrad,[1] and for the enormous casualties they are suffering. They are compelled to beg their overworked people to rally their weakened production. They even publicly admit, for the first time, that Germany can be fed only at the cost of stealing food from the rest of Europe.

They are proclaiming that a second front is impossible; but, at the same time, they are desperately rushing troops in all directions, and stringing barbed wire all the way from the coasts of Finland and Norway to the islands of the eastern Mediterranean. And meanwhile, they are driven to increase the fury of their atrocities.

The United Nations have decided to establish the identity of those Nazi leaders who are responsible for the innumerable acts of savagery. As each of these criminal deeds is committed, it is being carefully investigated; and the evidence is being relentlessly piled up for the future purposes of justice.

We have made it entirely clear that the United Nations seek no mass reprisals against the populations of Germany or Italy or Japan.

[1] Stalingrad (now called Volgograd) was the place where the Russians were making a desperate, costly, and courageous stand against a German force of half a million men. At the time of this speech, the Germans were advancing against the sixteen Russian divisions defending the city, and the fighting was house-to-house. Both Hitler and Stalin stubbornly insisted that there be no retreat. Finally, the exhausted Germans were caught in a pincers movement and encircled; they surrendered their army on February 2, 1943.

But the ringleaders and their brutal henchmen must be named and apprehended and tried in accordance with the judicial processes of criminal law.[2]

There are now millions of Americans in army camps, in naval stations, in factories, and in shipyards. Who are these millions upon whom the life of our country depends? What are they thinking? What are their doubts? What are their hopes? And how is the work progressing?

The commander in chief cannot learn all of the answers to these questions in Washington. And that is why I made the trip I did.

It is very easy to say, as some have said, that when the president travels through the country he should go with a blare of trumpets, with crowds on the sidewalks, with batteries of reporters and photographers—talking and posing with all of the politicians of the land.

But having had some experience in this war and in the last war, I can tell you very simply that the kind of trip I took permitted me to concentrate on the work I had to do without expending time, meeting all the demands of publicity. And—I might add—it is a particular pleasure to make a tour of the country without having to give a single thought to politics.

I expect to make other trips for similar purposes, and I shall make them in the same way.

In the last war, I had seen great factories; but until I saw some of the new present-day plants, I had not thoroughly visualized our American war effort. Of course, I saw only a small portion of all our plants, but that portion was a good cross-section, and it was deeply impressive.

The United States has been at war for only ten months, and is engaged in the enormous task of multiplying its armed forces many times. We are by no means at full production level yet. But I could not help asking myself on the trip, where would we be today if the government of the United States had not begun to build many of its factories for this huge increase more than two years ago—more than a year before war was forced upon us at Pearl Harbor.

We had also had to face the problem of shipping. Ships in every

[2]Following World War II there were well-publicized trials in Nuremberg, Germany, and in Tokyo, Japan, of Axis leaders who were accused of war crimes and atrocities and of crimes against peace and against humanity. Twelve Nazi officials were given the death sentence at Nuremberg, ten of whom were hanged in October 1946; seven Japanese were hanged in December 1948 as a result of the Tokyo trial.

part of the world continue to be sunk by enemy action. But the total tonnage of ships coming out of American, Canadian, and British shipyards, day by day, has increased so fast that we are getting ahead of our enemies in the bitter battle of transportation.

In expanding our shipping, we have had to enlist many thousands of men for our merchant marine. These men are serving magnificently. They are risking their lives every hour so that guns and tanks and planes and ammunition and food may be carried to the heroic defenders of Stalingrad and to all of the United Nations' forces all over the world.

A few days ago I awarded the first Maritime Distinguished Service Medal to a young man—Edward F. Cheney of Yeadon, Pennsylvania—who had shown great gallantry in rescuing his comrades from the oily waters of the sea after their ship had been torpedoed. There will be many more such acts of bravery.

In one sense my recent trip was a hurried one, out through the Middle West, to the Northwest, down the length of the Pacific coast, and back through the Southwest and the South. In another sense, however, it was a leisurely trip, because I had the opportunity to talk to the people who are actually doing the work—management and labor alike—on their own home grounds. And it gave me a fine chance to do some thinking about the major problems of our war effort on the basis of first things first.

As I told the three press association representatives who accompanied me, I was impressed by the large proportion of women employed—doing skilled manual labor, running machines. As time goes on, and many more of our men enter the armed forces, this proportion of women will increase. Within less than a year from now, I think, there will probably be as many women as men working in our war production plants.

I had some enlightening experiences relating to the old saying of us men that curiosity—inquisitiveness—is stronger among women. I noticed, frequently, that when we drove unannounced down the middle aisle of a great plant full of workers and machines, the first people to look up from their work were the men—and not the women. It was chiefly the men who were arguing as to whether that fellow in the straw hat was really the president or not.

So having seen the quality of the work and of the workers on our production lines—and coupling these firsthand observations with the reports of actual performance of our weapons on the fighting fronts—I can say to you that we are getting ahead of our enemies in the battle of production.

Of great importance to our future production was the effective and rapid manner in which the Congress met the serious problem of the rising cost of living. It was a splendid example of the operation of democratic processes in wartime.

The machinery to carry out this act of the Congress was put into effect within twelve hours after the bill was signed. The legislation will help the cost-of-living problems of every worker in every factory and on every farm in the land.

In order to keep stepping up our production, we have had to add millions of workers to the total labor force of the nation. And as new factories come into operation, we must find additional millions of workers.

This presents a formidable problem in the mobilization of manpower.

It is not that we do not have enough people in this country to do the job. The problem is to have the right numbers of the right people in the right places at the right time.

We are learning to ration materials; and we must now learn to ration manpower.

The major objectives of a sound manpower policy are:

First, to select and train men of the highest fighting efficiency needed for our armed forces in the achievement of victory over our enemies in combat.

Second, to man our war industries and farms with the workers needed to produce the arms and munitions and food required by ourselves and by our fighting allies to win this war.

In order to do this, we shall be compelled to stop workers from moving from one war job to another as a matter of personal preference; to stop employers from stealing labor from each other; to use older men, and handicapped people, and more women, and even grown boys and girls, wherever possible and reasonable, to replace men of military age and fitness; to train new personnel for essential war work; and to stop the wastage of labor in all nonessential activities.

There are many other things that we can do, and do immediately, to help meet this manpower problem.

The school authorities in all the states should work out plans to enable our high school students to take some time from their school year, to use their summer vacations, to help farmers raise and harvest their crops, or to work somewhere in the war industries. This does not mean closing schools and stopping education. It does mean giving older students a better opportunity to contribute their bit to the war effort. Such work will do no harm to the students.[3]

People should do their work as near their homes as possible. We cannot afford to transport a single worker into an area where there's already a worker available to do the job.

In some communities, employers dislike to employ women. In others they are reluctant to hire Negroes. In still others, older men are not wanted. We can no longer afford to indulge such prejudices or practices.

Every citizen wants to know what essential war work he can do the best. He can get the answer by applying to the nearest United States Employment Service office, and there are 4,500 of these offices throughout the nation. They form the corner grocery stores of our manpower system. This network of employment offices is prepared to advise every citizen where his skills and labors are needed most, and to refer him to an employer who can utilize them to the best advantage in the war effort.

Perhaps the most difficult phase of the manpower problem is the scarcity of farm labor in many places. I have seen evidences of the fact, however, that the people are trying to meet it as well as possible.

In one community that I have visited, a perishable crop was harvested by turning out the whole of the high school for three or four days.

And in another community of fruit growers the usual Japanese labor was not available; but when the fruit ripened, the banker, the butcher, the lawyer, the garage man, the druggist, the local editor, and in fact every able-bodied man and woman in town, left their occupations, went out, gathered the fruit, and sent it to market.

Every farmer in the land must realize fully that his production is part of war production, and that he is regarded by the nation as essential to victory. The American people expect him to keep his production up, and even to increase it. We will use every effort to

---

[3] This sentence was spoken by the president jocularly, with a bit of a chuckle.

help him to get labor; but, at the same time, he and the people of his community must use ingenuity and cooperative effort to produce crops, and livestock and dairy products.

It may be that all of our volunteer effort—however well intentioned and well administered—will not suffice wholly to solve this problem. In that case, we shall have to adopt new legislation. And if this is necessary, I do not believe that the American people will shrink from it.

In a sense, every American, because of the privilege of his citizenship, is a part of the Selective Service.

The nation owes a debt of gratitude to the Selective Service boards. The successful operation of the Selective Service system and the way it has been accepted by the great mass of our citizens give us confidence that, if necessary, the same principle could be used to solve any manpower problem.

And I want to say also a word of praise and thanks to the more than 10 million people, all over the country, who have volunteered for the work of civilian defense—and who are working hard at it. They are displaying unselfish devotion in the patient performance of their often tiresome and always anonymous tasks. In doing this important neighborly work they are helping to fortify our national unity and our real understanding of the fact that we are all involved in this war.

Naturally, on my trip I was much interested in watching the training of our fighting forces.

All of our combat units that go overseas must consist of young, strong men who have had thorough training. An Army division that has an average age of twenty-three or twenty-four is a better fighting unit than one which has an average age of thirty-three or thirty-four. The more of such troops we have in the field, the sooner this war will be won, and the smaller will be the cost in casualties.

Therefore, I believe that it will be necessary to lower the present minimum age limit for Selective Service from twenty years down to eighteen. We have learned how inevitable that is—and how important to the speeding up of victory.

I can very thoroughly understand the feelings of all parents whose sons have entered our armed forces. I have an appreciation of that feeling—and so has my wife.[4]

[4] All four sons of Franklin and Eleanor Roosevelt were in military service.

I want every father and every mother who has a son in the service to know—again, from what I have seen with my own eyes—that the men in the Army, Navy, and Marine Corps are receiving today the best possible training, equipment, and medical care. And we will never fail to provide for the spiritual needs of our officers and men under the chaplains of our armed services.

Good training will save many, many lives in battle. The highest rate of casualties is always suffered by units comprised of inadequately trained men.

We can be sure that the combat units of our Army and Navy are well manned, well equipped, well trained. Their effectiveness in action will depend upon the quality of their leadership, and upon the wisdom of the strategic plans on which all military operations are based.

I can say one thing about these plans of ours: They are not being decided by the typewriter strategists who expound their views in the press or on the radio.

One of the greatest of American soldiers, Robert E. Lee, once remarked on the tragic fact that in the war of his day all of the best generals were apparently working on newspapers instead of in the Army. And that seems to be true in all wars.

The trouble with the typewriter strategists is that, while they may be full of bright ideas, they are not in possession of much information about the facts or the problems of military operations.

We, therefore, will continue to leave the plans for this war to the military leaders.

The military and naval plans of the United States are made by the joint staff of the Army and Navy which is constantly in session in Washington. The chiefs of this staff are Admiral Leahy, General Marshall, Admiral King, and General Arnold.[5] They meet and confer regularly with representatives of the British joint staff, and with representatives of Russia, China, the Netherlands, Poland, Norway, the British Dominions, and other nations working in the common cause.

Since this unity of operations was put into effect last January, there has been a very substantial agreement between these planners, all of whom are trained in the profession of arms—air, sea,

[5] Admiral William D. Leahy (1875–1959); General George C. Marshall (1880–1959); Admiral Ernest J. King (1878–1956); and General Henry ("Hap") Arnold (1886–1950).

and land—from their early years. As commander in chief I have at all times also been in substantial agreement.

As I have said before, many major decisions of strategy have been made. One of them—on which we have all agreed—relates to the necessity of diverting enemy forces from Russia and China to other theaters of war by new offensives against Germany and Japan. An announcement of how these offensives are to be launched, and when, and where, cannot be broadcast over the radio at this time.

We are celebrating today the exploit of a bold and adventurous Italian—Christopher Columbus—who with the aid of Spain opened up a New World where freedom and tolerance and respect for human rights and dignity provided an asylum for the oppressed of the Old World.

Today, the sons of the New World are fighting in lands far distant from their own America. They are fighting to save for all mankind, including ourselves, the principles which have flourished in this New World of freedom.

We are mindful of the countless millions of people whose future liberty and whose very lives depend upon permanent victory for the United Nations.

There are a few people in this country who, when the collapse of the Axis begins, will tell our people that we are safe once more; that we can tell the rest of the world to "stew in its own juice"; that never again will we help to pull "the other fellow's chestnuts from the fire"; that the future of civilization can jolly well take care of itself insofar as we are concerned.

But it is useless to win battles if the cause for which we fight these battles is lost. It is useless to win a war unless it stays won.

We, therefore, fight for the restoration and perpetuation of faith and hope and peace throughout the world.

The objective of today is clear and realistic. It is to destroy completely the military power of Germany, Italy, and Japan to such good purpose that their threat against us and all the other United Nations cannot be revived a generation hence.

We are united in seeking the kind of victory that will guarantee that our grandchildren can grow and, under God, may live their lives, free from the constant threat of invasion, destruction, slavery, and violent death.

DEALING WITH STRIKING COAL MINERS

THE SPRING OF 1943 was a time of labor discontent in the United States. Representatives of labor and management had agreed on December 23, 1941, that there would be no strikes or lockouts for the duration of the war. Increasingly, however, it appeared to labor leaders as well as to the rank and file that the pledge was serving to enrich employers and penalize labor. Wage increases had been held to roughly 15 percent over the period since January 1941, the estimated rise in the cost of living. But low paid workers benefited only marginally from such modest percentage increases while others complained that rises in food, clothing, and housing costs far exceeded wage increases. In March 1943 a strike took place among shipyard machinists in San Francisco; in April some 55,000 members of the rubber workers union walked off the job in Akron; and in May nearly 30,000 Chrysler workers in Detroit struck for higher pay. All of this activity troubled Roosevelt, but none of it as much as the action of the United Mine Workers (UMW) under the direction of their leader, John L. Lewis. Lewis led 400,000 bituminous miners out on four separate strikes during 1943.

Legitimate as the mine workers' grievances and the interests of the nation might have been, they soon became submerged in a bitter contest of wills between Roosevelt and Lewis, both of whom possessed sizable egos. Lewis pointed out, correctly, that prices had never been effectively controlled in mining towns across the nation while wages had averaged only a little over $1,700 for 1942. In March 1943 he informed the mine operators that the union was demanding a two-dollar-per-day wage increase, better vacation pay, increased safety equipment at the expense of the owners, and portal-to-portal pay (i.e., pay from the time of entering the mine to the place of work and back again). At the end of April, Lewis called a general strike throughout the industry.

Roosevelt and Lewis had been feuding since 1940 when Lewis supported Wendell Willkie for the presidency. Roosevelt never forgot, and in November 1941 he referred to the union leader as a psychopath. By 1943 he so despised Lewis that he allegedly proposed a deal: he would resign as president of the United States if Lewis would commit suicide! When Roosevelt took over the mines and threatened to end the miners' Selective Service deferments, he gained the upper hand; the miners went back to work. The Fireside Chat of May 2, 1943, helped Roosevelt win the popularity contest with Lewis (opinion polls showed that Lewis was one of the most hated men in America), but it did not bring lasting peace in the coalfields.

MY FELLOW AMERICANS, I am speaking tonight to the American people, and in particular to those of our citizens who are coal miners.

Tonight this country faces a serious crisis. We are engaged in a war on the successful outcome of which will depend the whole future of our country.

This war has reached a new critical phase. After the years that we have spent in preparation, we have moved into active and continuing battle with our enemies. We are pouring into the worldwide conflict everything that we have—our young men, and the vast resources of our nation.

I have just returned from a two weeks' tour of inspection on which I saw our men being trained and our war materials made. My trip took me through twenty states. I saw thousands of workers on the production line, making airplanes and guns and ammunition.

Everywhere I found great eagerness to get on with the war. Men and women are working long hours at difficult jobs and living under difficult conditions without complaint.

Along thousands of miles of track I saw countless acres of newly plowed fields. The farmers of this country are planting the crops that are needed to feed our armed forces, our civilian population, and our allies. Those crops will be harvested.

On my trip, I saw hundreds of thousands of soldiers. Young men who were green recruits last autumn have matured into self-assured and hardened fighting men. They are in splendid physical condition.

They are mastering the superior weapons that we are pouring out of our factories.

The American people have accomplished a miracle.

However, all of our massed effort is none too great to meet the demands of this war. We shall need everything that we have and everything that our allies have to defeat the Nazis and the Fascists in the coming battles on the continent of Europe, and the Japanese on the continent of Asia and in the islands of the Pacific.

This tremendous forward movement of the United States and the United Nations cannot be stopped by our enemies.

And equally, it must not be hampered by any one individual or by the leaders of any one group here back home.

I want to make it clear that every American coal miner who has stopped mining coal—no matter how sincere his motives, no matter how legitimate he may believe his grievances to be—every idle miner directly and individually is obstructing our war effort. We have not yet won this war. We will win this war only as we produce and deliver our total American effort on the high seas and on the battle fronts. And that requires unrelenting, uninterrupted effort here on the home front.

A stopping of the coal supply, even for a short time, would involve a gamble with the lives of American soldiers and sailors and the future security of our whole people. It would involve an unwarranted, unnecessary, and terribly dangerous gamble with our chances for victory.

Therefore, I say to all miners—and to all Americans everywhere, at home and abroad—the production of coal will not be stopped.

Tonight, I am speaking to the essential patriotism of the miners, and to the patriotism of their wives and children. And I am going to state the true facts of this case as simply and as plainly as I know how.

After the attack at Pearl Harbor, the three great labor organizations—the American Federation of Labor, the Congress of Industrial Organizations, and the Railroad Brotherhoods—gave the positive assurance that there would be no strikes as long as the war lasted. And the president of the United Mine Workers of America[1] was a party to that assurance.

That pledge was applauded throughout the country. It was a forcible means of telling the world that we Americans—135 million of

---

[1] John L. Lewis (1880–1969) had been the president of the UMW since 1920.

us—are united in our determination to fight this total war with our total will and our total power.

At the request of employers and of organized labor—including the United Mine Workers—the War Labor Board was set up for settling any disputes which could not be adjusted through collective bargaining.[2] The War Labor Board is a tribunal on which workers and employers and the general public are equally represented.

In the present coal crisis, conciliation and mediation were tried unsuccessfully.

In accordance with the law, the case was then certified to the War Labor Board, the agency created for this express purpose with the approval of organized labor. The members of the board followed the usual practice which has proved successful in other disputes. Acting promptly, they undertook to get all the facts of this case from both the miners and the operators.

The national officers of the United Mine Workers, however, declined to have anything to do with the fact-finding of the War Labor Board, and the only excuse that they offer is that the War Labor Board is prejudiced.

The War Labor Board has been and is ready to give the case a fair and impartial hearing and I have given my assurance that if any adjustment of wages is made by the board, it will be made retroactive to April 1. But the national officers of the United Mine Workers refused to participate in the hearing, when asked to do so last Monday.

On Wednesday of this past week, while the board was proceeding with the case, stoppages began to occur in some mines. On Thursday morning I telegraphed to the officers of the United Mine Workers asking that the miners continue mining coal on Saturday morning. However, a general strike throughout the industry became effective on Friday night.

The responsibility for the crisis that we now face rests squarely on these national officers of the United Mine Workers, and not on the government of the United States. But the consequences of this arbitrary action threaten all of us everywhere.

At ten o'clock yesterday morning, Saturday, the government took over the mines. I called upon the miners to return to work for their

[2]Established in January 1942, the War Labor Board had the authority to enforce arbitration terms in any dispute. If these terms were rejected, the board could request that the president take over the industry or the plant in question.

government. The government needs their services just as surely as it needs the services of our soldiers and sailors and marines—and the services of the millions who are turning out the munitions of war.

You miners have sons in the Army and Navy and Marine Corps. You have sons who at this very minute—this split second—may be fighting in New Guinea or in the Aleutian Islands or Guadalcanal or Tunisia or China, or protecting troop ships and supplies against submarines on the high seas. We have already received telegrams from some of our fighting men overseas, and I only wish they could tell you what they think of the stoppage of work in the coal mines.

Some of your own sons have come back from the fighting fronts, wounded. A number of them, for example, are now here in an Army hospital in Washington. Several of them have been decorated by their government.

I could tell you of one from Pennsylvania. He was a coal miner before his induction, and his father is a coal miner. He was seriously wounded by Nazi machine-gun bullets while he was on a bombing mission over Europe in a Flying Fortress.

Another boy, from Kentucky, the son of a coal miner, was wounded when our troops first landed in North Africa six months ago.

There's another, from Illinois. He was a coal miner—his father and two brothers are coal miners. He was seriously wounded in Tunisia while attempting to rescue two comrades whose jeep had been blown up by a Nazi mine.

These men do not consider themselves heroes. They'd probably be embarrassed if I mentioned their names over the air. They were wounded in the line of duty. They know how essential it is for the tens of thousands, hundreds of thousands, and ultimately millions of other young Americans to get the best of arms and equipment into the hands of our fighting forces—and get them there quickly.

The fathers and mothers of our fighting men, their brothers and sisters and friends—and that includes all of us—are also in the line of duty—the production line. Any failure in production may well result in costly defeat on the field of battle.

There can be no one among us—no one faction—powerful enough to interrupt the forward march of our people to victory.

You miners have ample reason to know that there are certain basic rights for which this country stands, and that those rights are worth fighting for and worth dying for. That is why you have sent your sons and brothers from every mining town in the nation to join in the great struggle overseas. That is why you have contributed so generously, so willingly, to the purchase of war bonds and to the many funds for the relief of war victims here and[3] in foreign lands. That is why, since this war was started in 1939, you have increased the annual production of coal by almost 200 million tons a year.

The toughness of your sons in our armed forces is not surprising. They come of fine, rugged stock. Men who work in the mines are not unaccustomed to hardship. It has been the objective of this government to reduce that hardship, to obtain for miners and for all who do the nation's work a better standard of living.

I know only too well that the cost of living is troubling the miners' families, and troubling the families of millions of other workers throughout the country as well.

A year ago it became evident to all of us that something had to be done about living costs. Your government determined not to let the cost of living continue to go up as it did in the First World War.

Your government has been determined to maintain stability of both prices and wages—so that a dollar would buy, so far as possible, the same amount of the necessities of life. And by necessities I mean just that—not the luxuries, not the fancy goods that we have learned to do without in wartime.

So far, we have not been able to keep the prices of some necessities as low as we should have liked to keep them. That is true not only in coal towns but in many, many other places.

Wherever we find that prices of essentials have risen too high, they will be brought down. Wherever we find that price ceilings are being violated, the violators will be punished.

Rents have been fixed in most parts of the country. In many cities they have been cut to below where they were before we entered the war. Clothing prices have generally remained stable.

These two items make up more than a third of the total budget of the worker's family.

As for food, which today accounts for about another third of the family expenditure on the average, I want to repeat again: your government will continue to take all necessary measures to eliminate unjustified, avoidable price increases. And we are today taking measures to "roll back" the prices of meats.

This war is going to go on. Coal will be mined no matter what any

---

[3] Roosevelt added the words "here and" to the prepared version of the text.

individual thinks about it. The operation of our factories, our power plants, our railroads will not be stopped. Our munitions must move to our troops.

And so, under these circumstances, it is inconceivable that any patriotic miner can choose any course other than going back to work and mining coal.

The nation cannot afford violence of any kind at the coal mines or in coal towns. I have placed authority for the resumption of coal mining in the hands of a civilian, the secretary of the interior.[4] If it becomes necessary to protect any miner who seeks patriotically to go back and work, then that miner must have and his family must have—and will have—complete and adequate protection. If it becomes necessary to have troops at the mine mouths or in coal towns for the protection of working miners and their families, those troops will be doing police duty for the sake of the nation as a whole, and particularly for the sake of the fighting men in the Army, the Navy, and the Marines—your sons and mine—who are fighting our common enemies all over the world.

I understand the devotion of the coal miners to their union. I know of the sacrifices they have made to build it up. I believe now, as I have all my life, in the rights of workers to join unions and to protect their unions. I want to make it absolutely clear that this government is not going to do anything now to weaken those rights in the coalfields.

Every improvement of the conditions of the coal miners of this country has had my hearty support, and I do not mean to desert them now. But I also do not mean to desert my obligations and responsibilities as president of the United States and commander in chief of the Army and Navy.

The first necessity is the resumption of coal mining. The terms of the old contract will be followed by the secretary of the interior. If an adjustment in wages results from a decision of the War Labor Board, or from any new agreement between the operators and miners, which is approved by the War Labor Board, that adjustment as I have said before will be made retroactive to April 1.

In the Message that I delivered to the Congress four months ago, I expressed my conviction that the spirit of this nation is good.

[4] Harold L. Ickes (1874–1952), an outspoken reform lawyer from Chicago, served as secretary of the interior from 1933 to 1946. Ickes also administered the PWA.

Since then, I have seen our troops in the Caribbean area, in bases on the coasts of our ally, Brazil, and in North Africa. Recently I have again seen great numbers of our fellow countrymen—soldiers and civilians—from the Atlantic seaboard to the Mexican border and to the Rocky Mountains.

Tonight, in the face of a crisis of serious proportions in the coal industry, I say again that the spirit of this nation is good. I know that the American people will not tolerate any threat offered to their government by anyone. I believe the coal miners will not continue to strike against their government. I believe that the coal miners as Americans will not fail to heed the clear call to duty. Like all other good Americans, they will march shoulder to shoulder with our armed forces to victory.

Tomorrow the Stars and Stripes will fly over the coal mines, and I hope that every miner will be at work under that flag.[5]

[5] This speech did not solve the labor difficulties in the nation's coal mines. There were additional stoppages of work in June and in October of 1943, when the government gave up running the mines. In November Roosevelt stepped in again and took control of the industry, this time until 1944, when all coal mines were returned to their private owners.

THE FIRST CRACK IN THE AXIS: THE FALL OF MUSSOLINI

PRESIDENT ROOSEVELT was in high spirits as he spoke to the American people on July 28, 1943; he was celebrating the fall of Mussolini from power in Italy and anticipating Allied victory in Sicily. Having defeated German and Italian armies in North Africa, Allied forces had landed on July 10, along the southeastern coast of Sicily. By the end of the month they were advancing on Messina, across the strait from Italy, and within three weeks after that, had completed the conquest of the island. Unfortunately, during the thirty-eight day campaign a large number of German and Italian forces escaped into the Italian peninsula, thereby limiting the extent of the victory.

Allied successes in North Africa and then in Sicily caused the Fascist regime in Italy to fall apart. As early as March 1943 there had been a series of anti-Fascist strikes that resulted in government concessions to the strikers. Then a committee of anti-Fascist parties was formed to seek the overthrow of the government. When the Italians suffered an embarrassing defeat in Sicily, military officers began urging Mussolini's removal, action that was accomplished after the Fascist Grand Council, on July 24, denounced the *Duce* and then voted against him; and on July 25, King Victor Emmanuel III dismissed him from power. The police promptly arrested him and whisked him off to prison. "The first crack in the Axis has come," President Roosevelt announced. "The criminal, corrupt Fascist regime in Italy is going to pieces." What the president did not mention in his speech was that the Italian government had already begun to put out peace feelers. After lengthy negotiations between the Allies and the new government of Italy under the former chief of staff, Marshal Pietro Badoglio, an Italian surrender document was agreed upon on September 3, and the Italians came over to the Allied side. This occurred simultaneously with Allied landings on the Italian peninsula.

As usual during the war, Roosevelt's Fireside Chat carried a mixed message. He combined his report on military progress with fresh appeals for greater domestic efforts; and he outlined a postwar "G.I. Bill of Rights."

MY FELLOW AMERICANS. Over a year and a half ago I said this to the Congress: "The militarists in Berlin and Rome[1] and Tokyo started this war. But the massed, angered forces of common humanity will finish it."

Today that prophecy is in the process of being fulfilled. The massed, angered forces of common humanity are on the march. They're going forward—on the Russian front, in the vast Pacific area, and into Europe—converging upon their ultimate objectives: Berlin and Tokyo.

I think the first crack in the Axis has come. The criminal, corrupt Fascist regime in Italy is going to pieces.

The pirate philosophy of the Fascists and the Nazis cannot stand adversity. The military superiority of the United Nations—on sea and land and in the air—has been applied in the right place and at the right time.

Hitler refused to send sufficient help to save Mussolini. In fact, Hitler's troops in Sicily stole the Italians' motor equipment, leaving Italian soldiers so stranded that they had no choice but to surrender. Once again the Germans betrayed their Italian allies, as they had done time and time again on the Russian front and in the long retreat from Egypt, through Libya and Tripoli, to the final surrender in Tunisia.

And so Mussolini came to the reluctant conclusion that the "jig was up"; he could see the shadow of the long arm of justice.

But he and his Fascist gang will be brought to book, and punished for their crimes against humanity. No criminal will be allowed to escape by the expedient of "resignation."

So our terms to Italy are still the same as our terms to Germany and Japan—"unconditional surrender."

We will have no truck with Fascism in any way, in any shape or manner. We will permit no vestige of Fascism to remain.

---

[1] Roosevelt added "Rome" to the prepared text, which had originally included only Berlin and Tokyo.

Eventually Italy will reconstitute herself. It will be the people of Italy who will do that, choosing their own government in accordance with the basic democratic principles of liberty and equality. In the meantime, the United Nations will not follow the pattern set by Mussolini and Hitler and the Japanese for the treatment of occupied countries—the pattern of pillage and starvation.

We're already helping the Italian people in Sicily. With their cordial cooperation, we are establishing and maintaining security and order, we are dissolving the organizations which have kept them under Fascist tyranny, we are providing them with the necessities of life until the time comes when they can fully provide for themselves.

Indeed, the people in Sicily today are rejoicing in the fact that for the first time in years they are permitted to enjoy the fruits of their own labor—they can eat what they themselves grow, instead of having it stolen from them by the Fascists and the Nazis.

In every country conquered by the Fascists and the Nazis, or the Japanese militarists, the people have been reduced to the status of slaves or chattels.

It is our determination to restore these conquered peoples to the dignity of human beings, masters of their own fate, entitled to freedom of speech, freedom of religion, freedom from want, and freedom from fear.

We have started to make good on that promise.

I am sorry if I step on the toes of those Americans who, playing party politics at home, call that kind of foreign policy "crazy altruism" and "starry-eyed dreaming."

Meanwhile, the war in Sicily and Italy goes on. It must go on, and will go on, until the Italian people realize the futility of continuing to fight in a lost cause—a cause to which the people of Italy themselves never gave their wholehearted approval and support.

It's a little over a year since we planned the North African campaign. It is six months since we planned the Sicilian campaign. I confess that I am of an impatient disposition, but I think that I understand and that most people understand the amount of time necessary to prepare for any major military or naval operation. We cannot just pick up the telephone and order a new campaign to start the next week.

For example, behind the invasion forces in North Africa, the invasion forces that went out of North Africa, were thousands of ships and planes guarding the long, perilous sea lanes, carrying the men, carrying the equipment and the supplies to the point of attack. And behind all these were the railroad lines and the highways here back home that carried the men and the munitions to the ports of embarkation—there were the factories and the mines and the farms here back home that turned out the materials—there were the training camps here back home where the men learned how to perform the strange and difficult and dangerous tasks which were to meet them on the beaches and in the deserts and in the mountains.

All this had to be repeated, first in North Africa and then in Sicily. Here in Sicily the factor of air attack was added—for we could use North Africa as the base for softening up the landing places and the lines of defense in Sicily and the lines of supply in Italy.

It is interesting for us to realize that every Flying Fortress that bombed harbor installations at, for example, Naples, bombed it from its base in North Africa, required 1,110 gallons of gasoline for each single flight and that this is the equal of about 375 "A" ration tickets—enough gas to drive your car five times across this continent. You will better understand your part in the war—and what gasoline rationing means—if you multiply this by the gasoline needs of thousands of planes and hundreds of thousands of jeeps and trucks and tanks that are now serving overseas.

I think that the personal convenience of the individual, or the individual family, back home here in the United States will appear somewhat less important when I tell you that the initial assault force on Sicily involved 3,000 ships which carried 160,000 men—Americans, British, Canadians, and French—together with 14,000 vehicles, 600 tanks, and 1,800 guns. And this initial force was followed every day and every night by thousands of reinforcements.

The meticulous care with which the operation in Sicily was planned has paid dividends. Our casualties in men, in ships, and matériel have been low—in fact, far below our estimate.

And all of us are proud of the superb skill and courage of the officers and men who have conducted and are conducting this operation. The toughest resistance developed on the front of the British Eighth Army, which included the Canadians. But that is no new experience for that magnificent fighting force which has made the Germans pay a heavy price for each hour of delay in the final victory. The American Seventh Army, after a stormy landing on the exposed beaches of southern Sicily, swept with record speed across the island into the capital at Palermo. For many of our troops this was their first battle experience, but they've carried themselves like veterans.

And we must give credit for the coordination of the diverse forces in the field, and for the planning of the whole campaign, to the wise and skillful leadership of General Eisenhower. Admiral Cunningham, General Alexander, and Air Marshal Tedder[2] have been towers of strength in handling the complex details of naval and ground and air activities.

You have heard some people say that the British and the Americans can never get along well together—you've heard some people say that the Army and the Navy and the Air Forces can never get along well together—that real cooperation between them is impossible. Tunisia and Sicily have given the lie, once and for all, to these narrow-minded prejudices.

The dauntless fighting of the British people[3] in this war has been expressed in the historic words and deeds of Winston Churchill—and the world knows how the American people feel about him.

Ahead of us are much bigger fights. We and our allies will go into them as we went into Sicily—together. And we shall carry on together.

Today our production of ships is almost unbelievable. This year we are producing over 19 million tons of merchant shipping and next year our production will be over 21 million tons. And in addition to our shipments across the Atlantic, we must realize that in this war we are operating in the Aleutians, in the distant parts of the Southwest Pacific, in India, and off the shores of South America.

For several months we have been losing fewer ships by sinkings, and we have been destroying more and more U-boats. We hope this will continue. But we cannot be sure. We must not lower our guard for one single instant.

An example, a tangible result of our great increase in merchant shipping—which I think will be good news to civilians at home—is that tonight we are able to terminate the rationing of coffee. And we

[2] In addition to Dwight D. Eisenhower, the U.S. commander of the European theater, President Roosevelt singles out for praise here three experienced English officers: Admiral Sir Andrew Cunningham (1883–1963), the British commander in chief of Allied naval forces in the Mediterranean; General Sir Harold Alexander (1891–1969), who supervised the evacuation of Dunkirk and then directed British forces in North Africa and in Sicily and Italy; and Air Marshal Arthur William Tedder (1890–1967), who was the British air chief in the Mediterranean and deputy commander of the invasion.

[3] The original text referred to "the dauntless fighting spirit of the British people."

also expect within a short time we shall get greatly increased allowances of sugar.

Those few Americans who grouse and complain about the inconveniences of life here in the United States should learn some lessons from the civilian populations of our allies—Britain and China and Russia—and of all the lands occupied by our common enemy.

The heaviest and most decisive fighting today is going on in Russia. I am glad that the British and we have been able to contribute somewhat to the great striking power of the Russian armies.

In 1941–42 the Russians were able to retire without breaking, to move many of their war plants from western Russia far into the interior, to stand together with complete unanimity in the defense of their homeland.

The success of the Russian armies has shown that it is dangerous to make prophecies about them—a fact which has been forcibly brought home to that mystic master of strategic intuition, Herr Hitler.

The short-lived German offensive, launched early this month, was a desperate attempt to bolster the morale of the German people. The Russians were not fooled by this. They went ahead with their own plans for attack—plans which coordinate with the whole United Nations' offensive strategy.

The world has never seen greater devotion, determination, and self-sacrifice than have been displayed by the Russian people and their armies, under the leadership of Marshal Joseph Stalin.

With a nation which, in saving itself, is thereby helping to save all the world from the Nazi menace, this country of ours should always be glad to be a good neighbor and a sincere friend in the world of the future.

In the Pacific, we are pushing the Japs around from the Aleutians to New Guinea. There too we have taken the initiative—and we are not going to let go of it.

It becomes clearer and clearer that the attrition, the whittling down process against the Japanese is working. The Japs have lost more planes and more ships than they have been able to replace.

The continuous and energetic prosecution of the war of attrition will drive the Japs back from their overextended line running from Burma and the Straits settlements and Siam through the Netherlands Indies to eastern New Guinea and the Solomons. And we have good reason to believe that their shipping and their air power cannot support such outposts.

Our naval and land and air strength in the Pacific is constantly growing. And if the Japanese are basing their future plans for the Pacific on a long period in which they will be permitted to consolidate and exploit their conquered resources, they'd better start revising their plans now. I give that to them merely as a helpful suggestion.

We are delivering planes and vital war supplies for the heroic armies of Generalissimo Chiang Kai-shek, and we must do more at all costs.

Our air supply line from India to China across enemy territory continues despite attempted Japanese interference. We have seized the initiative from the Japanese in the air over Burma and now we enjoy superiority. We are bombing Japanese communications, supply dumps, and bases in China, in Indochina, and Burma.

But we are still far from our main objectives in the war against Japan. Let us remember, however, how far we were a year ago from any of our objectives in the European theater. We are pushing forward to occupation of positions which in time will enable us to attack the Japanese Islands themselves from the north, from the south, from the east, and from the west.

You have heard it said that while we're succeeding greatly on the fighting front, we're failing miserably on the home front. I think this is another of those immaturities—a false slogan easy to state but untrue in the essential facts.

For the longer this war goes on the clearer it becomes that no one can draw a blue pencil down the middle of a page and call one side the fighting front and the other side the home front. For the two of them are inexorably tied together.

Every combat division, every naval task force, every squadron of fighting planes is dependent for its equipment and ammunition and fuel and food, as indeed it is for manpower, dependent on the American people in civilian clothes in the offices and in the factories and on the farms at home.

The same kind of careful planning that gained victory in North Africa and Sicily is required, if we are to make victory an enduring reality and do our share in building the kind of peaceful world that will justify the sacrifices made in this war.

The United Nations are substantially agreed on the general objectives for the postwar world. They are also agreed that this is not the time to engage in an international discussion of *all* the terms of peace and *all* the details of the future. Let us win the war first. We must not relax our pressure on the enemy by taking time out to define every boundary and settle every political controversy in every part of the world. The important thing, the all-important thing now is to get on with the war—and to win it.

While concentrating on military victory, we are not neglecting the planning of the things to come, the freedoms which we know will make for more decency and greater justice throughout the world.

Among many other things we are, today, laying plans for the return to civilian life of our gallant men and women in the armed services. They must not be demobilized into an environment of inflation and unemployment, to a place on a breadline, or on a corner selling apples. We must, this time, have plans ready—instead of waiting to do a hasty, inefficient, and ill-considered job at the last moment.

I have assured our men in the armed forces that the American people would not let them down when the war is won.

I hope that the Congress will help in carrying out this assurance, for obviously the executive branch of the government cannot do it alone. May the Congress do its duty in this regard. The American people will insist on fulfilling this American obligation to the men and women in the armed forces who are winning this war for us.

Of course, the returning soldier and sailor and marine are a part of the problem of demobilizing the rest of the millions of Americans who have been working and living in a war economy since 1941. That larger objective of reconverting wartime America to a peacetime basis is one for which your government is laying plans to be submitted to the Congress for action.

But the members of the armed forces have been compelled to make greater economic sacrifice and every other kind of sacrifice than the rest of us, and they are entitled to definite action to help take care of their special problems.

The least to which they are entitled, it seems to me, is something like this:

First, mustering-out pay to every member of the armed forces and merchant marine when he or she is honorably discharged;

mustering-out pay large enough in each case to cover a reasonable period of time between his discharge and the finding of a new job.

Secondly, in case no job is found after diligent search, then unemployment insurance if the individual registers with the United States Employment Service.

Third, an opportunity for members of the armed services to get further education or trade training at the cost of their government.

Fourth, allowance of credit to all members of the armed forces, under unemployment compensation and federal old-age and survivors' insurance, for their period of service. For these purposes they ought to be treated as if they had continued their employment in private industry.

Fifth, improved and liberalized provisions for hospitalization, for rehabilitation, for medical care of disabled members of the armed forces and the merchant marine.

And finally, sufficient pensions for disabled members of the armed forces.[4]

Your government is drawing up other serious, constructive plans for certain immediate forward moves. They concern food, and manpower, and other domestic problems that tie in with our armed forces.

Within a few weeks I shall speak to you again in regard to definite actions to be taken by the executive branch of the government, together with specific recommendations for new legislation by the Congress.

All our calculations for the future, however, must be based on clear understanding of the problems involved. And that can be gained only by straight thinking—not guesswork, not political manipulation.

I confess that I myself am sometimes bewildered by conflicting statements that I see in the press. One day I read an "authoritative" statement that we will win the war this year, 1943—and the next day comes another statement equally "authoritative," that the war will still be going on in 1949.

Of course, both extremes—of optimism and pessimism—are wrong.

---

[4] Roosevelt's comments here foreshadowed the so-called G.I. Bill of Rights, which Congress passed and the president signed into law in June 1944. The legislation provided, among other things, for mortgage loan guarantees, education benefits, and financial support while veterans adjusted to civilian life.

The length of the war will depend upon the uninterrupted continuance of all-out effort on the fighting fronts and here at home, and that effort is all one.

The American soldier doesn't like the necessity of waging war. And yet—if he lays off for a single instant he may lose his own life and sacrifice the lives of his comrades.

By the same token, a worker here at home may not like the driving, wartime conditions under which he has to work and live. And yet—if he gets complacent or indifferent and slacks on his job, he too may sacrifice the lives of American soldiers and contribute to the loss of an important battle.

The next time anyone says to you that this war is "in the bag," or says, "It's all over but the shouting," you should ask him these questions:

"Are you working full time on your job?

"Are you growing all the food you can?

"Are you buying your limit of war bonds?

"Are you loyally and cheerfully cooperating with your government in preventing inflation and profiteering, and in making rationing work with fairness to all?

"Because—if your answer is no—then the war is going to last a lot longer than you think."

The plans we made for the knocking out of Mussolini and his gang have largely succeeded. But we still have to knock out Hitler and his gang, and Tojo and his gang. No one of us pretends that this will be an easy matter.

We still have to defeat Hitler and Tojo on their own home grounds. But this will require a far greater concentration of our national energy and our ingenuity and our skill.

It's not too much to say that we must pour into this war the entire strength and intelligence and willpower of the United States. We are a great nation—a rich nation—but we are not so great or so rich that we can afford to waste our substance or the lives of our men by relaxing along the way.

We shall not settle for less than total victory. That is the determination of every American on the fighting front. That must be, and will be, the determination of every American here at home.

ARMISTICE IN ITALY
AND THE THIRD WAR LOAN DRIVE

THIS FIRESIDE CHAT—one of the shortest—combines an announcement of the Allied armistice in Italy with the launching of the third
war loan drive. On August 19–20, following the Italian defeat in Sicily, General Giuseppe Castallano contacted American and British
representatives in Portugal with an offer: Italy would repudiate its alliance with Germany and join the Allied side. What the new Italian
government hoped to achieve by this move was Allied protection
against Germany, which had begun pouring forces into Italy as the
Fascist regime there collapsed. Italian surrender meant, in practice,
that they would cease all military activity against Great Britain and
the United States and resist attacks from Germany—if they could.
They could not. The Italian army, except for seven divisions that
joined the Allies, effectively evaporated. The Allies did gain access to
the Italian navy, which found safe haven in Allied ports. President
Roosevelt was correct in announcing that the armistice represented
"a great victory for the United Nations." He was also correct in pointing out that "we should not delude ourselves that this armistice
means the end of the war in the Mediterranean. We still have to drive
the Germans out of Italy."

To guarantee adequate funding for the military effort and, more
important, to siphon off consumers' money that would otherwise
cause inflationary pressure, the administration promoted the sale of
Treasury bonds in low denominations. The first war loan drive, which
raised about $13 billion, had begun in December 1942. Six other
drives occurred during the course of the war, each one about a month
in duration. Each was voluntary and accompanied by a presidential
appeal, a great deal of hoopla, and Madison Avenue–type promo-
tions. Advertising rather than coercion was the approach to the sale
of war bonds: everyone from politicians to movie stars to comic book
characters pitched in to help in the campaigns. Altogether the govern-

ment raised about $135 billion through the war loan drives, roughly one-quarter of it coming from the pockets of individual purchasers.

MY FELLOW AMERICANS. Once upon a time, a few years ago, there was a city in our Middle West which was threatened by a destructive flood in the great river. The waters had risen to the top of the banks. Every man, woman, and child in that city was called upon to fill sandbags in order to defend their homes against the rising waters. For many days and nights, destruction and death stared them in the face.

As a result of the grim, determined community effort, that city still stands. Those people kept the levees above the peak of the flood. All of them joined together in the desperate job that had to be done—businessmen, workers, farmers and doctors and preachers—people of all races.

To me, that town is a living symbol of what community cooperation can accomplish.

Today, in the same kind of community effort, only very much larger, the United Nations and their peoples have kept the levees of civilization high enough to prevent the floods of aggression and barbarism and wholesale murder from engulfing us all. The flood has been raging for four years. At last we are beginning to gain on it; but the waters have not yet receded enough for us to relax our sweating work with the sandbags. In this war bond campaign we are filling bags and placing them against the flood—bags which are essential if we are to stand off the ugly torrent which is still trying to sweep us all away.

Today, it is announced that an armistice with Italy has been concluded.

This was a great victory for the United Nations—but it was also a great victory for the Italian people. After years of war and suffering and degradation, the Italian people are at last coming to the day of liberation from their real enemies, the Nazis.

But let us not delude ourselves that this armistice means the end of the war in the Mediterranean. We still have to drive the Germans out of Italy as we have driven them out of Tunisia and Sicily; we must drive them out of France and all other captive countries; and we must strike them on their own soil from all directions.

Our ultimate objectives in this war continue to be Berlin and Tokyo.

I ask you to bear these objectives constantly in mind—and do not forget that we still have a long way to go before we attain them.

The great news that you have heard today from General Eisenhower[1] does not give you license to settle back in your rocking chairs and say, "Well, that does it. We've got 'em on the run. Now we can start the celebration."

The time for celebration is not yet. And I have a suspicion that when this war does end, we shall not be in a very celebrating mood, a very celebrating frame of mind. I think that our main emotion will be one of grim determination that this shall not happen again.

During the past weeks, Mr. Churchill and I have been in constant conference with the leaders of our combined fighting forces. We have been in constant communication with our fighting allies, Russian and Chinese, who are prosecuting the war with relentless determination and with conspicuous success on far-distant fronts. And Mr. Churchill and I are here together in Washington at this crucial moment.

We have seen the satisfactory fulfillment of plans that were made in Casablanca last January and here in Washington last May.[2] And lately we have made new well-considered[3] plans for the future. But throughout these conferences we have never lost sight of the fact that this war will become bigger and tougher, rather than easier, during the long months that are to come.

This war does not and must not stop for one single instant. Your fighting men know that. Those of them who are moving forward through jungles against lurking Japs—those who are landing at this moment, in barges moving through the dawn up to strange enemy coasts—those who are diving their bombers down on the targets at roof-top level at this moment—every one of these men knows that this war is a full-time job and that it will continue to be that until total victory is won.

---

[1] News of the Italian armistice was announced by General Eisenhower.

[2] The president refers to the Casablanca conference of January 12–25, 1943, and its follow-up meetings where plans were made for the invasion of Sicily and Italy.

[3] Roosevelt substituted the words "well-considered" for the "extensive" that appeared in the prepared text.

And, by the same token, every responsible leader in all the United Nations knows that the fighting goes on twenty-four hours a day, seven days a week, and that any day lost may have to be paid for in terms of months added to the duration of the war.

Every campaign, every single operation in all the campaigns that we plan and carry through must be figured in terms of staggering material costs. We cannot afford to be niggardly with any of our resources, for we shall need all of them to do the job that we have put our shoulder to.

Your fellow Americans have given a magnificent account of themselves—on the battlefields and on the oceans and in the skies all over the world.

Now it is up to you to prove to them that you are contributing your share and more than your share. It is not sufficient simply to put into war bonds money which we would normally save. We must put into war bonds money which we would not normally save. Only then have we done everything that good conscience demands. So it is up to you, up to you the Americans in the American homes—the very homes which our sons and daughters are working and fighting and dying to preserve.

I know I speak for every man and woman throughout the Americas when I say that we Americans will not be satisfied to send our troops into the fire of the enemy with equipment inferior in any way. Nor will we be satisfied to send our troops with equipment only equal to that of the enemy. We are determined to provide our troops with overpowering superiority—superiority of quantity and quality in any and every category of arms and armaments that they may conceivably need.

And where does this, our dominating power come from? Why, it can come only from you. The money you lend and the money you give in taxes buys that death-dealing, and at the same time life-saving, power that we need for victory. This is an expensive war—expensive in money. You can help it; you can help to keep it at a minimum cost in lives.

The American people will never stop to reckon the cost of redeeming civilization. They know there never can be any economic justification for failing to save freedom.

And we can be sure that our enemies will watch this drive with the keenest interest. They know that success in this undertaking will shorten the war. They know that the more money the American people lend to their government, the more powerful and relentless will be the American forces in the field. They know that only a united and determined America could possibly produce on a voluntary basis so huge a sum of money as $15 billion.

The overwhelming success of the second war loan drive last April showed that the people of this democracy stood firm behind their troops.

This third war loan, which we are starting tonight, will also succeed—because the American people will not permit it to fail.

I cannot tell you how much to invest in war bonds during this third war loan drive. No one can tell you. It is for you to decide under the guidance of your own conscience.

I will say this, however. Because the nation's needs are greater than ever before, our sacrifices too must be greater than they have ever been before.

Nobody knows when total victory will come—but we do know that the harder we fight now, the more might and power we direct at the enemy now, the shorter the war will be and the smaller the sum total of sacrifice.

Success of the third war loan will be the symbol that America does not propose to rest on its arms—that we know the tough, bitter job ahead and will not stop until we have finished it.

Now it is your turn!

Every dollar that you invest in the third war loan is your personal message of defiance to our common enemies—to the ruthless savages of Germany and Japan—and it is your personal message of faith and good cheer to our allies and to all the men at the front. God bless them!

REPORT ON THE CAIRO AND TEHERAN CONFERENCES

EARLY ON THE MORNING of November 12, 1943, President Roosevelt boarded the USS *Iowa,* a battleship anchored five miles outside the mouth of the Potomac River, for the beginning of a lengthy trip that would take him across the Atlantic Ocean, through the straits of Gibraltar, on to Oran on the Barbary Coast, and then by air and automobile to Tunis, Carthage, and Cairo. From Cairo, where he met with Prime Minister Churchill of Great Britain and Generalissimo Chiang Kai-shek of China, he flew on to Teheran, Iran, where he and Churchill conferred with Josef Stalin, the leader of the Soviet Union. From Teheran he returned to Cairo, and he and Churchill and their military staffs held a second conference. He then flew to Malta and on to Sicily where he once again boarded the *Iowa* for the trip home. He arrived in Washington just before Christmas, tired but exhilarated. He presented his report on this trip to the American people in a Fireside Chat delivered from the library of his home in Hyde Park, New York, on Christmas Eve.

This accounting omitted many important details of the conferences. The main decisions reached at Cairo were that Japan would be stripped of territories it had taken from China—Manchuria, Taiwan, and the Pescadores Islands—and that Korea would become free and independent at the war's end. Apart from these items, military-diplomatic discussions included considerations of an offensive in Burma, further support for China, and inclusion of the latter as one of the Big Four powers in the postwar period. At Teheran, arguably one of the most important of the wartime meetings, Churchill, Roosevelt, and Stalin agreed that a cross-channel invasion, which Stalin had been impatiently demanding since 1942, would begin in May or June of 1944 and would be supported by a simultaneous Allied landing in the south of France and a Soviet offensive on the eastern front. Stalin promised—repeating a comment made to Secretary of State Hull at the Moscow conference—to enter the war against Japan soon after the defeat of Germany for a price that would be determined later (the price was determined at the Yalta conference, February 4–11, 1945). The three major allies also reached informal agreement on the boundaries of Poland: the eastern boundary to be the Curzon Line, stripping Poland of territory in the east that it had controlled between 1921 and 1939; the western boundary to be the Oder river, giving Poland territory to be taken from Germany. Other than this, the leaders discussed but did not reach formal agreement on the dismemberment of Germany. At the second Cairo conference Roosevelt and Churchill and their military aides discussed a number of military issues, including President Roosevelt's decision to name General Eisenhower as commander of operation Overlord, the June 1944 landing across the English Channel.

MY FRIENDS. I have recently returned from extensive journeyings in the region of the Mediterranean and as far as the borders of Russia. I have conferred with the leaders of Britain and Russia and China on military matters of the present—especially on plans for stepping up our successful attack on our enemies as quickly as possible and from many different points of the compass.

On this Christmas Eve there are over 10 million men in the armed forces of the United States alone. One year ago 1,700,000 were serving overseas. Today, this figure has been more than doubled to 3,800,000 on duty overseas. And by next July 1 that number overseas will rise to over 5 million men and women.

That this is truly a world war was demonstrated to me when arrangements were being made with our overseas broadcasting agencies for the time for me to speak today to our soldiers and sailors and marines and merchant seamen in every part of the world. In fixing the time for this broadcast, we took into consideration that at this moment here in the United States, and in the Caribbean, and on the northeast coast of South America, it is afternoon. In Alaska and in Hawaii and the mid-Pacific, it is still morning. In Iceland, in Great Britain, in North Africa, in Italy and the Middle East, it is now evening.

In the Southwest Pacific, in Australia, in China and Burma and

India, it is already Christmas Day. So we can correctly say that at this moment, in those Far Eastern parts where Americans are fighting, today is tomorrow.

But everywhere throughout the world—through this war that covers the world—there is a special spirit that has warmed our hearts since our earliest childhood—a spirit that brings us close to our homes, our families, our friends and neighbors—the Christmas spirit of "peace on earth, goodwill toward men." It is an unquenchable spirit.

During the past years of international gangsterism and brutal aggression in Europe and in Asia, our Christmas celebrations have been darkened with apprehension for the future. We have said, "Merry Christmas and happy new year," but we have known in our hearts that the clouds which have hung over our world have prevented us from saying it with full sincerity and conviction.

But even this year, we still have much to face in the way of further suffering, and sacrifice, and personal tragedy. Our men, who have been through the fierce battles in the Solomons and the Gilberts and Tunisia and Italy know, from their own experience and knowledge of modern war, that many bigger and costlier battles are still to be fought.

But on Christmas Eve this year I can say to you that at last we may look forward into the future with real, substantial confidence that, however great the cost, "peace on earth, goodwill toward men" can be and will be realized and ensured. This year I *can* say that. Last year I could *not* do more than express a hope. Today I express a certainty—though the cost may be high and the time may be long.

Within the past year—within the past few weeks—history has been made, and it is far better history for the whole human race than any that we've known, or even dared to hope for, in these tragic times through which we pass.

A great beginning was made in the Moscow conference last October by Mr. Molotov, Mr. Eden, and our own Mr. Hull.[1] There and then the way was paved for the later meetings.

At Cairo and Teheran we devoted ourselves not only to military matters; we devoted ourselves also to consideration of the future—

[1]Vyacheslav Molotov (1890–1986), the Soviet foreign minister; Sir Anthony Eden (1897–1977), the British foreign minister; and Cordell Hull (1871–1955), the American secretary of state.

to plans for the kind of world which alone can justify all the sacrifices of this war.

Of course, as you all know, Mr. Churchill and I have happily met many times before, and we know and understand each other very well. Indeed, Mr. Churchill has become known and beloved by many millions of Americans, and the heartfelt prayers of all of us have been with this great citizen of the world in his recent serious illness.[2]

The Cairo and Teheran conferences, however, gave me my first opportunity to meet the Generalissimo, Chiang Kai-shek, and Marshal Stalin—and to sit down at the table with these unconquerable men and talk with them face to face. We had planned to talk to each other across the table at Cairo and Teheran; but we soon found that we were all on the same side of the table. We came to the conferences with faith in each other. But we needed the personal contact. And now we have supplemented faith with definite knowledge.

It was well worth traveling thousands of miles over land and sea to bring about this personal meeting, and to gain the heartening assurance that we are absolutely agreed with one another on all the major objectives—and on the military means of obtaining them.

At Cairo, Prime Minister Churchill and I spent four days with the Generalissimo, Chiang Kai-shek. It is the first time that we'd had an opportunity to go over the complex situation in the Far East with him personally. We were able not only to settle upon definite military strategy, but also to discuss certain long-range principles which we believe can assure peace in the Far East for many generations to come.

Those principles are as simple as they are fundamental. They involve the restoration of stolen property to its rightful owners, and the recognition of the rights of millions of people in the Far East to build up their own forms of self-government without molestation. Essential to all peace and security in the Pacific and in the rest of the world is the permanent elimination of the Empire of Japan as a potential force of aggression. Never again must our soldiers and sailors and marines—and other soldiers and sailors and marines— be compelled to fight from island to island as they are fighting so gallantly and so successfully today.

[2]While in the Middle East Churchill contracted a severe case of pneumonia, from which he was then recovering.

Increasingly powerful forces are now hammering at the Japanese at many points over an enormous arc which curves down through the Pacific from the Aleutians to the jungles of Burma. Our own Army and Navy, our Air Forces, the Australians and New Zealanders, the Dutch, and the British land, air, and sea forces are all forming a band of steel which is slowly but surely closing in on Japan.

And on the mainland of Asia, under the Generalissimo's leadership, the Chinese ground and air forces, augmented by American Air Forces, are playing a vital part in starting the drive which will push the invaders into the sea.

Following out the military decisions at Cairo, General Marshall has just flown around the world and has had conferences with General MacArthur and Admiral Nimitz[3]—conferences which will spell plenty of bad news for the Japs in the not-too-far-distant future.

I met in the Generalissimo a man of great vision, great courage, and a remarkably keen understanding of the problems of today and tomorrow. We discussed all the manifold military plans for striking at Japan with decisive force from many directions, and I believe I can say that he returned to Chungking with the positive assurance of total victory over our common enemy. Today we and the Republic of China are closer together than ever before in deep friendship and in unity of purpose.

After the Cairo conference, Mr. Churchill and I went by airplane to Teheran. There we met with Marshal Stalin. We talked with complete frankness on every conceivable subject connected with the winning of the war and the establishment of a durable peace after the war.

Within three days of intense and consistently amicable discussions, we agreed on every point concerned with the launching of a gigantic attack upon Germany.

The Russian army will continue its stern offensives on Germany's eastern front, the Allied armies in Italy and Africa will bring relentless pressure on Germany from the south, and now the encirclement will be complete as great American and British forces attack from other points of the compass.

The commander selected to lead the combined attack from these other points is General Dwight D. Eisenhower. His performances in

[3] Admiral Chester W. Nimitz (1885–1966) was the commander of the United States Pacific Fleet.

Africa, in Sicily, and in Italy have been brilliant. He knows by practical and successful experience the way to coordinate air, sea, and land power. All of these will be under his control. Lieutenant General Carl Spaatz[4] will command the entire American strategic bombing force operating against Germany.

General Eisenhower gives up his command in the Mediterranean to a British officer whose name is being announced by Mr. Churchill.[5] We now pledge that new commander that our powerful ground, sea, and air forces in the vital Mediterranean area will stand by his side until every objective in that bitter theater is attained.

Both of these new commanders will have American and British subordinate commanders whose names will be announced to the world in a few days.

During the last two days in Teheran, Marshal Stalin, Mr. Churchill, and I looked ahead, ahead to the days and months and years that will follow Germany's defeat. We were united in determination that Germany must be stripped of her military might and be given no opportunity within the foreseeable future to regain that might.

The United Nations have no intention to enslave the German people. We wish them to have a normal chance to develop, in peace, as useful and respectable members of the European family. But we most certainly emphasize that word "respectable"—for we intend to rid them once and for all of Nazism and Prussian militarism and the fantastic and disastrous notion that they constitute the "master race."

We did discuss international relationships from the point of view of big, broad objectives, rather than details. But on the basis of what we did discuss, I can say even today that I do not think any insoluble differences will arise among Russia, Great Britain, and the United States.

In these conferences we were concerned with basic principles—principles which involve the security and the welfare and the standard of living of human beings in countries large and small.

To use an American and somewhat ungrammatical colloquialism, I may say that I "got along fine" with Marshal Stalin. He is a man who combines a tremendous, relentless determination with a stalwart good humor. I believe he is truly representative of the heart

---

[4] General Spaatz (1891–1974) was commander of the Eighth Air Force.
[5] The appointment went to Henry Maitland Wilson (1881–1964), who had commanded troops in Egypt and Greece.

and soul of Russia; and I believe that we are going to get along very well with him and the Russian people—very well indeed.

Britain, Russia, China, and the United States and their allies represent more than three-quarters of the total population of the earth. As long as these four nations with great military power stick together in determination to keep the peace there will be no possibility of an aggressor nation arising to start another world war.

But those four powers must be united with and cooperate with the freedom-loving peoples of Europe and Asia and Africa and the Americas. The rights of every nation, large or small, must be respected and guarded as jealously as are the rights of every individual within our own republic.

The doctrine that the strong shall dominate the weak is the doctrine of our enemies—and we reject it.

But, at the same time, we are agreed that if force is necessary to keep international peace, international force will be applied—for as long as it may be necessary.

It has been our steady policy—and it is certainly a commonsense policy—that the right of each nation to freedom must be measured by the willingness of that nation to fight for freedom. And today we salute our unseen allies in occupied countries—the underground resistance groups and the armies of liberation. They will provide potent forces against our enemies, when the day of the counterinvasion comes.

Through the development of science the world has become so much smaller that we have had to discard the geographical yardsticks of the past. For instance, through our early history the Atlantic and Pacific Oceans were believed to be walls of safety for the United States. Time and distance made it physically possible, for example, for us and for the other American republics to obtain and maintain independence against infinitely stronger powers. Until recently very few people, even military experts, thought that the day would ever come when we might have to defend our Pacific coast against Japanese threats of invasion.

At the outbreak of the First World War relatively few people thought that our ships and shipping would be menaced by German submarines on the high seas or that the German militarists would ever attempt to dominate any nation outside of central Europe.

After the armistice in 1918, we thought and hoped that the militaristic philosophy of Germany had been crushed; and being full of the milk of human kindness we spent the next twenty years disarming, while the Germans whined so pathetically that the other nations permitted them—and even helped them—to rearm.

For too many years we lived on pious hopes that aggressor and warlike nations would learn and understand and carry out the doctrine of purely voluntary peace.

The well-intentioned but ill-fated experiments of former years did not work. It is my hope that we will not try them again. No—that is putting it too weakly—it is my intention to do all that I humanly can as president and commander in chief to see to it that these tragic mistakes shall not be made again.

There have always been cheerful idiots in this country who believed that there would be no more war for us if everybody in America would only return into their homes and lock their front doors behind them. Assuming that their motives were of the highest, events have shown how unwilling they were to face the facts.

The overwhelming majority of all the people in the world want peace. Most of them are fighting for the attainment of peace—not just a truce, not just an armistice—but peace that is as strongly enforced and as durable as mortal man can make it. If we are willing to fight for peace now, is it not good logic that we should use force if necessary, in the future, to keep the peace?

I believe, and I think I can say, that the other three great nations who are fighting so magnificently to gain peace are in complete agreement that we must be prepared to keep the peace by force. If the people of Germany and Japan are made to realize thoroughly that the world is not going to let them break out again, it is possible, and I hope, probable, that they will abandon the philosophy of aggression—the belief that they can gain the whole world even at the risk of losing their own souls.

I shall have more to say about the Cairo and Teheran conferences when I make my report to the Congress in about two weeks' time. And, on that occasion, I shall also have a great deal to say about certain conditions here at home.

But today I wish to say that in all my travels, at home and abroad, it is the sight of our soldiers and sailors and their magnificent achievements which have given me the greatest inspiration and the greatest encouragement for the future.

To the members of our armed forces, to their wives, mothers, and fathers, I want to affirm the great faith and confidence that we have in General Marshall and in Admiral King, who direct all of our armed might throughout the world. Upon them falls the responsibility of planning the strategy, of determining where and when we shall fight. Both of these men have already gained high places in American history, places which will record in that history many evidences of their military genius that cannot be published today.

Some of our men overseas are now spending their third Christmas far from home. To them and to all others overseas or soon to go overseas, I can give assurance that it is the purpose of their government to win this war and to bring them home at the earliest possible time.

And we here in the United States had better be sure that when our soldiers and sailors do come home they will find an America in which they are given full opportunities for education and rehabilitation and social security and employment and business enterprise under the free American system—and that they will find a government which, by their votes as American citizens, they have had a full share in electing.

The American people have had every reason to know that this is a tough and destructive war. On my trip abroad, I talked with many military men who had faced our enemies in the field. These hardheaded realists testify to the strengths and skill and resourcefulness of the enemy generals and men whom we must beat before final victory is won. The war is now reaching the stage where we shall all have to look forward to large casualty lists—dead, wounded, and missing.

War entails just that. There is no easy road to victory. And the end is not yet in sight.

I have been back only for a week. It is fair that I should tell you my impression. I think I see a tendency in some of our people here to assume a quick ending of the war, the war and the result means false reasoning. I think I discern an effort to resume or even encourage an outbreak of partisan thinking and talking.[6] I hope I am wrong. For, surely, our first and most foremost tasks are all concerned with winning the war and winning a just peace that will last for generations.

---

[6] Roosevelt stumbled at this point in the speech. The prepared text reads, "I think I see a tendency in some of our people here to assume a quick ending of the war—that we have already gained the victory. And, perhaps as a result of this false reasoning, I think I discern an effort to resume or even encourage an outbreak of partisan thinking and talking."

The massive offensives which are in the making—both in Europe and the Far East—will require every ounce of energy and fortitude that we and our allies can summon on the fighting fronts and in all the workshops at home. As I have said before, you cannot order up a great attack on a Monday and demand that it be delivered on Saturday.

Less than a month ago I flew in a big Army transport plane over the little town of Bethlehem, in Palestine.

Tonight, on Christmas Eve, all men and women everywhere who love Christmas are thinking of that ancient town and of the star of faith that shone there more than nineteen centuries ago.

American boys are fighting today in snow-covered mountains, in malarial jungles, on blazing deserts; they are fighting on the far stretches of the sea and above the clouds, fighting the thing that they, for which they struggle.[7] I think it's best symbolized by the message that came out of Bethlehem.

On behalf of the American people—your own people—I send this Christmas message to you, to you who are in our armed forces.

In our hearts are prayers for you and for all your comrades in arms who fight to rid the world of evil.

We ask God's blessing upon you—upon your fathers, mothers, and wives and children—all your loved ones at home.

We ask that the comfort of God's grace shall be granted to those who are sick and wounded, and to those who are prisoners of war in the hands of the enemy, waiting for the day when they will again be free.

And we ask that God receive and cherish those who have given their lives, and that He keep them in honor and in the grateful memory of their countrymen forever.

God bless all of you who fight our battles on this Christmas Eve.

God bless us all. Keep us strong in our faith that we fight for a better day for humankind—here and everywhere.

[7] Here again, the president, whose voice indicated weariness, stumbled. The prepared text reads, "they are fighting on the far stretches of the sea and above the clouds, and fighting for the thing for which they struggle."

A NATIONAL SERVICE LAW AND AN ECONOMIC BILL OF RIGHTS

THE AMERICAN EXPERIENCE in the First World War had been mercifully short—only about eighteen months. In January 1944, the United States was entering its third full year of participation in World War II, and there was still no clear end in sight. President Roosevelt confidently believed that his recent round of negotiations with the Allies at Cairo and Teheran had moved the world closer to a successful conclusion of the war and to a lasting peace. But he grew concerned upon his return to the United States—a feeling of "let down" was the way he put it—that Americans would not, in the face of a war of indeterminate length, hold together in the spirit of unity that had prevailed through 1942 and 1943. "Disunity at home," he said, "bickerings, self-seeking partisanship, stoppages of work, inflation, business as usual, politics as usual—these are the influences which can undermine the morale of the brave men ready to die at the front for us here."

On January 11, 1944, the president delivered his annual Message to Congress. At 9:00 P.M. that evening he delivered the same address—with even more extensive than usual emendations during the course of delivery—to the American people as a Fireside Chat. His comments included the introductory remarks printed below.

One distinctive feature of the address was its recommendation of a national service law. A product of the fertile brain of Roosevelt's friend Grenville Clark, Harvard Law School graduate and a member of Elihu Root's law firm, national service was an idea whose fortunes ebbed and flowed along with the state of the war and the size of the domestic pool of workers. In theory it made all Americans subject to conscription into designated war-related jobs. Labor opposed the idea from the start, and for the first two years of the war, President Roosevelt remained unenthusiastic about its merits. Three developments of 1943 revived it: a shortage of workers in aircraft plants in the Pacific Northwest caused by a dramatic increase in Selective Service quotas; strikes in vital economic areas, particularly those in the coalfields and on the nation's railroads; and concern by Roosevelt about complacency as the war dragged on. He urged Congress to enact national service as a part of a stabilization package, thinking that in view of antilabor attitudes such a law would make stabilization more palatable to Congress; and he urged that Congress pass stabilization measures along with a national service law, thinking that stabilization would make national service more palatable to labor. Despite the president's support, national service did not strike a sympathetic chord (it was unpopular even with American business) and over the next year and a half it died a slow death.

Another important part of this address appeared near the end. Roosevelt attempted to define nothing less than an economic Bill of Rights and to link those rights to the political ones enshrined in the Constitution's first ten amendments. It was a clarion call for the revival of the New Deal as soon as the war was over. Historian James MacGregor Burns called this speech a declaration of war and "a dramatic reassertion of American liberalism even at the height of war." Because of the bold joining of economic to political freedoms Burns insisted that of all of Franklin Roosevelt's speeches this was "the most radical speech of his life."

LADIES AND GENTLEMEN. Today I sent my annual Message to the Congress, as required by the Constitution. It has been my custom to deliver these annual Messages in person, and they have been broadcast to the nation. I intended to follow this same custom this year.

But, like a great many other people, I have had the flu, and although I am practically recovered, my doctor simply would not let me leave the White House to go up to the Capitol.

Only a few of the newspapers of the United States can print the Message in full, and I am anxious that the American people be given an opportunity to hear what I have recommended to the Congress for this very fateful year in our history—and the reasons for these recommendations. Here is what I said:

This nation in the past two years has become an active partner in the world's greatest war against human slavery.

We have joined with like-minded people in order to defend ourselves in a world that has been gravely threatened with gangster rule.

But I do not think that any of us Americans can be content with mere survival. Sacrifices that we and our allies are making impose upon all of us a sacred obligation to see to it that out of this war we and our children will gain something better than mere survival.

We are united in determination that this war shall not be followed by another interim which leads to new disaster—that we shall not repeat the tragic errors of ostrich isolationism.[1]

When Mr. Hull went to Moscow in October, when I went to Cairo and Teheran in November, we knew that we were in agreement with our allies in our common determination to fight and win this war. There were many vital questions concerning the future peace, and they were discussed in an atmosphere of complete candor and harmony.

In the last war such discussions, such meetings, did not even begin until the shooting had stopped and the delegates began to assemble at the peace table. There had been no previous opportunities for man-to-man discussions which lead to meetings of minds and the result was a peace which was not a peace.[2]

And right here I want to address a word or two to some suspicious souls who are fearful that Mr. Hull or I have made "commitments" for the future which might pledge this nation to secret treaties or to enacting the role of a world Santa Claus.[3]

Of course we made commitments. For instance we most certainly committed ourselves to very large and very specific military plans which require the use of all Allied forces to bring about the defeat of our enemies at the earliest possible time.

But there were no secret treaties or political or financial commitments.

The one supreme objective for the future, which we discussed for each nation individually, and for all the United Nations, can be summed up in one word: security.

---

[1] At this point Roosevelt deleted the following line from the version that had gone to Congress earlier in the day: "that we shall not repeat the excesses of the wild twenties when this Nation went for a joy ride on a roller coaster which ended in a tragic crash."

[2] Here Roosevelt deleted the line "That was a mistake which we are not repeating in this war."

[3] Here the president omitted from his radio address the following words: "To such suspicious souls—using a polite terminology—I wish to say that Mr. Churchill and Marshal Stalin and Generalissimo Chiang Kai-shek are all thoroughly conversant with the provisions of our Constitution. And so is Mr. Hull. And so am I."

And that means not only physical security which provides safety from attacks by aggressors. It means also economic security, social security, moral security—in a family of nations.

In the plain down-to-earth talks that I had with the Generalissimo and Marshal Stalin and Prime Minister Churchill, it was abundantly clear that they are all most deeply interested in the resumption of peaceful progress by their own peoples—progress toward a better life.[4]

All our allies have learned by bitter experience that real development will not be possible if they are to be diverted from their purpose by repeated wars—or even threats of wars.[5]

The best interests of each nation, large and small, demand that all freedom-loving nations shall join together in a just and durable system of peace. In the present world situation, evidenced by the actions of Germany and Italy and Japan, unquestioned military control over disturbers of the peace is as necessary among nations as it is among citizens in any community. And an equally basic essential to peace, permanent peace, is a decent standard of living for all individual men and women and children in all nations. Freedom from fear is eternally linked with freedom from want.

There are, of course, people who burrow, burrow through the nation like unseeing moles, and attempt to spread the suspicion that if other nations are encouraged to raise their standards of living, our own American standard of living must of necessity be depressed.

The fact is the very contrary. It has been shown time and again that if the standard of living of any country goes up, so does its purchasing power—and that such a rise encourages a better standard of living in neighboring countries with whom it trades. That is just plain common sense—and is the kind of plain common sense that provided the basis of our discussions at Moscow and Cairo and Teheran.

Returning from my journeyings, I must confess to a sense of being "let down" when I found many evidences of faulty perspectives here in Washington. The faulty perspective consists in overemphasizing

---

[4] From the printed version that went to Congress, the president here omitted the following: "All our allies want freedom to develop their lands and resources, to build up industry, to increase education and individual opportunity, and to raise standards of living."

[5] Here Roosevelt omitted the lead into the next paragraph: "China and Russia are truly united with Britain and America in recognition of this essential fact:"

lesser problems and thereby underemphasizing the first and greatest problem.

The overwhelming majority of our people have met the demands of this war with magnificent courage and a great deal of understanding. They have accepted inconveniences; they have accepted hardships; they have accepted tragic sacrifices.[6]

However, while the majority goes on about its great work without complaint, we all know that a noisy minority maintains an uproar, an uproar of demands for special favors for special groups. There are pests who swarm through the lobbies of the Congress and the cocktail bars of Washington, representing these special groups, as opposed to the basic interest of the nation as a whole. They have come to look upon the war primarily as a chance to make profits for themselves at the expense of their neighbors—profits in money or profits in terms of political or social preferment.

Such selfish agitation can be and is highly dangerous in wartime. It creates confusion. It damages morale. It hampers our national effort, it[7] prolongs the war.[8]

In this war, we have been compelled to learn how interdependent upon each other are all groups and sections of the whole population of America.

Increased food costs, for example, will bring new demands for wage increases from all war workers, which will in turn raise all prices of all things, including those things which the farmers themselves have to buy. Increased wages or prices will each in turn produce the same results. They all have a particularly disastrous result on all fixed-income groups.

And I hope you will remember that all of us in this government including myself represent the fixed-income group just as much as

[6]Roosevelt omitted the following sentence from the end of this paragraph: "And they are ready and eager to make whatever further contributions are needed to win the war as quickly as possible—if only they are given the chance to know what is required of them."

[7]Here Roosevelt omitted the phrase "muddies the waters and therefore."

[8]The version of the speech that went to Congress contained a history lesson that Roosevelt chose to omit as he talked over the radio: "If we analyze American history impartially, we cannot escape the fact that in our past we have not always forgotten individual and selfish and partisan interests in time of war—we have not always been united in purpose and direction. We cannot overlook the serious dissensions and the lack of unity in our war of the Revolution, in our War of 1812, or in our War Between the States, when the survival of the Union itself was at stake.

"In the first World War we came closer to national unity than in any previous war. But that war lasted only a year and a half, and increasing signs of disunity began to appear during the final months of the conflict."

we represent business owners or workers or farmers. This group of fixed-income people includes teachers and clergy and policemen and firemen and widows and minors who are on fixed incomes, wives and dependents of our soldiers and sailors, and old-age pensioners. They and their families add up to more than a quarter of our 130 million people. They have few or no high-pressure representatives at the Capitol. And in a period of gross inflation they would be the worst sufferers. Let us give them an occasional thought.[9]

If ever there was a time to subordinate individual or group selfishness to the national good, that time is now. Disunity at home—bickerings, self-seeking partisanship, stoppages of work, inflation, business as usual, politics as usual, luxury as usual, and sometimes a failure to tell the whole truth,[10] these are the influences which can undermine the morale of the brave men ready to die at the front for us here.

Those who are doing most of the complaining, I do not think that they are deliberately striving to sabotage the national war effort. They are laboring under the delusion that the time is past when we must make prodigious sacrifices—that the war is already won and we can begin to slacken off. But the dangerous folly of that point of view can be measured by the distance that separates our troops from their ultimate objectives in Berlin and Tokyo—and by the sum of all the perils that lie along the way.

Overconfidence and complacency are among our deadliest of all enemies.[11]

That attitude on the part of anyone—government or management or labor—can lengthen this war. It can kill American boys.

Let us remember the lessons of 1918. In the summer of that year the tide turned in favor of the Allies. But this government did not relax, nor did the American people.[12] In fact, our national effort was stepped up. In August 1918, the draft age limits were broadened

[9] This sentence, absent from the congressional version, Roosevelt added for the radio audience.

[10] Roosevelt also added the words "and sometimes a failure to tell the whole truth" to the printed version.

[11] At this point Roosevelt chose to omit the following lines from the radio address: "Last spring—after notable victories at Stalingrad and in Tunisia and against the U-boats on the high seas—overconfidence became so pronounced that war production fell off. In two months, June and July, 1943, more than a thousand airplanes that could have been made and should have been made were not made. Those who failed to make them were not on strike. They were merely saying, The war's in the bag—so let's relax."

[12] For the radio address, Roosevelt added the phrase "nor did the American people."

from twenty-one to thirty-one, all the way to eighteen to forty-five. The president called for "force to the utmost," and his call was heeded. And in November, only three months later, Germany surrendered.

That is the way to fight and win a war—all out—and not with half an eye on the battlefronts abroad and the other eye and a half on personal, selfish, or political interests here at home.

Therefore, in order to concentrate all of our energies, all of our resources on winning this war, and to maintain a fair and stable economy at home, I recommend that the Congress adopt:

First, a realistic and simplified [13] tax law—which will tax all unreasonable profits, both individual and corporate, and reduce the ultimate cost of the war to our sons and our daughters. The tax bill now under consideration by the Congress does not begin to meet this test. [14]

Secondly, a continuation of the law for the renegotiation of war contracts—which will prevent exorbitant profits and assure fair prices to the government. For two long years I have pleaded with the Congress to take undue profits out of war.

Third, a cost of food law—which will enable the government to place a reasonable floor under the prices the farmer may expect for his production; and to place a ceiling on the prices a consumer will have to pay for the necessary food he buys. This should apply, as I have intimated, to necessities only and this will require public finds to carry it out. It will cost in appropriations about 1 percent of the present annual cost of the war.

Fourth, an early reenactment of the stabilization statute of October 1942. This expires this year, June 30, 1944, and if it is not extended well in advance, the country might just as well expect price chaos by summertime.

We cannot have stabilization by wishful thinking. We must take positive action to maintain the integrity of the American dollar.

And fifth, a national service law—which, for the duration of the war, will prevent strikes, and, with certain appropriate exceptions,

[13] For the radio audience, the president added the words "and simplified."

[14] The tax law bill passed by Congress was disappointing to Roosevelt—both because it raised too little money and because it contained, in his view, too many favors for special interests. In a major revolt against Roosevelt's authority, the Congress overrode the veto overwhelmingly.

will make available for war production or for any other essential services every able-bodied adult in this whole nation.

These five measures together form a just and equitable whole. I would not recommend a national service law unless the other laws were passed to keep down the cost of living, to share equitably the burdens of taxation, to hold the stabilization line, and to prevent undue profits.

The federal government already has the basic power to draft capital and property of all kinds for war purposes on the basis of just compensation.

And as you know, I have for three years hesitated to recommend a national service act. Today, however, with all the experience we have behind us and with us,[15] I am convinced of its necessity. Although I believe that we and our allies can win the war without such a measure, I am certain that nothing less than total mobilization of all our resources of manpower and capital will guarantee an earlier victory, and reduce the toll of suffering and sorrow and blood. As some of my advisers wrote me the other day:[16]

> When the very life of a nation is in peril the responsibility for service is common to all men and women. In such a time there can be no discrimination between the men and women who are assigned by the government to its defense at the battlefront and the men and women assigned to producing the vital materials that are essential to successful military operations. A prompt enactment of a National Service Law would be merely an expression of the universality of this American responsibility.

I believe the country will agree that these statements are the solemn truth.

National service is the most democratic way to wage a war. Like Selective Service for the armed forces, it rests on the obligation of each citizen to serve his nation, to his utmost, where he is best qualified.

---

[15] Roosevelt added the phrase "with all the experience we have behind us and with us" to the radio talk.

[16] In the written speech to Congress, Roosevelt was more specific: "I have received a joint recommendation for this law from the heads of the War Department, the Navy Department, and the Maritime Commission. These are the men who bear responsibility for the procurement of the necessary arms and equipment, and for the successful prosecution of the war in the field. They say."

It does not mean reduction in wages. It does not mean loss of retirement and seniority rights and benefits. It does not mean that any substantial numbers of war workers will be disturbed in their present jobs. Let this fact be wholly clear.[17]

But there are millions of American men and women who are not in this war at all. It is not because they do not want to be in it. But they want to know where they can best do their share. National service provides that direction.[18]

I know that all civilian war workers will be glad to be able to say many years hence to their grandchildren: "Yes, I, too, was in service in the great war. I was on duty in an airplane factory, and I helped to make hundreds of fighting planes. The government told me that in doing that I was performing my most useful work in the service of my country."

It is argued that we have passed the stage in the war where national service is necessary. But our soldiers and sailors know that this is not true. We are going forward on a long, rough road—and, in all journeys, the last miles are the hardest. And it is for that final effort—for the total defeat of our enemies—that we must mobilize our total resources. The national war program calls for the employment of more people in 1944 than in 1943.

And it is my conviction that the American people will welcome this win-the-war measure which is based on the eternally just principle of "fair for one, fair for all."

It will give our people at home the assurance that they are standing four-square behind our soldiers and sailors. And it will give our enemies demoralizing assurance that we mean business—that we, 130 million Americans, are on the march to Rome and Berlin and Tokyo.

I hope that the Congress will recognize that, although this is a political year, national service is an issue which transcends politics. Great power must be used for great purposes.

---

[17] In the written address to Congress, the president had included this paragraph: "Experience in other democratic Nations at war—Britain, Canada, Australia, and New Zealand—has shown that the very existence of national service makes unnecessary the widespread use of compulsory power. National service has proven to be a unifying moral force—based on an equal and comprehensive legal obligation of all people in a Nation at war."

[18] Here Roosevelt had also told Congress "It will be a means by which every man and woman can find that inner satisfaction which comes from making the fullest possible contribution to victory."

And as to the machinery for this measure, the Congress itself should determine its nature—as long as it is wholly nonpartisan in its make-up.[19]

Several alleged reasons have prevented the enactment of legislation which would preserve for our soldiers and sailors and marines the fundamental prerogative of citizenship, in other words, the right to vote. No amount of legalistic argument can becloud this issue in the eyes of these 10 million American citizens. Surely the signers of the Constitution did not intend a document which, even in wartime, would be construed to take away the franchise of any of those who are fighting to preserve the Constitution itself.

Our soldiers and sailors and marines know that the overwhelming majority of them will be deprived of the opportunity to vote, if the voting machinery is left exclusively to the states under existing state laws—and that there is no likelihood of these laws being changed in time to enable them to vote at the next election. The Army and Navy have reported that it will be impossible effectively to administer forty-eight different soldier-voting laws. It is the duty of the Congress to remove this unjustifiable discrimination against the men and women in our armed forces—and to do it just as quickly as possible.[20]

It is our duty now to begin to lay the plans and determine the strategy for more than the winning of the war, it is time to begin the plans and determine the strategy for winning a lasting peace and the establishment of an American standard of living higher than ever known before.[21]

This republic had its beginning, and grew to its present strength, under the protection of certain inalienable political rights—among

---

[19] At this point in the written address, Roosevelt had included this paragraph: "Our armed forces are valiantly fulfilling their responsibilities to our country and our people. Now the Congress faces the responsibility for taking those measures which are essential to national security in this the most decisive phase of the Nation's greatest war." Despite this strong endorsement, the national service bill died in committee.

[20] Congress was deeply suspicious that Roosevelt was proposing this measure merely to line up votes for himself in the approaching election of 1944. By the time the bill permitting a federal ballot was sent to the White House, it was so watered down that Roosevelt decided to let it become law without his signature. Only about 85,000 servicemen voted under its provisions, fewer than voted by the traditional, state-ballot method.

[21] At this point in the radio version Roosevelt omitted the following lines: "We cannot be content, no matter how high that general standard of living may be, if some fraction of our people—whether it be one-third or one-fifth or one-tenth—is ill-fed, ill-clothed, ill-housed, and insecure."

them the right of free speech, free press, free worship, trial by jury, freedom from unreasonable searches and seizures. They were our rights to life and liberty.[22]

We have come to a clearer realization of the fact, however, that true individual freedom cannot exist without economic security and independence. "Necessitous men are not free men." People who are hungry, people who are out of a job are the stuff of which dictatorships are made.

In our day these economic truths have become accepted as self-evident. We have accepted, so to speak, a second Bill of Rights under which a new basis of security and prosperity can be established for all—regardless of station or race or creed.

Among these are:

the right to a useful and remunerative job in the industries or shops or farms or mines of the nation;

the right to earn enough to provide adequate food and clothing and recreation;

the right of farmers to raise and sell their products at a return which will give them and their families a decent living;

the right of every businessman, large and small, to trade in an atmosphere of freedom from unfair competition and domination by monopolies at home or abroad;

the right of every family to a decent home;

the right to adequate medical care and the opportunity to achieve and enjoy good health;

the right to adequate protection from the economic fears of old age and sickness and accident and unemployment; and, finally,

the right to a good education.

All of these rights spell security. And after this war is won, we must be prepared to move forward in the implementation of these rights, to new goals of human happiness and well-being.

America's own rightful place in the world depends in large part upon how fully these and similar rights have been carried into practice for all our citizens. For unless there is security here at home there cannot be lasting peace in the world.

One of the great American industrialists of our day—a man who has rendered yeoman service to his country in this crisis—recently

[22] Roosevelt also omitted this paragraph from the radio address: "As our Nation has grown in size and stature, however—as our industrial economy expanded—these political rights proved inadequate to assure us equality in the pursuit of happiness."

emphasized the grave dangers of "rightist reaction" in this nation. All clear-thinking businessmen share that concern. Indeed, if such reaction should develop—if history were to repeat itself and we were to return to the so-called normalcy of the 1920s—then it is certain that even though we shall have conquered our enemies on the battlefields abroad, we shall have yielded to the spirit of Fascism here at home.

I ask the Congress to explore the means for implementing this economic bill of rights—for it is definitely the responsibility of the Congress so to do, and the country knows it.[23] Many of these problems are already before committees of the Congress in the form of proposed legislation. I shall from time to time communicate with the Congress with respect to these and further proposals. In the event that no adequate program of progress is evolved, I am certain that the nation will be conscious of the fact.

Our fighting men abroad—and their families at home—expect such a program and have the right to insist on it. It is to their demands that this government should pay heed rather than to the whining demands of selfish pressure groups who seek to feather their nests while young Americans are dying.[24]

I have often said that there are no two fronts for America in this war. There is only one front. There is one line of unity which extends from the hearts of the people at home to the men of our attacking forces in our farthest outposts. When we speak of our total effort, we speak of the factory and the field and the mine as well as of the battlefield—we speak of the soldier and the civilian, the citizen and his government.

Each and every one of us has a solemn obligation under God to serve this nation in its most critical hour—to keep this nation great—to make this nation greater in a better world.

[23] The president added the words "and the country knows it" to the the the radio version of the speech.

[24] Roosevelt deleted, at this point, the following paragraph: "The foreign policy that we have been following—the policy that guided us at Moscow, Cairo, and Teheran—is based on the commonsense principle which was best expressed by Benjamin Franklin on July 4, 1776: We must all hang together, or assuredly we shall all hang separately."

REPORT ON THE CAPTURE OF ROME

NEVER BEFORE had President Roosevelt presented a Fireside Chat while being so thoroughly preoccupied. He had spent the weekend near Charlottesville, Virginia, on the farm of General Edwin ("Pa") Watson, one of his aides, nervously awaiting the launching of operation Overlord. Weather delayed the invasion: it did not begin on Sunday, or on Monday, Washington time. But even as the president spoke to the American people about the fall of Rome on Monday evening, June 5, ships and troops were moving across the English Channel toward the coast of Normandy.

The capture of Rome may be appropriately viewed against the background of the Normandy invasion, though no one could have known from the president's message. As the Allies had prepared for the cross-channel attack they had also begun planning for an offensive, termed Anvil, in the south of France. The British were highly skeptical of Anvil, particularly if that offensive drained equipment away from the Italian campaign. The issue precipitated heated debate between British and American military chiefs. Ultimately, American officials gave in to British insistence, and on April 19, the combined chiefs of staff authorized General Henry M. Wilson to direct an all-out offensive in Italy, even if it meant the postponement of Anvil.

It is interesting to note that the showdown over Italy coincided with a medical evaluation of President Roosevelt and with his subsequent "vacation" in South Carolina. On March 27, a physical examination at the Bethesda, Maryland Medical Center revealed that Roosevelt was gravely ill with a dangerously enlarged heart and extremely high blood pressure. Although never informed of the extent of his illness, he was persuaded to take a rest—beginning on April 8—away from the strenuous activities of the White House. Thus through April of 1944 the president was not in a position to assist in the battle with Churchill and his subordinates over military strategy.

On May 11, General Harold R. Alexander, in command of some

twenty-eight Allied divisions, began the large offensive in Italy. On June 4, Allied forces captured Rome. Roosevelt did not minimize the significance of this victory in his Fireside Chat; but neither did he portray it as central to the successful conclusion of the war: "From a strictly military standpoint, we had long ago accomplished certain of the main objectives of the Italian campaign. . . . It would be unwise to inflate in our own minds the military importance of the capture of Rome." While he was talking to the American people, a far more important and decisive operation was underway.

MY FRIENDS. Yesterday on June 4, 1944, Rome fell to American and Allied troops. The first of the Axis capitals is now in our hands. One up and two to go!

It is perhaps significant that the first of these capitals to fall should have the longest history of all of them. The story of Rome goes back to the time of the foundations of our civilization. We can still see there monuments of the time when Rome and the Romans controlled the whole of the then-known world. That, too, is significant, for the United Nations are determined that in the future no one city and no one race will be able to control the whole of the world.

In addition to the monuments of the older times, we also see in Rome the great symbol of Christianity, which has reached into almost every part of the world. There are other shrines and other churches in many places, but the churches and the shrines of Rome are visible symbols of the faith and determination of the early saints and martyrs that Christianity should live and become universal. And tonight it will be a source of deep satisfaction that the freedom of the Pope and the Vatican City is assured by the armies of the United Nations.

It is also significant that Rome has been liberated by the armed forces of many nations. The American and British armies—who bore the chief burdens of battle—found at their side our own North American neighbors, the gallant Canadians. The fighting New Zealanders from the far South Pacific, the courageous French and the French Moroccans, the South Africans, the Poles, and the East Indians—all of them fought with us on the bloody approaches to the city of Rome.

The Italians, too, forswearing a partnership in the Axis which they never desired, have sent their troops to join us in our battles against the German trespassers on their soil.

The prospect of the liberation of Rome meant enough to Hitler and his generals to induce them to fight desperately at great cost of men and materials and with great sacrifice to their crumbling eastern line and to their western front. No thanks are due to them if Rome was spared the devastation which the Germans wreaked on Naples and other Italian cities. The Allied generals maneuvered so skillfully that the Nazis could only have stayed long enough to damage Rome at the risk of losing their armies.

But Rome is of course more than a military objective.

Ever since before the days of the Caesars, Rome has stood as a symbol of authority. Rome was the republic. Rome was the empire. Rome was and is in a sense the Catholic Church, and Rome was the capital of a united Italy. Later, unfortunately, a quarter of a century ago, Rome became the seat of Fascism—and still later one of the three capitals of the Axis.

For this quarter-century the Italian people were enslaved. They were degraded by the rule of Mussolini from Rome. They will mark its liberation with deep emotion. In the north of Italy, the people are still dominated, threatened by the Nazi overlords and their Fascist puppets.

Somehow in the back of my head, I still remember a name, Mussolini.[1]

Our victory comes at an excellent time, while our Allied forces are poised for another strike at Western Europe—and while the armies of other Nazi soldiers nervously await our assault. And in the meantime our gallant Russian allies continue to make their power felt more and more.

From a strictly military standpoint, we had long ago accomplished certain of the main objectives of our Italian campaign—the control of the islands, the major islands—the control of the sea lanes of the Mediterranean to shorten our combat and supply lines, and the capture of the airports, such as the great airports of Foggia, south of Rome, from which we have struck telling blows on the con-

---

[1] This short paragraph was added spontaneously by the president as he spoke.

tinent—the whole of the continent all the way up to the Russian front.

It would be unwise to inflate in our own minds the military importance of the capture of Rome. We shall have to push through a long period of greater effort and fiercer fighting before we get into Germany itself. The Germans have retreated thousands of miles, all the way from the gates of Cairo, through Libya and Tunisia and Sicily and southern Italy. They have suffered heavy losses, but not great enough yet to cause collapse.

Germany has not yet been driven to surrender. Germany has not yet been driven to the point where she will be unable to recommence world conquest a generation hence.

Therefore, the victory still lies some distance ahead. That distance will be covered in due time—have no fear of that. But it will be tough and it will be costly, as I have told you many, many times.

In Italy the people had lived so long under the corrupt rule of Mussolini that, in spite of the tinsel at the top—you have seen the pictures of him[2]—their economic condition had grown steadily worse. Our troops have found starvation, malnutrition, disease, and deteriorating education, a lowered public health—all by-products of the Fascist misrule.

The task of the Allies in occupation has been stupendous. We have had to start at the very bottom, assisting local governments to reform on democratic lines. We have had to give them bread to replace that which was stolen out of their mouths by the Germans. We have had to make it possible for the Italians to raise and use their own local crops. We've had to help them cleanse their schools of Fascist trappings.

I think the American people as a whole approve the salvage of these human beings, who are only now learning to walk in a new atmosphere of freedom.

Some of us may let our thoughts run to the financial cost of it. Essentially it is what we can call a form of relief. And at the same time, we hope that this relief will be an investment for the future—an investment that will pay dividends by eliminating Fascism, by ending any Italian desires to start another war of aggression in the future. And that means that they are dividends which justify

---

[2] The words "you have seen the pictures of him" were also added spontaneously by President Roosevelt.

such an investment, because they are additional supports for world peace.

The Italian people are capable of self-government. We do not lose sight of their virtues as a peace-loving nation.

We remember the many centuries in which the Italians were leaders in the arts and sciences, enriching the lives of all mankind.

We remember the great sons of the Italian people—Galileo, Marconi, Michelangelo, Dante—and incidentally that fearless discoverer who typifies the courage of Italy, Christopher Columbus.

Italy cannot grow in stature by seeking to build up a great militaristic empire. Italians have been overcrowded within their own territories, but they do not need to try to conquer the lands of other peoples in order to find the breadth[3] of life. Other peoples may not want to be conquered.

In the past, Italians have come by the millions into the United States. They have been welcomed, they have prospered, they have become good citizens, community and government leaders. They are not Italian-Americans. They are Americans—Americans of Italian descent.

Italians have gone in great numbers to the other Americas—Brazil and the Argentine, for example—hundreds and hundreds of thousands of them. They have gone to many other nations in every continent of the world, giving of their industry and their talents, and achieving success and the comfort of good living, and good citizenship.

Italy should go on as a great mother nation, contributing to the culture and the progress and the good will of all mankind—developing her special talents in the arts and crafts and sciences, and preserving her historic and cultural heritage for the benefit of all peoples.

We want and expect the help of the future Italy toward lasting peace. All the other nations opposed to Fascism and Nazism ought to help to give Italy a chance.

The Germans, after years of domination in Rome, left the people in the Eternal City on the verge of starvation. We and the British will do and are doing everything we can to bring them relief. Anticipating the fall of Rome, we made preparations to ship food supplies to the city, but, of course, it should be borne in mind that the needs

---

[3] In the printed version of the speech, this word is given as "breath."

are so great, the transportation requirements of our armies are so heavy, that improvement must be gradual. But we have already begun to save the lives of the men, women, and children of Rome.

This, I think, is an example of the efficiency of your machinery of war. The magnificent ability and energy of the American people in growing crops, in building the merchant ships, in making and collecting the cargoes, in getting the supplies over thousands of miles of water, and thinking ahead to meet emergencies—all this spells, I think, an amazing efficiency on the part of our armed forces, all the various agencies working with them, and American industry and labor as a whole.

No great effort like this can be a hundred percent perfect, but the batting average is very, very high.

And so I extend the congratulation and the thanks tonight of the American people to General Alexander, who has been in command of the whole Italian operation; to our General Clark; to General Leese of the Fifth and the Eighth Armies; to General Wilson, the supreme Allied commander of the Mediterranean theater; to General Devers, his American deputy; to General Eaker; to Admirals Cunningham and Hewitt; and to all their brave officers and men.[4]

May God bless them and watch over them and over all of our gallant, fighting men.

[4] Roosevelt refers to General Mark W. Clark (1896–1984), commander of the Fifth Army; General Sir Oliver Leese (1894–1978), commander of the Eighth Army; General Sir Henry Maitland Wilson; General Jacob L. Devers (1887–1979); General Ira C. Eaker (1896–1987), Allied air commander in chief; Admiral Sir Andrew Cunningham (1883–1963), Allied naval commander in chief; and Vice Admiral H. Kent Hewitt (1887–1972), commander of U.S. naval forces.

LAUNCHING THE FIFTH
WAR LOAN DRIVE

THE STORY of D day and the days immediately following has been told many times. Bad weather, rough seas, confusion, miscommunication, fierce German resistance, heavy Allied casualties—all marked the landings. But so, too, did overwhelming Allied numbers and careful preparation for the offensive, which soon resulted in the seizure of key points along the coast. American forces pushed southward and westward from Utah and Omaha beaches to capture Cherbourg and the Cotentin Peninsula. British forces attacked Caen. Canadian troops shut off access along the route from Caen westward. By July, the Allies had put ashore a million fighting men.

Meanwhile in the Pacific, the invasion of Saipan was moving ahead. On June 15, over five hundred warships and landing craft moved into position to disgorge artillery and men—men in numbers exceeding 125,000. The magnitude of all of this is difficult to envision except in terms of total, global war.

In launching the fifth war loan drive, the ostensible purpose of this Fireside Chat of June 12, President Roosevelt called attention to the extensive activity of Allied operations and asked for additional sacrifice: "While I know that the chief interest tonight is centered on the English Channel and on the beaches and farms and the cities of Normandy, we should not lose sight of the fact that our armed forces are engaged on other battlefronts all over the world." The president then went on to say that there was "a direct connection between the bonds you have bought and the stream of men and equipment now rushing over the English Channel for the liberation of Europe." While these war loan drives were voluntary, the exhortation to buy bonds was often less than subtle, sometimes bordering on coercion. Roosevelt closed his message with one of those appeals: "There are still many people in the United States who have not bought war bonds," he said, "or who have not bought as many as they can afford. Everyone knows for himself whether he falls into that category or not. In some cases his neighbors know too. To the consciences of those people, this appeal by the president of the United States is very much in order."

LADIES AND GENTLEMEN. All our fighting men overseas today have their appointed stations on the far-flung battlefronts of the world. And we at home have ours too. We need, we are proud of, our fighting men—most decidedly. But, during the anxious times ahead, let us not forget that they need us too.

It goes almost without saying that we must continue to forge the weapons of victory—the hundreds of thousands of items, large and small, essential to the waging of the war. This has been the major task from the very start, and it is still a major task. This is the very worst time for any war worker to think of leaving his machine or to look for a peacetime job.

And it goes almost without saying, too, that we must continue to provide our government with the funds necessary for waging war not only by the payment of taxes—which, after all, is an obligation of American citizenship—but also by the purchase of war bonds— an act of free choice which every citizen has to make for himself under the guidance of his own conscience.

Whatever else any of us may be doing, the purchase of war bonds and stamps is something all of us can do and should do to help win the war.

I am happy to report tonight that it is something which nearly everyone seems to be doing. Although there are now approximately 67 million persons who have or earn some form of income, including the armed forces,[1] 81 million persons or their children have already bought war bonds. They have bought more than 600 millon individual bonds. Their purchases have totaled more than $32 billion. These are the purchases of individual men and women and children. Anyone who would have said that this was possible a few years ago would have been put down as a starry-eyed visionary. But of such visions is the stuff of America.[2]

[1] The words "including the armed forces" were not in the prepared text of the speech.
[2] In the prepared version, this sentence read, "But of such visions is the stuff of America fashioned."

Of course, there are always pessimists with us everywhere, a few here and a few there. I am reminded of the fact that after the fall of France in 1940, I asked the Congress for the money for the production by the United States of 50,000 airplanes per year. Well, I was called crazy—it was said that the figure was fantastic, that it could not be done. And yet today we are building airplanes at the rate of 100,000 a year.

There is a direct connection between the bonds you have bought and the stream of men and equipment now rushing over the English Channel for the liberation of Europe. There is a direct connection between your bonds and every part of this global war today.

Tonight, therefore, on the opening of this fifth war loan drive, it is appropriate for us to take a broad look at this panorama of world war, for the success or the failure of the drive is going to have so much to do with the speed with which we can accomplish victory and then peace.

While I know that the chief interest tonight is centered on the English Channel and on the beaches and the farms and the cities of Normandy, we should not lose sight of the fact that our armed forces are engaged on other battlefronts all over the world, and that no one front can be considered alone without its proper relation to all.

It is worth while, therefore, to make overall comparisons with the past. Let us compare today with just two years ago—June 1942. At that time Germany was in control of practically all of Europe, and was steadily driving the Russians back toward the Ural Mountains. Germany was practically in control of North Africa and the Mediterranean, and was beating at the gates of the Suez Canal and the route to India. Italy was still an important military and supply factor—as subsequent, long campaigns have proved.

Japan was in control of the western Aleutian Islands, and in the South Pacific was knocking at the gates of Australia and New Zealand—and also was threatening India. Japan had seized control of most of the Central Pacific.

American armed forces on land and sea and in the air were still very definitely on the defensive, and in the building-up stage. Our allies were bearing the heat and the brunt of the attack.

In 1942 Washington heaved a sigh of relief that the first war bond issue had been cheerfully oversubscribed by the American people. Way back in those days, two years ago, America was still hearing from many "amateur strategists" and political critics, some of whom were doing more good for Hitler than for the United States. Two years ago.

But today we are on the offensive all over the world—bringing the attack to our enemies.

In the Pacific, by relentless submarine and naval attacks, amphibious thrusts, and ever-mounting air attacks, we have deprived the Japs of the power to check the momentum of our ever-growing and ever-advancing military forces. We've reduced the Japs' shipping by more than 3 million tons. We have overcome their original advantage in the air. We have cut off from a return to the homeland tens of thousands of beleaguered Japanese troops who now face starvation or ultimate surrender. And we have cut down their naval strength, so that for many months they have avoided all risk of encounter with our naval forces.

True, we still have a long way to go to Tokyo. But, carrying out our original strategy of eliminating our European enemy first and then turning all our strength to the Pacific, we can force the Japanese to unconditional surrender or to national suicide much more rapidly than has been thought possible.

Turning now to our enemy who is first on the list for destruction, Germany has her back against the wall—in fact three walls at once!

In the south—we have broken the German hold on central Italy. On June 4, the city of Rome fell to the Allied armies. And allowing the enemy no respite, the Allies are now pressing hard on the heels of the Germans as they retreat northwards in ever-growing confusion.

On the east—our gallant Soviet allies have driven the enemy back from the lands which were invaded three years ago and the great Soviet armies are now initiating crushing blows.

Overhead—vast Allied air fleets of bombers and fighters have been waging a bitter air war over Germany and Western Europe. They have had two major objectives: to destroy German war industries which maintain the German armies and air forces; and to shoot the German Luftwaffe out of the air. As a result, German production has been whittled down continuously, and the German fighter forces now have only a fraction of their former power.

This great air campaign, strategic and tactical, is going to continue—with increasing power.

And on the west—the hammer blow which struck the coast of France last Tuesday morning, less than a week ago, was the culmination of many months of careful planning and strenuous preparation.

Millions of tons of weapons and supplies, hundreds of thousands of men assembled in England, are now being poured into the great battle in Europe.

I think that from the standpoint of our enemy we have achieved the impossible. We have broken through their supposedly impregnable wall in northern France. But the assault has been costly in men and costly in materials. Some of our landings were desperate adventures; but from advices received so far, the losses were lower than our commanders had estimated would occur. We have established a firm foothold. We are now prepared to meet the inevitable counterattacks of the Germans—with power and with confidence. And we all pray that we will have far more, soon, than a firm foothold.

Americans have all worked together to make this day possible.

The liberation forces now streaming across the channel, and up the beaches and through the fields and the forests of France, are using thousands and thousands of planes and ships and tanks and heavy guns. They are carrying with them many thousands of items needed for their dangerous, stupendous undertaking. There is a shortage of nothing—nothing! And this must continue.

What has been done in the United States since those days of 1940—when France fell—in raising and equipping and transporting our fighting forces, and in producing weapons and supplies for war, has been nothing short of a miracle. It was largely due to American teamwork—teamwork among capital and labor and agriculture, between the armed forces and the civilian economy—indeed among all of them.

And every one—every man or woman or child—who bought a war bond helped—and helped mightily!

There are still many people in the United States who have not bought war bonds, or who have not bought as many as they can afford. Everyone knows for himself whether he falls into that category or not. In some cases his neighbors know too. To the consciences of those people, this appeal by the president of the United States is very much in order.

For all of the things which we use in this war, everything we send to our fighting allies, costs money—a lot of money. One sure way every man, woman, and child can keep faith with those who have given, and are giving, their lives, is to provide the money which is needed to win the final victory.

I urge all Americans to buy war bonds without stint. Swell the mighty chorus to bring us nearer to victory!

WORK OR FIGHT

IN JANUARY 1945, President Roosevelt was a troubled man: troubled by the recent German offensive in Belgium which, though being successfully countered, had pushed a gigantic bulge in Allied lines; troubled also that his countrymen would not remain committed to internationalism at the end of the war. Although so far no one had the courage to tell him the extent of his illness, he must have recognized, too, the serious decline in his physical condition.

To meet the issue of continued devotion to the war, the president decided, on the advice of Secretary of War Stimson and Secretary of the Navy James V. Forrestal to push Congress once again to enact national service legislation—the so-called work-or-fight bill. He also proposed that Congress authorize the mobilization for war-related work of over 4 million men classified as unfit to serve in the military. The effects of these measures, the president argued, would be salutary: they would create a larger labor supply for the war and would boost the morale of those already in military service. To counter the fickleness of the American people toward foreign commitments, he believed it necessary to continue extolling the virtues of the Atlantic Charter and the projected United Nations. He articulated all of these points in his annual Message to Congress, and, in an abridged version, in the Fireside Chat of January 6, the last one he would ever deliver.

As he addressed the above issues, he was thinking ahead to his summit conference with Churchill and Stalin at Yalta, where a number of thorny military and diplomatic questions awaited decision: what to do about the boundaries of Poland and the composition of the Polish government, how to deal with Germany, what to do about China, how to satisfy Soviet aspirations in northeast Asia, and how to guarantee Soviet participation in the United Nations. The successful conclusion of the war and construction of the peace depended on a satisfactory resolution of these and other questions. To the overwhelming sorrow of the people of the nation, the people to whom he had talked so frankly and so often over the past twelve years, President Franklin Roosevelt would no longer be their leader when the time came to search for and implement the solutions.

LADIES AND GENTLEMEN. Today, in pursuance of my constitutional duty, I sent to the Congress a Message on the state of the union—and this evening I am taking the opportunity to repeat to you some parts of that Message.

This war must be waged—it is being waged—with the greatest and most persistent intensity. Everything we are, everything we have is at stake. Everything we are, and have, will be given.

We have no question of the ultimate victory. We have no question of the cost. Our losses will be heavy.

But—we and our allies will go on fighting together to ultimate total victory.

We have seen a year marked, on the whole, by substantial progress toward victory, even though the year ended with a setback for our arms, when the Germans launched a ferocious counterattack into Luxembourg and Belgium with the obvious objectives of cutting our line in the center.[1]

Our men have fought with indescribable and unforgettable gallantry under most difficult conditions.

The high tide of this German attack was reached two days after Christmas. Since then we have reassumed the offensive, we have rescued the isolated garrison at Bastogne, and forced a German withdrawal along most of the line[2] of the salient.

The speed with which we recovered from this savage attack was possible primarily because we have one supreme commander in complete control of all the Allied armies in France. General Eisenhower has faced this period of trial with admirable calm and resolution and is steadily increasing success.[3] He has my complete confidence.

---

[1] The so-called Battle of the Bulge.
[2] The printed version of this speech read "along the whole line of the salient."
[3] The printed version read "with steadily increasing success."

Further desperate attempts may well be made, and are being made, to break our lines, to slow our progress. We must never make the mistake of assuming the Germans are beaten until the last Nazi has surrendered.

And I would express a most serious warning against the poisonous effects of enemy propaganda.

The wedge that the Germans attempted to drive in Western Europe was less dangerous in terms of winning the war than the wedges which they are continually attempting to drive between ourselves and our allies.

Every little rumor which is intended to weaken our faith in our Allies is like an actual enemy agent in our midst—seeking to sabotage our war effort. There are, here and there, evil and baseless rumors against the Russians, rumors against the British, rumors against our own American commanders in the field. And when you examine these rumors closely, you will observe that every one of them bears the same trademark—"Made in Germany."

We must resist this propaganda—we must destroy it—with the same strength and the same determination that our fighting men are displaying as they resist and destroy the panzer divisions.

In all of the far-flung operations of our own armed forces—on land and sea and in the air—the final job, the toughest job, has been performed by the average, easygoing, hard-fighting, young American who carries the weight of battle on his own shoulders.

It is to him that we and all future generations of Americans must pay grateful tribute.

But—it is of small satisfaction to him to know that monuments will be raised to him in the future. He wants and he needs and he's entitled to insist upon our full and active support now.

Although unprecedented production figures have made possible our victories, we shall have to increase our goals in certain weapons even more.

Our armed forces in combat have steadily increased their expenditure of ammunition, for example. As we continue the decisive phases of this war, the munitions that we expend will mount everyday.

I shall not go into the details of war production and the requirements of war materials. They are contained in the Message that I sent today, and I hope that many of you will have an opportunity to read that in full.

But there is one very human need that I do want to mention.

We need twenty thousand more trained nurses for our Army and Navy.

Those nurses that we have are rendering gallant service to our sick and wounded men, but they have been called upon to do more than their share. More than a thousand nurses are now hospitalized themselves—and part of this is due to overwork. At Army hospitals in the United States there is only one nurse to twenty-six beds, instead of one to fifteen beds, as there should be.

Since volunteering has not produced the number of nurses required, I asked the Congress in my Message to amend the Selective Service Act to provide for the induction of registered nurses into the armed forces.

The need is too pressing to await the outcome of further efforts at recruiting. However, I urge registered nurses throughout the country, and there are several hundred thousand of them,[4] to volunteer immediately for this great service.

The only way to meet our increased needs for more weapons and new weapons is for every American now engaged in war work to stay on his job, his war job—for additional American civilians, men and women not now engaged in essential work, to go out and get a war job. Workers who are released because their war production is cut back should get another war job where war production is being increased. I think that this is no time to quit or change to less essential jobs.

There's an old and true saying that the Lord hates a quitter. And this nation must pay for all those who leave their essential jobs—for all those who lay down on their essential jobs for nonessential reasons. And that payment must be made with the life's blood of our own sons.

Last year, after much consideration, I recommended that the Congress adopt a national service act as the most efficient and democratic way of ensuring full production for our war requirements. But this recommendation was not adopted.

So I have again called upon the Congress today to enact this measure for the total mobilization of all our human resources—men and women—for the prosecution of the war. I urge that this be done at the earliest possible moment.

---

[4]The phrase "and there are several hundred thousand of them" did not appear in the prepared text.

It is not too late in the war. In fact, bitter experience has shown that, in this kind of mechanized warfare where new weapons are constantly being created by our enemies and by ourselves, the closer we come to the end of the war, the more pressing becomes the need for sustained war production with which to deliver the final blow to the enemy.

There are three basic arguments for a national service law.

First, it would assure that we have the right numbers of workers in the right places at the right times.

Second, it would provide supreme proof to all our fighting men that we are giving them what they are entitled to, which is nothing less than our total effort back home.

And third, it would be the final, unequivocal answer to the hopes of the Nazis and the Japanese that we may become half-hearted about this war, and that they can get from us a negotiated peace.

National service legislation would be used only to the extent absolutely required by military necessities. In fact, experience in Great Britain and in other nations at war indicates that use of the compulsory powers of national service is necessary only in very rare instances.

National service would provide against loss of retirement and seniority rights and benefits. It would not mean reduction in wages.

The contribution of our workers in this war has been beyond measure. We must now build on the foundations that have already been laid, and supplement the measures now in operation, in order to guarantee the production that may be necessary in the critical period that lies ahead.

The secretary of war and the secretary of the navy have written me a letter in which, speaking of present war needs, they said:

> In our considered judgment, which is supported by General 'Marshall and Admiral King, this requires total mobilization of our manpower by the passage of a national war service law. The armed forces need this legislation to hasten the day of final victory, and to keep to a minimum the cost in lives.

That is the testimony of those best qualified to know the situation which confronts us.

Pending action by the Congress on the broader aspects of national service, I have recommended that the Congress immediately enact legislation which will be effective in using the services of the

4 million men now classified as 4-F[5] in whatever capacity is best for the war effort.

In the field of foreign policy, we propose to stand together with the United Nations not for the war alone but for the victory for which the war is fought.

It is not only a common danger that unites us, but a common hope. Ours is an association not of governments but of peoples—and the peoples' hope is peace. Here, as in England; in England, as in Russia; in Russia, as in China; in France, and through the continent of Europe, and throughout the world: wherever men love freedom, the hope and purpose of the people are for peace—a peace that is durable and secure.

Now, it will not be easy to create this peoples' peace. We have seen already, in areas liberated from the Nazi and the Fascist tyranny, what problems peace will bring. And we delude ourselves if we attempt to believe wishfully that all these problems can be solved overnight.

The firm foundation can be built—and it will be built. But the continuance and assurance of a living peace must, in the long run, be the work of the people themselves.

We ourselves, like all peoples who have gone through the difficult processes of liberation and adjustment, know of our own experience how great the difficulties can be. We know that they are not difficulties that are peculiar to any country or any nation. Our own Revolutionary War left behind it, in the words of one American historian, "an eddy of lawlessness and disregard of human life." Why, there were separatist movements of one kind or another in Vermont and Pennsylvania and Virginia and Tennessee and Kentucky and Maine. There were insurrections, open or threatened, in Massachusetts and New Hampshire. We worked out for ourselves these difficulties—as the people of the liberated areas of Europe, faced with complex problems of adjustment, and, over a period, will work out their difficulties for themselves.

Peace can be made and kept only by the united determination of free and peace-loving peoples who are willing to work together—willing to help one another, willing to respect and tolerate and try to understand one another's opinions and feelings.

In the future world the misuse of power, as implied in the term

[5] 4-F was the Selective Service classification for those deemed unfit for active duty.

"power politics," must not be a controlling factor in international relations. That is the heart of the principles to which we have subscribed. In a democratic world, as in a democratic nation, power must be linked with responsibility, and obliged to defend and justify itself within the framework of the general good.

After our disillusionment after the last war, we gave up the hope of achieving a better peace because we had not the courage to fulfill our responsibilities in an admittedly imperfect world.

We must not let that happen again, or we shall follow the same tragic road again—the road to a third world war.

We can fulfill our responsibilities for maintaining the security of our own country only by exercising our power and our influence to achieve the principles in which we believe, and for which we have fought.

It is true that the statement of principles in the Atlantic Charter does not provide rules of easy application to each and every one of the tangled situations in this war-torn world. But it is a good and a useful thing; in fact, it's an essential thing to have principles toward which we can aim.

And we shall not hesitate to use our influence—and to use it now—to secure so far as it is humanly possible the fulfillment of the principles of the Atlantic Charter. We have not shrunk from the military responsibilities brought on by this war. We cannot and will not shrink from the political responsibilities that follow in the wake of battle.

But to do this we must be on our guard not to exploit and exaggerate the differences between us and our allies, particularly with reference to the peoples who have been liberated from Fascist tyranny. That is not the way to secure a better settlement of those differences, or to secure international machinery which can rectify mistakes which may be made.

I must admit concern about many situations—the Greek and the Polish for example. But those situations are not as easy or as simple to deal with as some spokesmen, whose sincerity I do not question, would have us believe. We have obligations, not necessarily legal, to the exiled governments, to the underground leaders, and to our major allies who came much nearer to the shadows than we did.

We and our allies have declared that it is our purpose to respect the right of all peoples to choose the form of government under which they will live and to see sovereign rights and self-government restored to those who have been forcibly deprived of them. But with internal dissensions, with many citizens of liberated countries still prisoners of war or forced to labor in Germany, it is difficult to guess the kind of self-government the people really want.

During the interim period, until conditions permit a genuine expression of the peoples' will, we and our allies have a duty, which we cannot ignore, to use our influence to the end that no temporary or provisional authorities in the liberated countries block the eventual exercise of the peoples' right freely to choose the government and the institutions under which, as free men, they are to live.

It is our purpose to help the peace-loving peoples of Europe to live together as good neighbors, to recognize their common interests, and not to nurse their traditional grievances against one another.

But we must not permit the many specific and immediate problems of adjustment connected with the liberation of Europe to delay the establishment of permanent machinery for the maintenance of peace. Under the threat of a common danger, the United Nations joined together in war to preserve their independence and their freedom. They must now join together to make secure the independence and the freedom of all peace-loving states, so that never again shall tyranny be able to divide and conquer.

International peace and well-being, like national peace and well-being, require constant alertness, continuing cooperation, organized effort.

International peace and well-being, like national peace and well-being, can be secured only through institutions that are capable of life and growth.

One of the most heartening events of the year in the international field has been the renaissance of the French people and the return of the French nation to the ranks of the United Nations. Far from having been crushed by the terror of Nazi domination, the French people have emerged with stronger faith than ever in the destiny of their country and in the soundness of the democratic ideals to which the French nation has contributed so greatly.

Today, French armies are again on the German frontier and are again fighting shoulder to shoulder with our sons.

Since our landings in Africa, we have placed in French hands all the arms and material of war which our resources and the military situation permitted. And I am glad to say that we are now about to equip large new French forces with the most modern weapons for combat duty.

I am clear in my own mind that, as an essential factor in the maintenance of world peace in the future, we must have universal military training after this war, and I shall send a special message to the Congress on this subject a little later on.

An enduring peace cannot be achieved without a strong America—strong in the social sense, strong in the economic sense as well as in the military sense.

I have already set forth what I consider to be an American economic Bill of Rights, and the most fundamental of these is the "right to a useful and remunerative job in the industries or shops or farms or mines of the nation."

In turn, others of the economic rights of American citizenship such as the right to a decent home, to a good education, to good medical care, to social security, to reasonable farm income, will, if fulfilled, make major contributions to achieving adequate levels of employment.

In the Message that I sent to the Congress today I discussed the general approach to the program that we have in mind for the provision of close to 60 million jobs.

Although we must plan now for our postwar economy, and enact the necessary legislation, and set up the appropriate agencies for reconversion from war to peace, and lay the foundations for that transition period—all of which we are doing now—it is obviously impossible for us to do anything which might possibly hinder the production for war at this time, when our men are fighting on the frontiers of Germany and dropping bombs on the war industries of Japan.

In these days, our thoughts and our hopes and our prayers are with our sons and brothers, our loved ones who are far from home.

We can and we will give them all the support of which this great nation is capable. But—no matter how well they may be equipped with weapons and munitions—their magnificent fight will have been in vain if this war should end in the breaking of the unity of the United Nations.

We need the continuing friendship of our allies in this war. Indeed, that need is a matter of life and death. We shall need that friendship in the peace.

I quote from an editorial in the *Stars and Stripes,* our soldiers' own newspaper in Europe:

"For the holy love of God let's listen to the dead. Let's learn from the living. Let's join ranks against the foe. The bugles of battle are heard again above the bickering."

That is the demand of our fighting men. We cannot fail to heed it.

This new year of 1945 can be the greatest year of achievement in human history.

Nineteen forty-five can see the final ending of the Nazi-Fascist reign of terror in Europe.

Nineteen forty-five can see the closing in of the forces of retribution about the center of the malignant power of imperialistic Japan.

Most important of all, 1945 can, and must, see the substantial beginning of the organization of world peace—for we all know what such an organization means in terms of security, and human rights and religious freedom.

We Americans of today, together with our allies, are making history—and I hope it will be a better history than ever has been made before.

We pray that we may be worthy of the unlimited opportunities that God has given us.

INDEX

Adams, John: 195
Administrative Reorganization Act (1939): 126n.
Adowa, battle of (1895): 142
Agricultural Adjustment Act (1933): 19, 40, 42n., 83, 112, 126
Agriculture and agricultural policy: 3, 19, 22, 32, 40–41, 47–48, 73–79, 96, 100–101, 115, 178, 232–36; *see also* Agricultural Adjustment Act
Alcohol, tax on: 22
Alexander, Gen. Harold: 261n., 294–95
Allied cooperation and wartime conferences: 145, 261, 269, 272, 274–79, 284–85, 306, 308, 311–13; *see also* Cairo, Casablanca, Moscow, Quebec, Teheran, Yalta conferences
America First Committee: 144
American Expeditionary Force (1981): 170
American Federation of Labor: 95n., 251; *see also* Labor policy
American Red Cross: 153
Antitrust policy: 24, 29, 54, 96, 103–104, 127
Anvil, operation: 294
Archduke Maximilian: 181n.
Argentina: 192
Arnold, Gen. Henry ("Hap"): 247n.
"Asia-firsters": 206
Atlantic, battle of (1940–41): 181
Atlantic Charter (1941): 217 & n., 312
Australia: 209
Austria: 169, 199
Axis powers: 140, 147
Azores (Portugal): 168, 179, 181

Badoglio, Pietro: 257
Bankhead (Cotton Control) Act: 47n.
Bankhead-Jones Farm Tenant Act: 126n.
Banking Act 1935: 64
Banking system: 4–5, 11–16 19–20, 30–31, 42, 55–56, 71, 115, 117, 164
Bank runs: 11
Barbary pirates: 181n., 196 & n.
Bastogne, Belgium: 307
Beer-Wine Revenue Act (1933): 18
Belgium: 152–53, 167, 169, 199
Bethesda, Maryland (Medical Center): 294
Bill of Rights: 46, 49